Mastering
Basic management

1/5

Palgrave Master Series

Accounting
Accounting Skills
Advanced English Language
Advanced Poetry
Advanced Pure Mathematics
Arabic
Basic Management
Biology
British Politics
Business Communication
Business Environment
C Programming
C++ Programming
Chemistry
COBOL Programming
Communication
Computing
Counselling Skills
Counselling Theory
Customer Relations
Database Design
Delphi Programming
Desktop Publishing
e-Business
Economic and Social History
Economics
Electrical Engineering
Electronics
Employee Development
English Grammar
English Language
English Literature
Fashion Buying and Merchandising
  Management
Fashion Styling
Financial Management
French
Geography
German

Global Information Systems
Globalization of Business
Human Resource Management
Information Technology
International Trade
Internet
Italian
Java
Language of Literature
Management Skills
Marketing Management
Mathematics
Microsoft Office
Microsoft Windows, Novell
  NetWare and UNIX
Modern British History
Modern European History
Modern United States History
Modern World History
Networks
Novels of Jane Austen
Organisational Behaviour
Pascal and Delphi Programming
Philosophy
Physics
Practical Criticism
Psychology
Public Relations
Shakespeare
Social Welfare
Sociology
Spanish
Statistics
Strategic Management
Systems Analysis and Design
Team Leadership
Theology
Twentieth-Century Russian History
Visual Basic
World Religions

www.palgravemasterseries.com

Palgrave Master Series
Series Standing Order ISBN 0–333–69343–4
(outside North America only)

You can receive future titles in this series as they are published by placing a standing order. Please contact your bookseller or, in case of difficulty, write to us at the address below with your name and address, the title of the series and the ISBN quoted above.

Customer Services Department, Macmillan Distribution Ltd
Houndmills, Basingstoke, Hampshire RG21 6XS, England

Mastering

Basic management

Third Edition

E. C. Eyre

and

Richard Pettinger

palgrave

First edition 1982
Revised 1985
Reprinted four times
Second edition 1993
Reprinted four times
Third edition 1999

Published by
PALGRAVE
Houndmills, Basingstoke, Hampshire RG21 6XS and
175 Fifth Avenue, New York, N. Y. 10010
Companies and representatives throughout the world

PALGRAVE is the new global academic imprint of
St. Martin's Press LLC Scholarly and Reference Division and
Palgrave Publishers Ltd (formerly Macmillan Press Ltd).

ISBN 0–333–77240–7

This book is printed on paper suitable for recycling and
made from fully managed and sustained forest sources.

A catalogue record for this book is available
from the British Library.

Typeset by EXPO Holdings, Malaysia

Printed and bound by Antony Rowe Ltd, Eastbourne

Contents

■ ⓨ Preface to the second edition

My aims in this second edition of *Mastering Basic Management* have not changed since the work was first published. What I have done is to examine very carefully changes in the syllabuses of the professional bodies and in the types of questions set. These changes I have endeavoured to reflect in this revision and I hope the work will continue to be found useful to those seeking an introduction to the increasingly important subject of management, whether through a professional qualification, BTEC Certificate in Management or simply by personal study.

Because this work is heavily orientated to the requirements of the professional bodies I have continued to append to the appropriate chapters questions from recent past examination papers. Where the book finds favour with lecturers conducting BTEC courses I hope these questions can be used as a basis for the assignment required for these courses.

In Britain industry has been concerned to raise the standard of management and to this end in 1988 the Management Charter Initiative (known as MCI) was launched. To quote from its brochure 'The Management Charter Initiative is an employer-led drive to improve the performance of U.K. managers'. Initiated by a group of major British companies it sets standards of achievement for management training. It does not, itself, provide management education and training, but by a system of networks assists member companies to achieve this effectively themselves. The training is essentially in-house and on the job.

MCI is viewed as a great step forward in management education and training and because of this BTEC has geared its Certificate in Management requirements to it.

It had been suggested that I should include some notes on the impact of the UK's membership of the EC on management practice. After careful thought I came to the conclusion that this warrants a special study much wider than can be encompassed in this current volume, particularly in view of the new-found single European market. This view is reinforced by the fact that at least one professional body has a special paper on this subject.

Acknowledgements for the use of past examination questions are given under that heading, but I must express my especial appreciation of the assistance I have received in carrying out this revision from Mr Brian Banks, Director-General of the Institute of Company Accountants, from the Institute of Administrative Management and from the Chartered Institute of Management Accountants, whose help has been invaluable.

I must also extend my thanks to the British Standards Institution who kindly read and corrected my text on quality assurance, to my editor, Mr John Winckler for his suggestion, patience and support, and to my wife Irene for her continued support, encouragement and forbearance.

1993   E. C. EYRE

■ ⌄ Preface to the third edition

It has been a great pleasure to update and revise the high-quality and enduring work of Edward Eyre. It is a measure of the excellence of the original that most of the revision has become necesssary as the result of changes in the law, the increased influence of the European Union, and external changes in management approaches. By and large the key principles identified still hold good.

Since the second editon was produced in 1993, there has been a vast increase in the number of people studying management at all levels. Undergraduate and postgraduate university courses in management have proliferated, together with high-quality organisation-based training and development schemes. This has occurred alongside the much greater recognition of the direct relationship between effective management and successful organisational performance – and the converse, the direct relationship between poor management and poor and declining organisational performance.

The book therefore continues to target those undertaking professional studies courses, especially those provided by professional bodies. It is intended to serve as a clear and direct introduction to the subject for students in the first-year or introductory stage of undergraduate courses. It will also be a valuable introductory reader for anyone (including postgraduates) wishing to gain an initial insight into the principles and practices of management.

1999   RICHARD PETTINGER

■ ∨   Acknowledgements

The authors and publishers acknowledge, with grateful thanks, permission from the following to quote copyright material:

Longman, for the quotation from the Preface from H. Johannsen and A. Robertson, *Management Glossary*, edited by E. F. L. Brech, in Chapter 1; and for the quotation from E. F. L. Brech, *Principles and Practice of Management* (1975, p. 19) in Chapter 1.

McGraw-Hill, for the quotation from Harold Koontz and Heinz Weirich, *Management* (1988, p. 15) in Chapter 1.

Scientific Methods, Inc., for Figure 16.3, the Leadership Grid, from Robert R. Blake and Anne Adams McCanse, *Leadership Dilemmas – Grid Solutions* (Gulf Publishing Co., 1991, p. 29) in Chapter 16.

Pentax (UK) Ltd, for the Pentax slogan 'Simply hold a Pentax' quoted in Chapter 18.

The following professional bodies for past examination questions: Chartered Association of Certified Accountants (ACCA); Institute of Administrative Management (IAM); Institute of Chartered Secretaries and Administrators (ICSA); Chartered Institute of Management Accountants (CIMA); Chartered Institute of Marketing (CIM); Institute of Company Accountants (IComA); Institute of Personnel Management (IPM).

The original sources of material for the theories of motivation given in Chapter 13 are also acknowledged; the interpretations of these are our own:

A. H. Maslow, *Motivation and Personality* (Harper & Row, 1987) in 13.6.

Douglas M. McGregor, *The Human Side of Enterprise* (McGraw-Hill, 1972) in 13.7.

F. Herzberg, *Work and the Nature of Man* (Crosby Lockwood, 1975) in 13.8.

W. G. Ouchi, *Theory Z* (Avon Books, 1982) in 13.9.

Ayer & Co., for the management scale quoted in Chapter 1, from E. T. Elbourne, *Fundamentals of Industrial Administration* (1980).

BSI Quality Assurance, Milton Keynes, for the extract on registration procedure and for Figure 25.1, both in Chapter 25.

Every effort has been made to trace all the copyright-holders, but if any have been inadvertently overlooked the publishers will be pleased to make the necessary arrangement at the first opportunity.

▪ ⌄   ▮ An introduction to management

The topic of management has become the subject of increased study and discussion over the past few decades and has indeed, forced itself into the examination schemes of a large number of professional bodies. Equally, it has become a field of study in its own right, above all through the great proliferation of business and management schools, and postgraduate qualifications in management, especially the Master of Business Administration (MBA). Certificate and diploma qualifications in management also continue to increase, as does the influence of institutes of management.

The would-be student of management is immediately beset by two potential problems: first, the vocabulary of management is by no means standardised and second, most books recommended for reading by examining bodies use specialist language and often have lengthy reading lists.

It seems that little can be done about the former. It is true to say that some people and authorities have tried to produce management glossaries. However, the problem has been greatly compounded in recent years by the proliferation of management 'techniques' an approaches such as Business Process Re-engineering (BPR), Total Quality Management (TQM), benchmarking, and so on.

It is hoped, however, that the second problem will have a partial solution in this volume.

1.1   Management and administration

- One of the first things a writer on management tries to do is to distinguish between what is meant by 'management' and what is meant by 'administration'. The definitions given for 'management' are many and include the following:

  'A social process entailing responsibility for the effective and economical planning and regulation of the operations of an enterprise, in fulfillment of a given purpose or task'. This responsibility includes:

  (a) Judgement and decision making, devising and determining plans and in using data to monitor performance against plans; and

  (b) The guidance, integration, motivation and supervision of the staff comprising the enterprise, and carrying out its operations.

  So said E. F. L. Brech in *Principles and Practice of Management*.

- In *Toward a Unified Theory of Management* Harold Koontz offered a simpler definition: 'Managing is the art of getting things done through and with people in formally organised groups'.
- E. F. L. Brech's definition seems to imply that management is a skill whereas Harold Koontz specifically states that it is an art. We could, therefore, take the essence of these two statements and create the definition that 'Management is the art or skill of directing human activities and physical resources in the attainment of predetermined goals'. Inherent in these definitions are the implications that management is about making decisions; and that it is concerned with coping with change and uncertainty. These views are universally accepted.
- Much greater difficulty occurs when it is required to define 'administration'. The problem is that the word 'administration' is used both to describe the activity of implementing policy decisions and also to describe the narrower activity of regulating the day-to-day operations of a section of an organisation such as the office. The word is also used to describe the very top functions in public service.
- It can safely be said that administration is part of management. It is certainly very much concerned with the implementation of policy, but its freedom of action will be limited by the decisions of policy laid down by those charged with directional responsibilities.
- In terms of management, it is much safer and more usual to concentrate on the key principles of leadership, decision-making, communication, co-ordination, control and consultation rather than on administrative processes.

1.2 The practice of management

- Managerial skills, qualities, attributes and expertise are quite distinct from other skills that a person calling himself a member of the management team might possess. For example, the chief accountant of a business enterprise is expert in the accounting function – the treatment of financial issues and measuring in financial terms various aspects of the enterprise for control purposes and decision-making. Such activities, however, demand only technical skill and knowledge. Similarly, production managers will be extremely knowledgeable about production processes and about the properties of the materials the department uses but the application of this technical knowledge does not necessarily imply that they are employing managerial skills.
- It is when the accountant, or the production manager, or the sales manager or any other manager directs and co-ordinates the activities of the team of people to achieve the required results through the use of finance, materials, marketing expertise and the like that each is managing.
- The sales manager may be an able salesperson, and be quite successful in converting a potential customer into an actual buyer: this displays technical skills. It is when they control teams of salespeople, organising their activities,

co-ordinating their efforts, planning their work-loads and directing and controlling their operations that they are acting as managers.

- It will be seen, therefore, that the ability to manage is an attribute quite apart from any technical skills. One school of thought states that a manager needs no specific skills and can therefore switch from job to job and still be a successful manager. This is particularly held to be the case in the upper echelons of both public and private organisations, where such managers move regularly between different areas of activity – and indeed between the public and private sectors. This approach is also gaining in importance at more junior organisational and functional levels. It is becoming increasingly apparent that the requirement for a holder of any managerial post is the ability to organise and direct the resources available, to make competent decisions based on the advice received from those with the technical knowledge and expertise.

- One authoritative writer on this subject, E. T. Elbourne, reinforces this view by suggesting that as the management scale ascends, the element of technical expertise used reduces and that of management expertise increases. He quantifies this as follows:

	% managing
Managing director	90
Principal officer or senior executive	50
Foreman or supervisor	35

From this, it can be seen that even at the most junior levels the need for managerial capability and expertise is critical.

1.3   The manager and the business

- The need to develop management as a separate field of study came about as a result of the increasing size of business and other undertakings since the latter part of the nineteenth century. At first there were only two divisions, capital and labour. The owner, who provided the physical and financial resources to promote industrial or commercial activity, was also the one who managed the enterprise, decided policy and directed the human and physical resources under his control to attain his objectives. His undertaking flourished or failed according to his business acumen, in other words according to his management flair or expertise. The attribute of management ability was looked upon as a natural talent and no training was expected or available except through experience on the job.

- In the smaller enterprise the owner was usually an active member of the working team, as today. In the larger enterprise the owner was normally present to oversee the diligence of senior staff who might, or might not, have been called managers. What training they received was at his hands, in his example and to his pattern. The need to develop some supervisory skills was recognised, but no formal training was given, or even envisaged.

- However, the rapid development of the joint-stock company and the increasing size of the capital investment required to operate competitively in the face of ever more complex manufacturing and other techniques eventually led to the position where the true owners of an enterprise were not personally involved in its management. It has also led to the curious situation that the true owners, or shareholders, are not in a technical legal sense, in fact, the owners since a limited liability company is a corporate entity in its own right. This came about by virtue of the decision in the *Salomon* case of 1897 and subsequent Companies Acts. However, it is convenient in the context of a discussion on capital and management to consider shareholders as owners, as is generally accepted by the community at large.
- Modern investors are almost entirely interested in the financial returns brought by their capital, either by way of income or by way of capital growth. Their contribution to industry and commerce in financial terms is just as great or greater then ever it was, but they are no longer in a position to exert very much influence on the actual management of the company. Unless the organisation is being grossly mismanaged, the average shareholder has only one chance a year to influence company affairs, and that is at the Annual General Meeting (AGM)
- The relationship between managers and their 'businesses' has been further complicated in recent years by the proliferation of alternative forms of organisation – especially privatisation, the creation of organisations with trust status, the increase in organisations of charitable status, the proliferation of multinational corporations and cross-border activities; and the deregulation of financial markets allowing foreign investors to invest in businesses in the UK, and UK investors to invest in foreign enterprises.

1.4   The structure of management

- Thus modern owners have to rely heavily on other people to manage and direct their enterprises, and so there has evolved the present-day system of three divisions:

  CAPITAL (mainly absentee)
  MANAGEMENT (largely salaried)
  LABOUR

- Of course, it is true to say that members of management are often shareholders and thus also have an interest in capital, many companies have this as a requirement for a directorship. However, this in no way diminishes the basic fact that there are now three levels.
- The management structure, itself stratified, has now become that shown in Figure 1.1
- It must be remembered that all management personnel do not act on one level only. For example, the managing director is a member of the board of directors and also the chief executive officer.

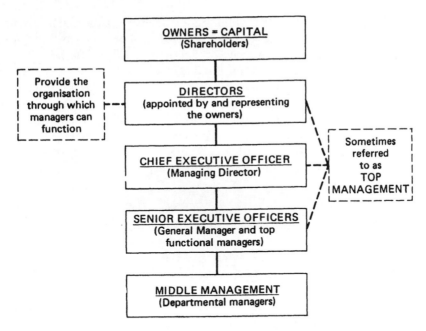

Figure 1.1 The structure of modern management

- This division into levels is important because each has special responsibilities, which can be quite easily seen in a large enterprise though they may be somewhat obscured in a small one. The responsibilities of the management structure with which we are concerned are:

1 THE SHAREHOLDERS provide the capital to finance the enterprise. They also select the directors who represent their interests. They have little, if any, control over the objectives of the organisation or its day-to-day management. They may use argument at the annual general meeting, which may or may not be effective. Their most effective power is that of being able to discharge directors and appoint new ones to their liking.

2 THE DIRECTORS are charged with the overall management of the undertaking on behalf of the owners. Acting as a board they are responsible for deciding the objectives of the enterprise and for determining its policies in pursuit of those objectives. The directors must make provision for a proper and adequate organisation, for authorising capital expenditure and for generally controlling the enterprise in the interests of the owners.

3 THE CHIEF EXECUTIVE OFFICER, or managing director, is the link between the board of directors and senior management, often by virtue of dual capacity as director and executive.

4 THE SENIOR EXECUTIVE OFFICERS are responsible for the detailed conduct of the undertaking in order to meet the objectives laid down within the policy framework. They are accountable to the chief executive – or, the managing director.

5 DEPARTMENTAL MANAGERS, sometimes known as middle management, are usually responsible of running departments or divisions, and are accountable to the senior executive officers on a functional basis.

6 SUPERVISORS are responsible for the day-to-day running of work groups within departments, divisions and functions, who normally report to departmental or middle managers. Supervisors are increasingly being asked to take ever-greater responsibilities for the results of their particular groups and organisations are becoming evermore aware that senior, long serving and expert functionaries can carry out adequate and effective supervision duties in addition to their technical or functional expertise.

QUESTIONS

1 Explain what is meant by the term 'management' and indicate its relationship with 'administration'.

2 Discuss the relationship between managerial and technical skills.

3 The practice of management has become a study in its own right. Explain why this has come about.

4 Describe and discuss the form of management structure that obtains in most modern organisations.

5 Many firms follow a policy of appointing the heads of the main functional departments – marketing, finance, production, etc. – to the board of directors.
   (a) Why do they do this?
   (b) In what ways would the nature of the responsibilities of a marketing manager change, when appointed to the board? (CIM)

2 The purpose and nature of management

The purpose of management can be stated to be the formulation of the objectives and policies of the firm and the pursuit of all the necessary activities that will bring those objectives and policies to satisfactory fruition.

- It is commonly stated that there is one main objective to be followed, and that is to maximise profits. Certainly the entrepreneurial urge usually initiates business activity. An opportunity to fill a market need, or indeed to create one, which will bring financial rewards frequently instigates the setting up of an organisation or causes an existing enterprise to diversify into a field other than its own. However, this is not always the case: often a business is formed because the original owner has a passionate interest in a certain activity, and so seeks to derive a livelihood; or they have an idea which they feel will benefit the community and at the same time provide an income. Many organisations were originally founded on individual personal passions, and have gone on to be extremely successful commercially.
- As enterprises grow so does the emphasis on profit maximisation. In particular, shareholders wish only to see the maximum possible return on their outlay; and this is particularly true of large institutional investors – insurance companies, pension funds, and others.
- However, other factors have also to be taken into consideration. The naked pursuit of profit has become socially unacceptable in many quarters, and the effect of business activity on the community at large, on the environment, on staff relations and on consumers has become of current concern socially, environmentally and politically. Pressure groups have been formed to protect the environment and the consumer. The law has been invoked through the passing of appropriate statutes in the areas of equal opportunities for all, consumer rights, environmental protection, and other aspects, in an attempt to safeguard the interests of the public at large. Because of these factors, management has a duty to include in its philosophy considerations other than the financial.
- Profit maximisation also has to be seen in terms of time. It is true to say that in recent years, profit maximisation has been a short-term activity – the goal was to make as much money in as short a time as possible by driving down costs and making short-terms cuts and savings. The alternative view is that profit maximisation can only be achieved over the extreme long term – by

investing and underpinning activities to an extent sufficient to ensure long-term viability of the firm.
- This is the basis on which objectives and policies are formulated. It might be said that objectives are what the firm is aiming to achieve, and that policies are how this is to be done.

2.1 The economic view of management objectives

The economic view of the firm is that it exists to make a profit and that all other considerations are very much subservient to this. It is in business to mix the factors of production – labour, materials and capital – in the proportions appropriate to its particular activities so as to produce an output of goods or services that it can sell at the maximum profit. The philosophy behind this view is that what benefits the entrepreneur ultimately benefits the community at large, as is enshrined in the maxim propagated by America's largest manufacturer of motor-cars, General Motors: 'what is good for General Motors is good for America'.

The revenue of the country is primarily derived from taxation, a large proportion of which comes from business enterprise, and hence if profits are maximised then so is the national revenue. Further, if customers fail to support an enterprise and consequently losses are incurred this is an indication that the resources being devoted to that particular activity need to be used in other ways and so made to produce profits.

This somewhat naive view of management objectives is derived from the theory of perfect competition, where only the efficient survive and the inefficient are forced to use their resources in other more profitable ways; where conditions of complete freedom of action obtain, coupled with a relatively compliant work-force. Further, there is the assumption that management is in the hands of the owner or very close to the owner, who is able to exert considerable influence on decisions as to objectives and policies. The fact is that nowadays this theory in its pure form must be questioned on the following grounds:

(a) By no stretch of the imagination can it be said that business has anything like complete freedom of action. Government intervention in the operations of business is considerable and growing. Business is controlled and restricted in its activities by a host of laws, relating to employment of staff, material usage, location of operations and many other areas of its activities. Such legislation increases costs without compensating opportunities for making extra profits to accommodate them, and affects small as well as large undertakings.

(b) Except in the smaller concerns businesses are no longer managed by, or close to, the owners. Indeed, for the most part the owners take no active part or interest in the actual management of the concern. Professional managers have their own personal interests to pursue as well as those of the owners. In consequence, improved working conditions, increases in earnings, perhaps by way of bonuses, and other personal factors are likely to weigh in their deliberations as well as the prime objective of making maximum profits.

(c) Competition is very restricted in some sections of the economy, for example in the utility, energy and defence sectors. Considerations other than competition influence the conduct of these large units. Both public and private monopolies, or near monopolies, also exist.

(d) The economic maxim of economies of scale, in which it is claimed that increases in the scale of operations bring increases in efficiency and better utilisation of resources, has proved to have severe limitations in practice. This is especially true in the case of mergers, acquisitions and takeovers; according to a survey carried out by the Institute of Management in 1996, only 13 per cent of those questioned stated that economies of scale had been achieved.

(e) The economic view tends towards realising efficiencies of operation, and profit maximisation, in the short term only. Again, it is becoming increasingly apparent that success is only to be achieved if profits are maximised – or optimised – over the long-term.

(f) The economic view also tends to rigidity. Unless one is very careful, it makes no allowances for changing circumstances, changes in markets, changes in the price of commodities, or changes in the price that customers and consumers are willing to pay.

2.2 The behavioural view of management objectives

The rather simplistic view of management objectives put forward by the economic theorists has been challenged by sociologist and psychologists – the behavioural scientists. They contend that because of the intervention of the salaried manager profit maximisation alone is not, and cannot be, the sole management objective. They believe that employed managers have as much interest in their own benefits as in benefits for the firm, and the behavioural theory suggests that:

(a) Managers will set objectives that fulfil their own interests and which will produce profits not at the maximum, but at the level that will satisfy the owners. The behavioural scientists term this 'satisficing'.

(b) Because of the fact that each manager has personal objectives, which can be achieved only through employment, and because they have at the same time to set acceptable company objectives, there is an essential element of bargaining and internal politics in the formulation of management objectives to reconcile these two elements. Since no manager is likely to be truly altruistic, some element of self-interest is bound to be present in all deliberations about setting objectives.

(c) Again, therefore, objectives cannot remain static, as they would if profit maximisation were achievable on economic grounds alone. Changes in objectives are therefore inevitable, because of changes in the size and scale of the concern, changes in the technical and social environment, and changes in personal and professional aspirations.

2.3 The stakeholder view of management objectives

In recent years, the behavioural view has become enlarged to include the influences of all those who have a vested interest in the performance of organisation – i.e. stakeholders. This view states that there are a number of interested parties to be considered in the formulation of objectives. It is usual to consider the stakeholders of an organisation as:

(a)   shareholders: those who have invested in an organisation; and this includes other backers (e.g. loan makers), and – for public concerns – the government and its instruments;
(b)   managers: responsible for delivering the benefits expected by other stakeholders, as well as having their own interests;
(c)   staff and workers: who seek long-term stability of employment, together with promotion and development prospects;
(d)   customers and consumers: who expect a long-term steady stream of ever-improving products and services;
(e)   suppliers: dependent upon the concern for its continued well-being;
(f)   distributors: dependent upon the concern for their continued well-being;
(g)   the local community: requiring concerns operating in their locality to provide work as well as products and services;
(h)   lobby groups, pressures groups and other vested interests: voicing particular concerns and points of view about the standard and conduct of particular problems; of especial current importance are environmental and ethical pressure groups;
(i)   the media and journalists: who report increasingly on the activities of particular concerns and organisations.

Every firm, and thus every management, has a different set of circumstances with which to contend, so its objectives will be influenced by those special circumstances. It is also important to recognise that managers may be affected by circumstances outside their control – and when this happens, time and resources have to be devoted to addressing the particular situation. In practice, therefore, organisational and management objectives cannot be seen from a purely economic point of view. In the long-term, profit maximisation – or optimisation – is only achieved if the different, and often conflicting, concerns of all those with a vested interest in the organisation are satisfied.

2.4 Policy-making

Policies are shaped out of a combination of organisational objectives, and social drives and demands. The greater the emphasis on economic objectives, the more likely it is that management policies will be based on financial gain rather than on social considerations. If, on the other hand, objectives are formulated on the basis of social obligations as well as the need to make profits, then the policies decided upon will reflect this concern. If the stakeholder approach is accepted by the firm then the policies adopted will tend to take a broad view, seeking to address the concerns of all those involved, as well as making long-term profits.

- Objectives and policies are the prerogative of top management – the board of directors in a company are guided and aided by their senior executive officers. In most cases, the board includes directors who are also executives and this liaison is thus easily accomplished. Senior executives not on the board also have their views taken into account through their close day-to-day association with their executive directors.
- Many boards of directors also include non-executive directors – members who do not take part in the actual operations of the company but who are included because of their knowledge and experience in certain fields and whose advice is useful to the board. Non-executive directors act as a mirror or sounding board when policies are being formulated; they also act as a curb on over-ambitious schemes and proposals.
- It is also true that the mix of economic and social factors taken into account by management in setting objectives and formulating policies, is dependent to a significant degree on the size of the undertaking. For example, smaller organisations may not be able to make such a significant social contribution

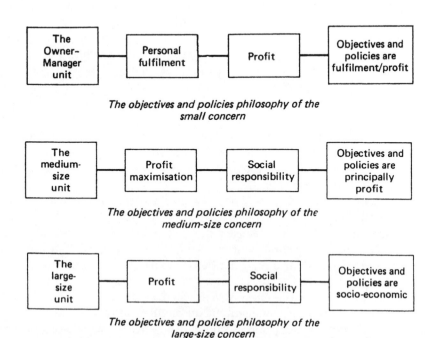

The objectives and policies philosophy of the
small concern

The objectives and policies philosophy of the
medium-size concern

The objectives and policies philosophy of the
large-size concern

Figure 2.1   A comparison of the objectives and policies/philosophies of different-size enterprises

as larger companies; it may take several years for a new company to become commercially viable, let alone contribute to society. The different approaches and philosophies are presented graphically in Figure 2.1.

- It must be said, however, that concern for the social and environmental aspects of running an organisation has not been arrived at entirely voluntarily in many cases. Some managements have had to have their attention brought to these responsibilities by law. In Britain, there are already many laws on the statue book to try to ensure that industry fulfils its social responsibilities concerning its workers and staff; and the community and the environment. New laws are constantly being enacted as new abuses or hazards come to light. The European Union has also produced very strong legislation, especially in the areas of the rights of individual workers, and health and safety at work, and this is certain to continue for the foreseeable future.

2.5 The concept of social responsibility

Legally and socially, management has duties outside its obligations to the owners of the business. However, to combine in one philosophy the need to make profits for dividends and continued investment; and to provide good pay, working conditions and job security for employees, as well as to ensure the protection of the environment, and to serve the interests of customers and of the community as a whole, is not easy.

- The ethical behaviour of business generally has become a matter of major public concern and different organisations have taken different approaches. For example, Nissan placed the quality of their staff at the top of their list of priorities, taking the view that excellent products and customer service can only be achieved through the employment of high quality staff. The Body-Shop requires all its employees to undertake some form of community activity one day per month. Mitsubishi has tried to ensure security of employment for its staff through requiring them to undertake extensive an continued training programmes so that they are ready for every eventuality. BMW (the owners of the British Rover Group) has engaged extended pay agreements (for up to three years) so that it knows to a greater extent their obligations on the wages bill.
- Many organisations and areas of activity have become the object of pressure groups and lobbies. One instance of this is the campaign to stop the transport of nuclear materials through densely populated districts. Another instance is the concern for the environment caused by the development of industrial and commercial activities on greenfield (i.e. fresh) sites, and through the building of major road schemes.
- Pressures also come: from employees for better pay and conditions and for greater participation in management decisions; from consumers for more product information and product safety; from environmentalists for restrictions on pollution and other matters possibly detrimental to the environment; from conservationists for the protection of the landscape and of various forms of animal and plant life.

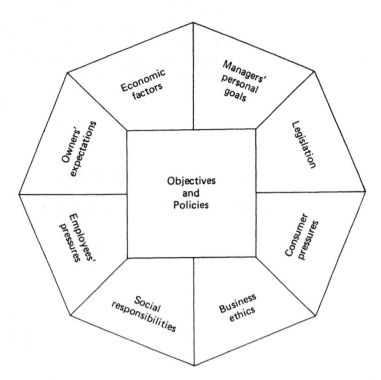

Figure 2.2 Elements influencing management philosophy on objectives and policies

- Pressures also come from the British government and European Union for changes in business practices and manufacturing standards; and again, both the British government and the European Union are increasingly resorting to legislation in areas where a shortfall is perceived.
- As a consequence, the nature and purpose of management is a matter for various interpretations and subject to constant change (see Figure 2.2). On the one hand, it can still be argued that the purpose of management is to max-imise profits to the benefit of the owners. On the other hand, the broadest possible view has to be taken; it can be asserted that management should be socially conscious and that only by taking this approach is it possible to create the conditions in which long-term profits can be maximised. Some organisations that have failed to take the broader view, and have tried to con-centrate purely on profit maximisation have paradoxically had their profits seriously affected; an example of this is where the Shell Oil Company's refusal to deal with the Brent Spar oil rig in an environmentally concerned manner led to a consumer boycott and serious loss of sales.
- Problems concerning the overall integrity of companies have also arisen where there is known, believed or perceived to be too great a differential between the pay of those at the top of the organisation, and those at lower levels. This has led in many instances to accusations of self-serving on the part of managers and, in extreme cases, to media stories about 'fat cats'.

- Problems also arise where the continued survival of the enterprise is no longer possible, or possible only by severe staff reductions. These situations result in grave repercussions for employees and the community. When redundancies and staff reductions do occur, there is always a knock-on effect on the other businesses in the particular community. When these situations arise, some employers try to mitigate the effects by setting up facilities and counselling to find jobs for those under threat of redundancy and job loss.

2.6   Management and environmental constraints

Increasingly, environmental questions concern management and these come from many sources.

- There is increasing British and EU legislation concerning planning regulations, the disposal of waste and effluent and concern for the environment, to which all organisations must conform.
- Organisations in sectors that have extreme effects on the environment – e.g. oil, construction, the nuclear industry – are required to take ever-increasing and long term account of the effect that their activities have on the environment.
- Inside the organisation concern for the welfare and employment conditions of the staff is paramount, induced by the goodwill of the employer or by employee pressure. External to the enterprise, government legislation and consumer pressures put constraints on the firm's behaviour. Less forcibly, social morals, ethics and justice may play a part.
- The increasing numbers of, and influence of, pressure groups such as Greenpeace also have an effect on management action.
- Besides management's concern for staff welfare and expectations internally, and for environmental matters externally, there is also the often forgotten social responsibility between the organisation and its suppliers. A large-scale purchaser has a very great commercial advantage over its suppliers even if they are also large-scale, but this is much more evident if the supplier is a small operator. Pressure from the buyer, particularly in terms of price, can cause financial embarrassment to the supplier who may have to adopt socially unattractive practices such as lowering working conditions and/or pay for the workforce. A large buyer can, and often does, also cause financial difficulties to small suppliers by delaying payment for purchases well beyond the normal credit period.
- On the other hand, a monopoly or near monopoly supplier can also trade in an unsocial manner to deprive the purchaser of freedom of choice in purchasing. In Britain 'tied' public houses whose managers or tenants are forced to serve only one brewer's wares are a case in point.

QUESTIONS

    1   'Whatever the theorists may say, a business in fact is run primarily for the benefit of its managers; any other parties are only considered in so far as they may be

able to threaten the well-being of the management.' Discuss the subject of this quotation, together with the difficulties encountered in the theoretical analysis of business. (ACCA)

2 In what ways may the need to exercise social responsibility shape the relationship of enterprise management to some of its internal and external stakeholders? (ACCA)

3 Social responsibility is expected from all types of organisations.
   (a) Discuss what, in a management context, is meant by 'social responsibility'.
   (b) State and explain the sources from which concepts of social responsibility may be derived. (IAM)

4 Research has identified the importance of particular external constraints related to the environment in which organisations operate.
   Discuss any THREE of the principal constraints identified. (IAM)

5 Organisations employ various resources (e.g. finance, raw materials, people, plant and equipment) in order to achieve objectives. Discuss the role of management in an organisation and assess the relative importance of management as a resource. (ICSA)

6 (a) Compare the characteristics of a sole trader, a partnership and a limited company, illustrating your answer with an example of each type of business.
   (b) Explain why, in each case, the structure is particularly suited to the nature of the firm's business. (CIM)

7 The responsibilities of managers include those to employees, customers or clients, shareholders, the local community and government. How may these responsibilities be discharged in the event of a decision to close a large factory or office involving a significant number of redundancies? In responding to this question you need not refer to the detailed provisions of redundancy legislation. (ICSA)

■ ⋎ 3 The directors

Before proceeding further into this study of management it is useful to examine the role and responsibilities of the directors, who are answerable not only to their shareholders but also to the law.

3.1 The board of directors

The directors of a company are elected by the owners of the enterprise and may act only as a committee, known as a board, and not individually. In the case of a new company they are either named in the articles of association of the company or are appointed by the subscribers (that is, the first shareholders) to the memorandum of association. Thereafter, their tenure of office is as laid down in the articles, which ensure that at regular intervals a stated proportion of the board must resign and offer themselves for re-election at the next annual general meeting. This gives the shareholders the opportunity to express their confidence in the retiring directors by re-electing them, or to show their dissatisfaction with the performance of the board by electing new directors. The shareholders also have other ways of changing the composition of the board, but these belong to the study of company law. The memorandum and the articles of association, also, are the subject of company law and it is sufficient to state in the present context that they regulate the powers and the proceedings of a company.

The responsibilities of the board of directors fall into two general categories, legal and domestic.

(a) The legal responsibilities of the directors

The board is responsible for ensuring that the company operates according to the law. Among the legal requirements are:
1 to comply with all the provisions of the Companies Acts;
2 liability to third parties on acts of the company and its servants, this being an implied responsibility;
3 to ensure that all operations of the company are within the general law, statute and common; for example, complying with the requirements of the Town and Country Planning Acts, the Finance Acts and other statutes, and ensuring that the company carries on no illegal activities.

4 to produce an accurate annual report, giving a true and fair reflection of the company's activities for the previous year.

(b)   The domestic responsibilities of the directors

The duties and responsibilities of the directors are as follows:

1 there is a trustee relationship between directors and shareholders. In effect, the board acts as trustee for the funds subscribed by members, and for the proper application of those funds

2 shareholders also have a right to expect the board to act primarily in their interests. The company is entitled to the unbiased advice of each director on any matter of concern to the company. These rights are of special importance in the case of projected takeovers, mergers, acquisitions, withdrawals or sell-offs.

- Sometimes impartiality on the part of a director is difficult because of a personal interest in a matter that has come up for discussion or action. For instance, they may be financially interested in another company with which a contract is being considered. In such cases it is usually required that the director concerned should declare an interest and refrain from joining in any discussion of the matter and from voting.
- As part of top management the directors are responsible for formulating the objectives of the enterprise, which was fully discussed in Chapter 2. To achieve these objectives the board has to formulate a policy which it considers will best serve to attain its goals. As both objectives and policy-making were discussed in Chapter 2 at this point it is sufficient to say simply that objectives are *what* is to be achieved and policy is *how* to go about achieving them. While flexibility must apply to both, it is self-evident that objectives must be fairly fixed in nature while policy is subject to easier modification. Agreeing objectives and formulating policy are probably the most onerous of the domestic responsibilities of directors.

3.2   The managing director or chief executive

Any discussion of the board of directors would not be complete without mention of the managing director or chief executive. The role is complex

- Managing directors partake in the activities of the board – the formulation of policy, decisions on capital expenditure and so on. Often in this capacity, because of the additional function as chief executive, views expressed at board meetings are looked upon with great respect, and considerable authority.
- Chief executives form a link between the board and fellow managers, and also the responsibility for seeing that management carries out the policies and decisions of the board.
- Thus they interpret and put into effect, through the management team, the decisions taken at board level, and can follow them through down the

organisation chain. This is done through the process of delegation and through the reporting and control systems set up to monitor company performance.

- Managing directors are involved in the day-to-day management work involved in implementing the board's wishes. Similarly, chief executives are aware of the day-to-day problems and requirements of the company in all significant areas such as capital requirements, staffing, liquidity and so on. They are in a unique position to bring these problems to the attention of the board, where necessary, for their advice and possible action.
- A strong managing director is likely to dominate the board of directors and also the management team. This is a type of quality most useful in fulfilling this exacting function. Firmness is most essential, tempered by the ability to analyse and discuss problems with colleagues, and to alter course where logically necessary.

3.3 The chairman

Every company, and board of directors, must have a chairman. The chairman is a member of the board of directors. However, the chairman is elected not by the shareholders but by the board of directors. They are usually chosen because of knowledge and experience and experience of the industry within which the organisation operates, though a proven record of success elsewhere may prove equally attractive to the board.

- If the enterprise is a major one the chairman will be the member of the board most in the public eye and must therefore present a suitable public image that encourages confidence in the company.
- Unless the enterprise is fairly small the chairman usually has no executive powers and is thus free from the day-to-day problems of running the organisation. They are therefore able to devote energies to those problems that concern top management, such as policy-making, where their expertise and advice are most valuable. The primary technical function is to control and regulate the proceedings at board meetings. As head of the organisation the chairman should have the capacity to lead the management team in a positive fashion and to stimulate it to develop new approaches to management problems.
- Because of the great responsibilities carried by the managing director and because of the strength of this authority it is essential that the chairman and the managing director work in harmony. Indeed, the offices are sometimes combined, especially in the smaller concern, and one person occupies the position of chairman and managing director. Whilst this may result in the avoidance of divided opinions at the top, there are two important reasons for not combining these two offices:

  (a) The task of the chairman is very onerous and requires a good deal of time devoted to it, particularly in considering matters coming up for discussion at board meetings. So far as is possible this needs detachment and the ability to take the broad view. This is difficult to achieve when a person has executive responsibilities and is thus constantly in contact with the day-to-day operations of the concern.

(b) Consultation between chairman and managing director on many matters is often helpful and fruitful because the chairman can be detached from the problem and can offer unbiased advice based on independent experience. The advantage of two opinions and two approaches is lost if the two offices are combined.

3.4 Executive and non-executive directors

Like the managing director, many directors on a board are also full-time executives of the company and have a functional managerial role in addition to their responsibilities as directors. They are, consequently, in daily contact with the progress of the business and are called upon to make decisions in relation to the policy of the board as a whole and to implement these decisions on a day-to-day basis. In his executive capacity as head of a division or function an executive director does, in fact, assume personal responsibility for running their division or function effectively within the framework of the objectives laid down at board level.

- The majority of executive directors are elected to the board on the recommendation of the managing director because of their functional expertise. There are two consequences. First, their technical background – the word 'technical' is here used in its widest sense – may cause them to have a narrow view of the business bounded by their specialist knowledge and experience. Second, being appointed by the managing director may cause some executive directors to follow their line. Many companies, therefore, find it useful to have non-executive directors on their boards. They are appointed for a variety of reasons. It may be to gain the experience and advice of an acknowledged expert who can bring to bear a wider view to the deliberations of the board. Or a company may be required to have a non-executive director appointed by a third party. Such a case might be where a company is being financed to a considerable degree by a merchant bank or other financial house; such an institution may only agree to provide the finance if a part-time director recommended by them is taken on.
- The main advantage to a company of expert non-executive directors is that they are relatively independent and therefore less likely to be influenced by pressures put on the board by the chairman, chief executive or other executive directors.

3.5 The board and industrial democracy

No discussion on the role and responsibilities of directors would be complete without mention of industrial democracy.

- As a result of the drive towards industrial democracy being felt in all Member States of the European Union, it is certain that both the constitution and remit of the board of directors will undergo a significant change. At present in such countries as Sweden and Germany there is a legal requirement for there to be worker directors in companies of above a certain size (in Sweden this is twenty-five employees). Sometimes the requirement is for the worker directors to sit on a single board with the other directors, the so-called unitary board. In these cases, the worker directors have the same powers as the other directors in voting on matters of policy, direction, objectives and other top management decisions.
- The other approach is the two-tier board of directors. This means, in effect, that two boards are set up. The top level is a supervisory board akin to present boards of directors. The second level is an executive board to which the supervisory board delegates the responsibility of running the day-to-day business of the concern. The supervisory board remains responsible for policy, direction and meeting shareholders' concerns, while the executive board is responsible for taking those decisions needed to put policies and direction into action. It is also particularly concerned with management/ employee affairs.
- The main area of contention is the manner in which worker representatives should be appointed or elected. Trade unions want worker directors to be drawn from their members. Others contend that this would be inequitable to those members of staff who did not belong to a trade union and indeed might operate to the detriment of such members of staff.
- There is no doubt that the introduction of employees on to the boards of directors of companies will have a profound effect on top management decisions. Shareholders' directors will inevitably experience some constraints on their freedom to make decisions, as broader interests come to prominence.

3.6 The influence of the European Union on company directors

The European Union and its forerunners – the European Economic Community, the European Coal and Steel Community – always took the view that worker participation and industrial harmony were prerequisites to organisational economic success. The view has therefore long since been held that workers should have a say in the decision-making and policy-formulation processes of their organisations.

- The most significant change in the area is the elevation of the staff and worker interest to that equivalent to the shareholder interest. This means a fundamental shift of attitude on the part of many British company directors, particularly in the area of reconciling shareholder with worker interest, and also on disclosures of company information which might hitherto have been regarded as sensitive.
- Since 1970, the European Union and its forerunners have proposed a European Company Statute. If this is implemented, companies constituting

themselves under the European Companies Statute must have between one third and one half of their supervisory boards consisting of employee representatives. It would require full staff consultation on matters concerning takeovers, mergers, acquisitions, withdrawals, divestments and sell-offs.

- The existence of worker directors, works councils and other forms of participation compels other directors to seek consensus with employee representatives on all important issues.
- On matters other than worker representation, company directors now have greater duties and responsibilities under European Union regulations. Products and services must now be delivered to European standards. Quality assurance is now produced to the European standard ISO9000/9001 rather than BS5750. Responsibilities for health and safety, product performance and advertising standards are increasingly being set to cover the entire European Union, as are matters relating to health and safety at work. There is tighter regulation on the movement of particular goods – especially toxic and hazardous substances.
- It is also certain that the periods of appointment of company directors will become more restricted. At present, the majority of European Union countries insist that directors be re-elected every six years, and this seems likely to be the standard adopted for all Member States.
- Whatever the course of developments in this area, there will be much of interest to those having any concern about management and its problems. There are certain to be changes in statutory duties; and certain to be requirements in the shift of attitudes and approaches, and the constitution of boards of directors.
- There is no doubt that the introduction of employees on to the boards of directors of companies will have a profound effect on top-management decisions, whether the unitary board system is adopted or whether the two-tier system finds favour. Certainly it seems inevitable that the shareholders' directors will experience some constraints on their freedom to make decisions. One major concern is that board meetings may become talking shops, perhaps centred chiefly around management-staff relations and other purely domestic matters, instead of being platforms for the discussion of the future objectives of the company and its prosperity.

QUESTIONS

1 Compare the role of non-executive directors with the role to be played by full-time employees (both management and worker) on the board of a company. (ACCA)
2 Discuss what is meant by the term 'two-tier board of directors', and suggest plausible functions for each tier. (ACCA)
3 In what ways would the marketing manager of a large company be able to do a more effective job, if appointed to the board as a marketing director? How would these responsibilities change? (CIM)

■ ✓ 4 Objectives and policy

It was stated in Chapter 2 that the setting of objectives was the prerogative of top management, and that these would be formulated according to the accepted philosophies of the firm and its management. The same remarks were also applied to the creation of policies, indicating that objectives must be formulated first because they are *what* is to be done, and policies to pursue these objectives are formulated afterwards because policies lay down *how* the objectives are to be achieved.

4.1 Defining objectives

To travel with certainty it is necessary to have a goal, otherwise effort and energy is wasted journeying along byways and side roads which do not lead directly to the final destination.

The same remarks apply to organisations: they must have specific goals in order to use all their resources in the most effective fashion. These goals are the objectives of the firm, the end-results that have to be achieved.

- Unfortunately, as with much of the terminology of management studies, the word 'objective' is open to more than one interpretation and it is even occasionally taken to be inseparable from policy. So far as this work is concerned, therefore, it is necessary to define what is meant by this term, which can be stated as follows: 'Objectives are the goals a firm seeks to attain, and which constitute the principal reasons for its existence.'
- An organisation's objectives should be set out as clearly and as precisely as possible: only in this way can a certain path for the future be laid down. However, the precision of their formulation will depend a great deal upon the time over which they are expected to be achieved. Given the imponderables of the future, it would be unrealistic to try to formulate precise long-term objectives; these must be expressed in terms of ambition rather than accurate prediction. On the other hand, short-term goals can be formulated with a high degree of expectation of achievement, and on these the longer-term objectives can be built. Suppose for example, it is an objective to capture 20 per cent of the market in a particular product in five years' time: this target will be achieved by shorter-term objectives of a smaller percentage expressed in yearly steps. The short-term objectives can be tackled with greater precision than the five year ones.

- In any case, it has become evermore difficult to set long-term objectives with any certainty. Market fluctuations, the globalisation of all areas of business, and ever-increasing drives to maximise the return on scarce resources, all mean that any objective that is set for a period of time greater than two years hence must be kept under constant review.

4.2   Deciding objectives

The decisions as to what objectives to pursue are influenced by five principal factors:

(a) The philosophy of top management, and the balance of social, economic and stakeholder approach desired.
(b) Opportunities that present themselves, or which may present themselves in the foreseeable future.
(c) The resources that are or can be made available.
(d) The size, nature and complexity of the organisation.
(e) The size and nature of the markets in which business is to be conducted.

- The philosophical outlook of management has a bearing on objectives and their formulation less in regard to what goals to pursue than in regard to the vigour and single-mindedness of their pursuit. It is in this area that objectives and policy become very much interrelated. For example, if the objective were ultimately to achieve 100 per cent of the market, the purely economic philosophy would see no detriment in this. However, market domination of this order brings the other issues out into the open. Because of its domination of the computer software market, Microsoft is currently facing a series of legal battles concerning its ability to act in customers' and consumers' best interests. The proposed merger between British Airways and American Airlines has run into difficulties over route domination – where the view is taken that customers would have little real choice other than to fly with one of the merged airlines. The currently prevailing view is that such monopolies, or near monopolies, undoubtedly prejudice the welfare of sections of the community.
- A business or an organisation of any kind exists only so long as it fills a need, either present or able to be created, and at a price attractive to the market. In considering acceptable objectives, therefore, management will have to consider what goals will be viable both in the immediate and in the long-term future. The setting of objectives in consideration of present or future opportunities, in the modern world of rapid technological development and change, is a difficult and challenging exercise. All businesses succeed or fail in the market-place, and consumer tastes and expectations change rapidly under the pressures of increasing sophistication of products and marketing campaigns. Objectives must be set, therefore, in the knowledge that constant service and product development will be called for to maintain the momentum to make achievement possible. Similarly, organisations engaged in providing services of all kinds will also have to take account of changing consumer requirements in assessing the viability of long-term objectives.

- These factors lead to the forming of appropriate objectives for staff training, staff recruitment and other associated programmes so that the personnel needed are ready and available when required. Objectives set by opportunity possibilities must, in fact, be supported by departmental objectives in all the relevant areas such as sales, production, purchasing, research and development, administration, and personal and industrial relations. All of these objectives are interdependent and vital to the achievement of the main, ultimate, goals.
- Management must also relate its objectives to the resources it has available or is willing and able to make available. It must, therefore, ascertain the extent of the commitment required in pursuance of its objectives in labour, plant, buildings and material resources, not forgetting the necessary supporting administrative services. It must then determine to what extent current resources match up to the requirements of the goals to be set. Short- and longer-term secondary objectives will then have to be set, if necessary, for the financing of any additional resources that will be required.
- It will be seen, then, that the main goals of an enterprise rest on the fulfillment of a number of secondary and short-term objectives being satisfactorily achieved. The fewer the principal objectives the more concentrated can be the effort to achieve them, but that is not to say that an organisation must have only one purpose to be sure of succeeding. On the contrary, provided objectives are interrelated they can work to their mutual assistance, particularly if they are socially orientated. Thus, an objective to achieve an increased market share can be helped along by a realistic programme of sales training with the objective of improving the performances of sales representatives, and by an objective to gain the best customer and supplier goodwill.

4.3   Objectives and profit

Whatever the objectives laid down for a firm, however, there is no doubt that the objective of profit must be recognised as being of prime importance because only from profit can come the financial resources to support other, more socially inclined, objectives previously discussed. It is useful, therefore, to examine the benefits that profit brings to the firm, and these may be set out as follows:

(a) Only by making adequate profits can the firm survive. If the firm fails, all objectives will fail, so profit is the foundation upon which all else is built.

(b) Profit provides a measure of how efficiently the firm's resources are being used. Comparison with other firms' profit results also gives an indication of the relative success of the firm against others in the same industry, which in turn may initiate an investigation into the use of resources if the comparison is unfavourable.

(c) The performance of the management of a firm, particularly top management, can be assessed very much by the profit earned, particularly when measured against the capital resources employed.

(d) Equally, the pursuit of profit provides an incentive to management to succeed, and a spur to greater effort.

(e) It is the source of dividends for the shareholders or owners, and also provides the revenue to pursue objectives that are considered to be of benefit to the community.

(f) When new capital is required the performance of the firm in regard to earning profits is an important item in the deliberations of potential investors. This is also true when it is necessary to borrow funds from any of the usual sources of finance.

(g) Adequate profits not only provide income for the owners and financial resources for furthering the more socially orientated objectives, they also provide internally generated capital for the expansion of the business: self-generated finance is the least expensive source of funds and should have a high priority when considering objectives.

(h) Finally, adequate profit goes a long way to ensuring job security, and thus high morale, for the work-force.

4.4　Objectives of different types of organisation

All organisations must therefore concern themselves with setting objectives that are measurable and achievable over particular time frames. One acronym that is used for this is SMART:

Specific
Measurable
Achievable
Results-orientated
Time constrained

While the principles of objective setting remain the same, whatever the organisation and its business, the application of those principles may differ widely from sector to sector. Examples are as follows.

(a) Banks: While the need to make profits is an important consideration, the primary objective of a bank could be said to be to ensure the safety of the funds entrusted to it by its customers. Without the confidence of its customers in this respect its scale of operations would be severely curtailed because of its consequent inability to attract adequate funds. A further objective of high priority could be seen to be the support of local industry by providing loan capital in various ways, the availability of which would depend upon the previous priority.

(b) Building societies: The main objective of building societies is enshrined in the reason for their invention over a century ago – that is, to provide finance at reasonable cost to enable ordinary members of the community to become owners of their own homes. This main objective has given rise to a highly important second objective, which is to provide a safe form of investment for the small investor, which in turn has established a third objective of ensuring security for investors' funds. Emphasis is on the small investor in that practically all societies put a limit on the total funds they will accept from one individual, and this can be seen as an objective to help the average member of the community rather than the wealthy. Recent legislation in Britain enables building societies to expand their activities beyond the home mortgage market, but this in no way detracts from their main objective.

(c) Hospitals: The primary objective of hospitals run under the National Health Service (NHS) is to maximise the number of successful treatments. This in turn gives rise to the secondary, but important, objectives of a quicker turnround of patients, an improved utilisation of resources such as beds, wards and staff, and a reduction in costs without detriment to patients.

Nursing homes or hospitals run by profit-making organisations, such as those existing in the private sector in Britain and in America, also have profit as an objective, though patient care will still be the primary objective. The profit motive will have no place in the deliberations of hospital managements in the National Health Service, however, though the need to conserve financial resources will be important. Nevertheless, the development of hospital trusts in Britain as a result of government reforms of the National Health Service in the late 1980s has led to a market approach to hospital patient care. Because these trusts are no longer under the jurisdiction of their regional health authorities, but are entirely responsible for managing their own affairs, the cost of services to patients has greater emphasis than hitherto.

(d) Local authorities: Local government's primary objective is the provision of adequate services to the local community. The second can be seen to be the most economical use of the funds available. The welfare of the community in all its aspects very much influences the formulation of the objectives of local authorities, and therefore there can arise severe conflicts between the two objectives just mentioned. Hence, the objectives finally decided upon are usually very much modified from the original proposals just because of these conflicts.

Each area of activity for which local government is responsible, for example, education, roadworks, social services and so on, will have its own set of objectives and thus claims on funds, and so inter-activity conflict also arises. Local authorities' objectives are also very much subject to the influence of central government, which provides a substantial proportion of the finance local government spends, and also to the influence of local political and other pressures.

(e) Privately owned industries: The primary objectives here are long-term profitability, and profit maximisation and optimisation, based on a supply of good quality products which can be sold to the public at large at whatever level of price is necessary to ensure commercial viability. Closely allied to this are objectives concerned with product improvement and development, innovation, quality assurance and enhancement, after-sales service and maintenance. If industrial companies fail to take note of these points, they will be caught up and overtaken by those that do. Another objective, or commitment, which must be accepted by industry is the need to invest in production plant which is capable of turning out the products to ever-greater quality, and ensuring ever-increasing levels of return on that investment. Industrial objectives will also be concerned with ensuring the necessary supply flows of components and raw materials, and of ensuring the quality and certainty of distribution and outlet facilities.

(f) **Publicly owned industries:** industries were originally taken into public ownership in order to provide a better service to the community than could be provided in the particular sector by private enterprise. The overriding objective of nationalised industries is to ensure that the country continues to enjoy some domestic capability in a particular sector, rather than having to buy the particular products on the world or commercial markets.

(g) **Privatised industries:** many previously publicly owned industries were privatised; this process started in the 1970s, peaked in the mid to late 1980s, and continues at present. The objective of privatisation was to try and ensure that customers and consumers received better value for money through exposing the industries to the market place, rather than having them under the protection of government. This has not always worked in practice.

In Britain, because of the nature of the privatised industries – overwhelmingly in the transport, energy, utilities, and telecommunications sectors – objectives have to be based on using resources, and generating income and profits, founded on rules and regulations laid down by regulatory bodies. Objectives also have to be concerned with customer and consumer satisfaction, improved levels of output, and improvements in public perceptions and customer confidence.

(h) **Charities and voluntary organisations:** charities and voluntary organisations are established with a view to providing specific services to particular members of the community (especially the disadvantaged) for which no commercial market exists. Many charities – e.g. Oxfam, Amnesty International – are multinational organisations in their own rights, commanding huge budgets. Others – e.g. NSPCC, Help the Aged – have been subcontracted to carry out work hitherto carried out by local authorities. Others still are very small and localised, often founded by those to whom a particular tragedy has happened, so that work can be carried out to prevent it happening again. All charities and voluntary organisations are bound by their own constitutions, and subject to regulation by the Charity Commissioners. Both direction, and operational objectives must be drawn up so as to be compatible with the purposes for which they were originally established. Whatever the objectives established, it should be noted that the voluntary and charity sectors have greatly expanded in Britain in recent years, and the management of these organisations is becoming increasingly professionalised.

Despite the differences that emerge as the principal objectives of the various types of organisation just examined, as compared with profit-making industry in the private sector, nevertheless overall secondary objectives must be seen to be common to all forms of activity. Concern for staff, for the environment and for the community figure in the objectives of all forms of enterprise.

4.5 Departmental objectives

The corporate objectives of any type of organisation cannot be decided in isolation; their achievement rests on the performances of the various sections or departments comprising the whole. Therefore it is just as important that there be departmental objectives as that there should be corporate ones.

- Departmental objectives are formulated in much the same way as corporate ones and are subject to much the same constraints. The main difference is that a division, department or other section of an organisation works within the environment of that organisation, and the philosophies and constraints on its goals are conditioned by this fact in the same way as the wider, corporate objectives are to a large extent conditioned by the world outside the organisation.
- For example, a departmental manager will be concerned with the need to run the department as economically as possible, thus contributing to the overall profitability of the firm; and will also be concerned with the welfare of staff (a social responsibility); and with the necessity of co-operating and co-ordinating with other departments and divisions. Every worker from the managing director down is a stakeholder whose interests must be safeguarded (see Chapter 2). Thus departmental objectives must be set within this framework. In addition, departmental managers will also be inclined to set objectives that will be appropriate to their own personal aspirations and for their furtherance, as mentioned in Section 2.2 above.
- Because of their overriding responsibility to ensure the success and continued survival of the organisation, the directors or top executives of a firm, or the governing body of other types of organisation, must approve the sectional objectives put up by the managers concerned to make sure that they are properly within the framework of the total organisational objectives, and that no conflicts are apparent or likely to arise.

4.6 Policy-making

Just as objectives are *what* the organisation seeks to achieve, so policies are *how* these objectives are to be pursued; and as with the formulation of objectives so with the formulation of policies, this is the ultimate responsibility of the board of directors. In fact, it is generally the case that overall policies are laid down solely by the board.

- Policy formulation may be considered to be the laying down of company attitudes in the achievement of objectives, and to this extent the board will set the overall attitudes to be adopted in relation to all the functions of the business. In doing this it may decide that some areas such as marketing require a conciliatory policy to be pursued with customers, whereas in regard to purchasing it might consider a very firm line with suppliers should be adopted. However, it is unlikely that the members of the board will be experts in all the functions of the enterprise. It is thus generally recognised that in the larger concerns at least policy committees should be set up for the various functions to deliberate on the policies that should be adopted relative to the objectives set. Members of these committees are expert in their fields and are usually principal executive officers and their senior staff. Their knowledge and experience enables them to deliberate expertly upon the relevant facts and trends and to advise top management, with authority, on suitable policies to be pursued. Policy committees do not, as a general rule, have executive powers but are required to report their recommendations to the board: it is the board of directors who will make the final policy decisions.

- The following are some of the policy committees that might be found in large organisations:

(a) **The finance committee,** who will discuss policies as to sources of funds, whether to borrow money or float shares, what proportion of loan capital there should be to equity capital (i.e. owners' capital), whether loans should be short- or long-term, and whether loan finance should come from a commercial bank, a merchant bank or by way of debentures.

Such a committee might also consider policy in regard to granting customers credit, the extent of leniency in time allowed for payment, and so on. Their experience in the area of finance will enable the committee members to put forward a prudent but sensible policy for consideration by the board, who will then be able to lay down the appropriate official company policy on this matter.

(b) **The marketing committee,** who will deliberate on marketing policy, what markets to penetrate, and the extent of the possible penetration; on policies concerning customers such as company practice as to contract conditions, exchange and return facilities and after-sales service; on the proportion of the marketing budget to be spent on publicity and advertising; on the kinds of public relations exercises to be undertaken; and on the many other facets of the marketing activity.

(c) **The personnel committee,** who will give consideration to matters of human relations policy concerning recruitment and training; on promotion and whether this should be entirely internal or otherwise; on staff welfare and on pay and pensions.

(d) **The production committee,** who will consider production programme policy, output levels, quality-control tolerances, whether various components should be manufactured within the factory or whether some should be bought outside the firm, and similar matters.

- It should be noted that some aspects for consideration by these committees overlap: thus finance and marketing are both interested in expenditure on publicity, and on terms of credit for customers. Consequently there must be adequate liaison by all committees formed for policy-making purposes.
- These examples are sufficient to illustrate what can be done by committees to assist the board to formulate general policies for the organisation as a whole and, if it is a group of companies, for the whole group. In fact, even the formation of a group is a matter of policy: if the board decides to expand, does it do so by natural growth or by acquiring other companies? Does it want to diversify? A policy of acquisition is particularly helpful in this case.
- Out of the policy decisions arrived at should flow the following:

  (a) The structuring of the organisation so that it has the ability to carry out the activities necessary to achieve the objectives of the company as laid down by the board.

  (b) The provision of a sound and workable financial structure adequate to adjust to future needs, both for investment and for working capital.

  (c) Consideration for the technical aspects of the company, and for adequate research and development facilities to keep abreast of technological change and to cope with competition.

  (d) Adequate provision for the training of all staff, both administrative and technical, and for retraining all types of worker where operations alter owing to technical change. Such changes are prone to lead to the deskilling of some work (computerisation of an operation for example) or may require the learning of new skills or the adaptation of old ones, such as a typist changing from a typewriter to a word-processor.

  (e) Co-ordination of the efforts of marketing with production and finance.

  (f) The provision of after-sales servicing and of maintenance, where necessary. The question of guarantees is an important issue, as is the question of how long to go on making spare parts for old and obsolete models of manufactured goods where this applies.

  (g) There must be an awareness of the social responsibilities the firm has to the world at large and in particular to its customers, its suppliers and its staff.

  (h) Management development and training should also be of considerable concern to policy-makers.

4.7   The flexibility of objectives and policies

The question of how flexible objectives and policies should be is an important one.

- So far as the objectives of an organisation are the reasons for its existence then they can be said to be relatively unalterable. If the objectives set are unattainable owing to lack of resources, collapse of a market or governmental intervention, then that firm ceases to be able to function as it was set up to do. A change of objectives could therefore be seen as a change of organisation, even though it continues with the same name and the same directors and staff. A company set up to deal in scrap metal does not remain the same company if it forsakes that activity to make electric train sets.

- That is not to say that external forces may not impinge on the organisation to make it modify its objectives, but such modification would not be substantial. In the short term temporary modification of objectives to cope with a temporary bad trading period may be justifiable but the long-term objectives should remain.
- Policies, on the other hand, are much more flexible. These can be adjusted to deal with problems that arise in the pursuit of the firm's objectives or according to immediate operating conditions. For example, if the firm's cash-flow position becomes difficult and a policy of allowing extended credit to be taken by customers has been pursued, this policy can readily be modified so that stricter limits on credit are imposed: this more stringent policy can then be relaxed again, if thought desirable, when the cash position improves.

4.8 Communicating objectives and policies

Objectives and policies cannot be formulated without being communicated to those who will be affected by them.

- Since, on the whole, objectives remain static then these are usually incorporated in a statement of objectives and published in the document defining the constitution of the body concerned. In the case of a limited company, for example, they will be embodied in the objects clause of the memorandum of association, one of the legal requirements for the formation of a company.
- Policies, on the other hand, being determined ultimately by the governing body of the organisation, the board of directors in the case of a company, will be written into the minutes of the meeting at which they were decided. This, however, is usually insufficient publication and it is not unusual for there to be a statement of policy published for the organisation's staff. Other means of ensuring that policies are known to those whom they concern are by statements in staff handbooks, in written operating procedures issued to those engaged in specific routines, and by information given during staff training sessions. Policies affecting customers and suppliers are normally incorporated in conditions of sale and conditions of purchase, printed on sales order acknowledgement forms, invoices and purchase orders.

4.9 Policies by consent

While it is true to say that the policies of an organisation are laid down by its governing body, using advice offered by various functional policy committees, it must be recognised that nowadays control is by consent. Consequently, policies that are at variance with the desires of those they affect will stand little chance of being fully accepted and thus of working as effectively as they should.

- For example, promotion policies that are seen by staff as being inequitable are likely to be the source of discontent at the very least, and may lead to bad management – staff relations and thus inefficient operation. The result may also be a high turnover of staff with the consequent disruption of work and the cost of recruitment and training of new staff.
- Thus, while policy formulation may be a high-level activity, in effect it is extremely important that the views of those likely to be affected by the policies laid down should be sought and given consideration. Imposed policies are unlikely to work effectively: policies formulated by consent are likely to have a very good chance of success.
- Even when the policies affect those outside the organisation they must be acceptable to be able to be implemented. A policy to tighten up credit may meet with resistance simply in the form of customers going elsewhere to satisfy their needs. It is therefore not possible to formulate policies in isolation from the environment in which they are required to work.

QUESTIONS

1 What would be the major factors you would consider if you were drawing up the objectives of one of the following organisations:
(a) a hospital
(b) a bank
(c) a manufacturing company
(d) a nationalised industry. (ICSA)

2 (a) Review the differences between objectives and policies of organisations.
(b) Why are both an essential part of the managing and organising process? (IAM)

3 'Objectives are needed in every area where performance and results directly and vitally affect the survival and prosperity of the business' (P. Drucker). Discuss this statement and identify those key objectives you consider to be most important to a business. (IAM)

4 What is meant by 'the policies of an organisation', and how are policies formulated? What influence do the objectives of an organisation have on the policies decided upon?

5 Why may an organisation's goals change over time? Discuss, making reference to an example from your own experience. (ICSA)

6 In the area of business planning it has been suggested that 'objectives' need to be thought of in terms of:
(i) a central purpose;
(ii) responsibilities which an organisation has to its many stakeholders; and
(iii) a field of activities within which the organisation intends to operate.
(a) Illustrate the extent to which a changing environment makes an impact upon 'objectives' thought of in this way.

(b) Give three examples, with appropriate details, of how 'happenings in the environment' might change such objectives. (CIMA)

7 (a) Explain the meaning of the term 'policy', in a business context.

(b) Describe four areas which could be expected to be covered in the marketing 'Policy' of a firm engaged in the manufacture of industrial products. (CIM)

◼ ⬙ 5 Short-range and long-range forecasting

Having decided upon what its objectives are, the firm must plan how these are to be achieved. However, plans can be made only on the basis of what is expected to happen in the future, both within the organisation and in the world outside. Likely events and conditions must be forecast before plans for the attainment of objectives can be laid down. It is essential that all forecasting is carried out from the broadest possible perspective, and based on the best quality information available in the circumstances.

Gathering information is based on time. The longer the time available, the better the quality and volume of information gathered. It is also based on asking the right questions. For example, many market researchers fall into the trap of asking *'Would you buy this product'* rather than *'Will you buy this product'*, thereby gaining a generally favourable response, but with very little indication as to how large the actual market is.

Forecasting also means consulting the right sources of information, and where necessary, asking the right people their opinions. Information on which forecasting is based may be classified as:

(a) primary: gathered by the organisation for its own stated purposes;
(b) secondary: using information available from other sources for given purposes.

Forecasting is normally carried out on short-range and long-range bases. Both are necessary if the firm is to be successful in achieving its objectives, and maintaining its long-term viability.

5.1 Short-range forecasts

Except for totally unforeseeable events, short-range forecasts, which are normally taken to be those of a year or less, can be reasonably accurate, and can be seen rather as a prediction than as a statement of probability. It can also be seen that the shorter the term involved the more accurate the forecast is likely to be: a forecast for a week ahead in a very high percentage of cases will be absolutely accurate; for a year ahead the chances of variance are much greater.

- The sources for information and data for short-range forecasting are partly internal and partly external, and can be enumerated as follows:

(a) Information from internal sources

1 The most obvious information on which to base short-range forecasts is that of the actual achievement of the firm for the previous year (or part of year if the period is shorter) and the current year to date. This information is, or should be, readily available from the records kept by the organisation. Data should be available for the separate functions of the firm, such as sales, production and so on, and these activities should have analysed data in their records, such as the sales and trends for each product and for each market in which it is sold.

2 The length of time the firm's present products have been on the market and the expected remaining life of each based on the projected life span when each was launched.

3 The probability of the launch of new products during the term of the forecast, and the development stage reached on all such new ventures.

4 The probable cash-flow requirements as suggested by management's financial policies.

5 The probability of bringing new and more efficient machinery into use as determined by management's capital investment policies.

6 The cost of labour per product unit and the trend shown by the records; the cost of administrative staff.

7 The state of industrial relations within the organisation, time lost because of disputes, and the trends in this area.

8 The way the firm has maintained its market share, or whether it has increased it or has suffered a reduction.

(b) Information from external sources

1 The outlook in the market or markets in which the firm is involved: is demand growing or declining?

2 The behaviour of the firm's competitors: have they been aggressive and increased their share of the market, perhaps at the expense of the firm? Have they launched up-dated competing products?

3 The behaviour of price levels: have competitors' prices fallen in comparison to the firm's own? Have competitors held their prices level while the firm's have risen?

4 The type of product offered by competitors in the immediate past: have completely new designs been introduced, perhaps utilising the most modern technology, which have made the firm's products seem out of date?

5 Has the company much loan capital, or is it likely to need it? In this case the cost of money on the market will be very significant. In times of high inflation and high-interest rates this area of forecasting is of very great importance when forward planning is being discussed.

6 The possibility of government interference in the industry, threats of nationalisation or government regulation; the possible influence of government fiscal policy: such possibilities can be of enormous significance in the exercise of formulating forecasts.

If the organisation is concerned with international trade, either as an exporter or an importer, or simply has to rely on the import of materials or components, the following further items of information are required:

7   The state of international trade: is it buoyant or depressed?
8   Is there the likelihood of political instability in the areas of the world where the firm's interests lie?
9   The state of the international currency market: are rates of exchange adverse or favourable? Are they stable?
10 The foreign competition: are overseas competitors developing new and more attractive products? What is their pricing policy?

- Much information about the external factors influencing forecasting can be obtained from various government reports and statistics, the reports of independent economic forecasting organisations, from trade organisations, trade journals, and from the more informative daily and weekly newspapers such as the *Financial Times*, which regularly includes business and financial supplements.
- While short-range forecasting cannot be absolutely accurate it can often be nearly so and, naturally, the shorter the term the more accurate it is likely to be, as previously pointed out. Even so, even the shortest forecast can be made to be hopelessly wrong if a totally unforeseeable event should happen. The unprecedented steep rise in the price of oil in 1974, after decades of cheap oil, upset all forecasts, as did the prolonged drought in Britain in 1976. Accurate forecasts about the weather of more than a day or two ahead are notoriously difficult, and industries very susceptible to weather conditions, such as farming and the civil engineering industry, find even short-range forecasting far from easy. Short-range forecasts where fuel is an important ingredient can also be less than reliable due to the instability of prices, but the certainty of price rises can be assumed; the only doubt is the extent of the rises.

5.2   Long-range forecasts

Any forecasts for periods in excess of a year may be said to be long-range forecasts, and are generally accepted as such, though periods of between six months and three years might more properly be called 'medium-term forecasts'. Most authorities, however, restrict their definitions to short-range and long-range, and for the latter it can be said that the type of activity will, in most cases, determine how long is 'long'.

- To make this clear an oil company will commonly forecast for twenty to thirty years ahead, whereas a manufacturer of women's fashion wear would find it difficult to make any forecast exceeding two or three years hence, and even then would stand a good chance of being very wrong. This is because of the different environments within which each operates.
- An oil company works in a relatively stable market environment and the life of any particular oil field can be predicted with reasonable certainty.

Whatever the fluctuations in world oil prices there is a minimum level of demand that will inevitably be maintained because of the reliance on oil as a fuel by much of the industrial activity of the developed world. Only if some revolutionary new fuel were to be developed would the demand for oil change radically, and even then it would take a considerable time for industry to change over to using the new fuel because of the vast capital investment already tied up in oil-burning plant. Thus an oil company can look ahead for ten, twenty, thirty or even more years: its chief uncertainty would probably be in the area of discovering new oil fields to replace those running out. Here again, however, it takes a decade or more to bring a new oil field to full production. In such an industry, therefore, long-range forecasting over very long periods, while not easy, can have a fair degree of certainty in it. Another factor affecting very long-range forecasting for an industry such as oil production is the unstable political state of the world. Regimes that were once stable have now become unstable politically. Where these regions are major producers of vital raw materials and fuels, such as the Middle East for oil, very long-range forecasting becomes very difficult.

- On the other hand, a manufacturer of women's wear is faced with a very volatile market in which taste changes in the very short term. Even the most highly proficient fashion house can go sadly wrong in predicting even next year's fashions, and long-term forecasting is a near-impossibility. Yet some forecasting for a period of about twelve months is necessary because garments must be designed and then samples made and be ready for showing at least six months before the goods are put on sale to the public.

- Project work is also extremely difficult to forecast. The defence industry commissions new hardware – fighter aircraft, submarines – that may take up to fifteen years to come to fruition. Much defence hardware commissioned in the early to mid 1980s as a consequence of the Cold War was obsolete by the time it came to production in the mid 1990s because the Cold War had ended. Some civil engineering projects also suffer from this: when the M25 London Orbital motorway was commissioned, it was deemed adequate to cope with the traffic flows; by the time it was completed, traffic had increased to the extent that it could not cope with the traffic flows and this has led to constant rewidening. The Channel Tunnel is operationally extremely profitable: on the other hand, it stands no chance of recouping the capital outlay or the interest charges accrued.

- Public services also suffer from the same degree of uncertainty. Hospitals have to be able to predict the nature and volume of patients that they are going to be required to treat; and clearly this will vary if, for example, there is a sudden influx of elderly people into the area; or if, as the result of a new business starting up, there is an attraction of younger people with families into the area. The same influx may cause sudden increases in demands for school places, with which the local education authority may not be able to comply.

These examples clearly indicate that long-range forecasting is different for different activities, concerning both timespan and the possibility of anything approaching accuracy. Long-range forecasting is therefore fraught with difficulties. There is very little firm information that can be used with confidence; and the use of projection and extrapolation techniques have to be viewed also with extreme care. There have been great improvements in long-range forecasting techniques, greatly aided by information technology. Information based on a large number of variables and hypothetical sets of circumstances can be produced. What is at issue is the capability of different organisations to analyse and collate the information and to use it for their own purposes. However, it is clear that some sort of prediction of probabilities is essential, and if it is applied flexibility, it can at least be used as an illustration and guide to the probable, likely and possible range of outcomes that may occur in the future.

5.3 The effects of forecasting on general objectives

It was seen in Chapter 4 that the main objectives of an organisation are formulated as the basis of its existence, and it follows therefore that these objectives must be seen to be reasonably attainable.

- Such a supposition, however, must be based on something more valid than guesswork or pious ambition: in fact the basis is forecasts prepared to ascertain what are the likely to be the future possibilities for the organisation.
- Consequently, general objectives are very much dependent on the forecast made, both short-range and long-range, but particularly the later. If, for example, an increase in the sales of bicycles is predicted over a period of years then it can be confidently forecast that there will be an increase in the demand for the many ancillary items for bicycles such as bells, locks and chains, carriers, safety helmets and the like. An opportunity in one or more of these products is thus presented and any one of many manufacturers may be tempted to set up a specialist department, or even a subsidiary company, with the main objective of satisfying the expected demand for such products. Without the forecast the special objective would not arise.
- Similarly, a forecast can lead to a change in objectives, or a modification of them, though, as pointed out in Chapter 4, a fundamental alteration in effect changes the organisation. Thus, a forecast of a severe decline in the birth-rate could persuade a baby-buggy maker to forsake the objective of being a major manufacturer of prams: instead they might change to the manufacture of trolleys for supermarkets where the forecast is of significant growth. Such a change of main objective need not, however, change the supplementary objectives such as total of turnover, required return on capital and so on, albeit the organisation is no longer a manufacturer of baby buggies but of supermarket trolleys.

5.4   The business cycle

In preparing forecasts for the long term the phenomenon of the *business cycle* must be taken into account.

- An organisation can be said to be organic, and like all organisms it begins, grows and can then decline. Unlike natural organisms, however, its decline can be retarded or can be prevented altogether; in fact a firm can continue into perpetuity. Continued existence, however, can be maintained only if management appreciates the fact of the business cycle. Normally this cycle is taken to relate to a firm's products; they are designed and developed, launched, have a period of popularity and then decline because of the entry into the market of newer, simpler, cheaper or more attractive substitutes. A similar pattern of growth and decline can be found in all aspects of a business. Methods of manufacture, from being modern and up to date become obsolescent and inefficient, causing high costs and hence high prices for the products, which result in customer resistance and a diminishing market. Personnel practices, from being enlightened and far-sighted become dated and less acceptable to workers, resulting in deteriorating industrial relations. The manner of the acquisition of capital may cease to achieve the results of the past and may lead to under-capitalisation with its attendant problems of reduced cash flow and insufficient funds to renew old equipment.
- Two problems, then, assail the preparation of long-range forecasts: the prediction of when changes are likely to be required to ensure a continuance of the existence of the organisation, and the fact that different activities in the business have different time cycles. Much of the influence on the organisation that results in the decline of any sector is external – change of customer taste, new technology, changing interest rates on money – and some of these are hard to predict, particularly as to when change is likely to happen. It is incumbent on those responsible for forecasting, therefore, to keep abreast of developments in all relevant areas through publications, conferences and similar sources of information. Much guidance on the course of the business cycle can also, however, be gained from internal records, internal statistics and so on. For example, falling sales can be seen from sales records, while the reasons for this can often be determined from the reports of the sales representatives in the field. Falling productivity can often be discovered through comparison of present and past records, and also by interfirm comparisons. A high labour turnover as indicated in the personnel records can mean unsatisfactory personnel practices, even though previously they had been accepted as very good.

5.5   Technological forecasting

Probably the most fluid circumstances that the forecaster has to deal with is the rapid changes taking place in technology and its application to manufacturing and other processes. This has led to the need for technological forecasting, which can be defined as 'forecasting the expected technological development in a given area of activity over a given time'. It differs from business forecasting (which has been the subject of discussion so far) in that it can be more certain than business forecasting. This is so because the aims of technological research and development are normally well-defined. The required outcomes have been determined and the chief problem is not 'what' but 'when'; in other words the main uncertainty is the time the development will take to reach the stage of application. Even this is controllable to some extent by simple measures such as overtime working on the project, reducing testing times and similar expediencies.

- Some examples of technological change which have occurred and which should have been taken account of in the forecasts of the appropriate organisations are:
  1. The change from mechanical to electronic office machines and cash registers (one well-known company in this field neglected this change and is no longer in business).
  2. The change from leather soles to plastic compounds in footwear.
  3. The change from paper to plastic sheeting in a wide range of products such as food bags, carrier bags and so on. Similarly, the change from glass to rigid and flexible plastic sheeting in such items as roofs for lean-to buildings, some greenhouses, agricultural cloches and other products.
  4. The use of special plastics instead of steel or other metals where strength is required.
  5. Non-silver imaging in photography.
  6. Total electronic automation in such activities as stock-keeping and warehousing.

5.6   Forecasting in the public sector

On the face of it, there is no fundamental difference in forecasting in the public sector from that in the private sector. As elsewhere, forecasting will be based on the nature, volume and quality of information available, and the timescale within which it has to be gathered, analysed and considered.

- Public sector forecasting is subject to political constraints, and political conditions, over which those responsible for service delivery have little or no control.
- In recent years, changes in funding arrangements and structures have occurred, causing particular public services to be radically altered and re-directed.
- The demands for public services may, in some circumstances, be predicted with a fair amount of accuracy – for example, the number of five-year-olds in school in a particular area may indicate the likely number of places required

for further and higher education in the area in 10–15 years' time. However, this demand may or may not be satisfied; in particular, it may not be satisfied by the instruments of government which have different and diverging priorities which, in turn, change from time to time.

● All parts of public service activities are affected by political and economic crises; when these occur, the usual effect is to cut budgets and to drop those objectives further down the priority list. These crises cannot be predicted with any accuracy, and neither can their immediate and lasting effects. All public service forecasting has therefore to take account of this.

5.7 Forecasting and error

Forecasting, as pointed out already in this chapter, is subject to the probability of error, and the longer the range of the forecast the more likelihood there is that it will prove to be incorrect to a lesser or greater degree.

● Nevertheless forecasts are essential for planning the activities of the organisation. What, then, can be done to reduce the incidence of error to the smallest possible degree? The answer lies in examining past forecasts and comparing them with what actually occurred. From these comparisons it is possible to assess the percentage error that has shown itself in each case: this can then be projected into future forecasts. This will not, by any means, make future predictions accurate, but will tend to reduce the amount of the variance between forecast and actual performance.

● There are many reasons for errors occurring in forecasts, most of them subjective. They include:
  1 Undue optimism or pessimism, which prejudice the forecaster's judgement.
  2 Unwillingness on the part of the forecaster to accept the conclusions that the data he has been using indicate.
  3 Faulty and inaccurate assumptions from the data and information the forecaster has been using. This may arise from a combination of 1 and 2 above.
  4 Unforeseen events, such as a significant change in government policy or a change of government, prolonged strikes, political or military activity abroad.
  5 Collapse of markets.
  6 Inability to satisfy market demand.
  7 Failure on the part of managers to accept the forecaster's judgements.
  8 Erroneous gathering of information.
  9 Not taking a broad enough perspective.
  10 Providing the 'required' answer (e.g. that which the forecast commissioner is seeking), rather than the actual information.
  11 Effects of merger, takeover, acquisition, divestment or withdrawal.

5.8 Mathematical methods of forecasting

In order to take some of the uncertainty out of forecasting, there has been a much greater emphasis on the use of mathematical methods of determining probability, and possible and likely outcomes of particular situations. As stated above, the use of these techniques is greatly assisted through computer and electronic information technology. However, these are properly the tools of the practitioner in operational and market research and forecasting, and can be mis-leading if used by the inexpert. What managers need in these situations is infor-mation presented in ways that make forecasting and analysis as straightforward as possible. Ultimate responsibility for the choice of courses of action based on forecasting remains with managers; they must therefore have confidence in those that they employ to carry out the forecasting, gather information and make analyses. Research specialists act in an advisory capacity to managers. Computer software for the purpose of information analysis and forecasting is available off the shelf; or it may be designed by specialists for use by particular organisations. Such software can greatly assist forecasting and planning in the following areas.

- Projects management: concerning the projected and possible usage of a par-ticular project (e.g. public facility) once it is completed.
- Market research: assessing the likely attractiveness, and therefore demand, for particular products and services.
- Human resource management: predicting skills, cuts and shortages; and the effects on work-force and labour availability if a major new employer was to move into the area, or if a major employer was to move out of the area.
- Investment forecasting: based on the availability of capital, future exchange rates, likely and possible interest rates; and based on the extent of competi-tion for that form of capital.
- Economic forecasting: based on projections of peoples' capability and will-ingness to spend in the areas under consideration; this is of especial import-ance in the white goods and motor-car industries.
- Marketing forecasting: projecting the likely effects of particular marketing, advertising and public relations campaigns.
- New product development: the effects of introducing new products on the existing product portfolio.
- Pricing policies: the effect on the market at large of price rises or reductions.
- Product and service extension: the projected effects of improving or reducing service levels offered in support of the firm's activities.

Those who are interested in the techniques of forecasting, quantitative analyses for managers and operational research, are advised to consult specialist textbooks on the subject, such as T. Lucey, *Quantitative Techniques* (D. P. Publications).

QUESTIONS

1 Discuss the ways in which short-range forecasting differs from long-range fore-casting, and explain the reasons for this.

2 What are the factors that forecasters normally take into account when developing short-range forecasts? How much reliance can be put on historical data in this connection?

3 Distinguish between business and technological forecasting. How does technological forecasting assist management to respond effectively to technological change? (ICSA)

4 What differences, if any, are there between the bases for long-range forecasting in the public sector as compared to the private sector? Do these differences hold good over all the public sector, and if not, why is this?

5 One of the essential tasks of a marketing department is to prepare a detailed forecast of sales for a future period. What is the purpose of such a forecast
(a) to a production department?
(b) to an accounting department? (CIM)

▪ Ⅿ 6 Planning

If an organisation is to achieve the objectives it has set itself then it must plan courses of action that will enable it to attain these goals. Without proper planning, the organisation is at the mercy of management whims and external pressures, and it will quickly lose sight of its objectives. Yet it is surprising how many businesses do not in fact have significant forward plans but are content to carry on operations virtually on a day-to-day basis. Conversely, in public services, planning is often far too rigid, taking no account of likely and possible political and economic changes.

- Lack of planning does not make for efficient use of resources. Some people take the view that, because economic and political world conditions are so turbulent, it is impossible to plan for anything except in the very short-term. Nothing could be further from the truth. The greater the uncertainties, the more important it is to plan what can be planned, and to be aware of those things that can upset the intended direction.
- The most important feature of planning is flexibility so that modifications can be made when necessary. Any changes that do become necessary can then themselves be properly planned for.
- Above all, if this flexible and forward-looking approach is taken, contingencies, crises and emergencies can be identified early and dealt with on a properly planned basis. It is also much easier to identify and assess the particular nature of risk in a given set of circumstances.

6.1   Short-range planning

- Plans that are to run for periods of up to 6–9 months come under the heading of short-range planning. Many of them fall into the category of everyday decisions, especially if they cover only a few days or weeks, and they can be expected to run precisely as predicted. Thus, the work-rate and material requirements for decorating an office suite over the span of three weeks can be planned with the virtual certainty that no divergence will occur to the plan, or will be needed. This would be a contract where the work would be done under cover, not subject to the vagaries of the weather, and the time span is so short as almost to obviate any contingency likely to upset the plan.
- If the contract were for a complex of office blocks and the work time a year, though the very length of time might mean contract planning would be

subject to some unforeseen circumstances, nevertheless it could be assumed that the work should be able to be carried out exactly according to plan.

- So, with short-range planning there is every possibility that few adverse contingencies will arise to upset the plan, and the shorter the period of the plan the less likelihood there will be of emergencies arising. Nevertheless, flexibility is still needed in even the shortest plans. In the first example the unexpected illness of a specialist supervisor might mean the work would not be able to continue. Two circumstances then arise which need attention. The first is the requirement to complete the work in the allotted time. The second is to find remunerative work for the staff who are unable to carry on at that site, because of the incapacity of their supervisors, until such time as they can again return to the interrupted contract. So contingency plans are required; that is, flexibility in planning, even for the shortest time span.

- A firm engaged on the three-week contract would, undoubtedly, redeploy the staff on another site in order that this valuable resource should be profitably employed. Plans to finish the contract in three weeks would have undoubtedly been made on the assumption of normal working hours. Depending upon the seriousness of the supervisor's illness, the management would either abandon work on the site if the indisposition were reckoned to last only a day or two and recommence on the supervisor's return, or would deploy another gang either of their own or of a sub-contractor if the illness were likely to be protracted. In either case the contract time would be met by working overtime; another deviation from the original plan.

- Over longer periods even more flexibility would be needed in connection with the planning exercise, and the more vulnerable the subject of the planning to outside influences the more flexible must be the plans drawn up in pursuance of any specific objective. In the second example cited, if this were exterior and not interior decoration the weather over a year would certainly interfere with the initial planning.

- In most cases of short-range planning contingency plans can be laid to cope with commonly experienced eventualities so that alternative action can be taken quickly if circumstances so require. Where the time span is relatively short the totally unforeseen eventuality is comparatively rare.

6.2 Long-range planning

- Long-range planning takes into account periods in excess of a year and may cover periods of any number of years according to circumstances. Circumstances include the type of industry concerned and the manner in which it operates. An engineering contractor, for instance, involved in the construction of off-shore oil rigs would plan on a contract basis, the term being the length of time it would normally take to construct a rig. These plans would be largely operational over, say, two or three years and would have to take account of the many imponderables likely to occur during that time, such as labour disputes, material shortages, economic climate and weather conditions. Experience gained on previous contracts would assist in formulating these plans.

- They would, of course, be concerned with other long-range planning, for instance the continued existence of the enterprise on the completion of the current work. So in such an industry long-range plans can be put into two categories. The first is where actions are severely circumscribed by contract conditions, particularly in regard to the time element, and flexibility of manoeuvre in the event of necessary deviation is severely limited. The second category is that where planning is in the longer term and, simply, is concerned with the survival of the organisation. In this case maximum flexibility is required. The goal is not the completion of a specific contract, but the continuing effort required to attain the organisation's major objectives.

- An oil company, on the other hand, would enjoy greater flexibility in both its short- and long-term planning. The engineering firm is bound by contract and has a specific cut-off point: failure to comply may attract severe cash penalties in favour of the oil company for which it is working. The oil company itself is not so tightly constrained. True, failure to achieve a planned date for the installation of a new oil rig would result in loss of revenue, but the oil company is answerable only to itself. Complete flexibility in the case of delays might mean that it could increase production at another oil field while the delays on the new one were resolved.

- These examples illustrate some of the difficulties encountered in long-range planning. Particularly for the oil industry, where long-range planning can mean period of up to ten, twenty or even thirty years, account has to be taken of changes in demands for the company product, changes in price, currency fluctuations, and world social, economic and political stability. In this, and other industries where the long range is so vital, companies work to a broad direction and strategy, which is the subject of constant monitoring, review and update.

- All planning activities must consider the nature or risk involved in particular activities. As well as considering the social, political and economic factors indicated above, it is also necessary to be aware of likely and potential developments in market size, customer and consumer demand, and changes in production technology over the period of time in question; and the longer the range of planning, the greater the necessity to be aware of these factors.

6.3 The relationship between forecasting and planning

Successful short-range and long-range planning are both based on accurate forecasting. Those responsible for developing plans for an organisation's future will inevitably rely heavily on forecasts. These are then combined with their own experience and knowledge of their firm, its industry, and its markets. All planning and forecasting has therefore to be seen in its own particular context. All planning and forecasting techniques require adaptation to the particular set of circumstances if they are to work effectively.

- When plans are implemented, performance must be monitored and compared with what was intended, and the reasons for deviations and differences discovered and analysed. Forecasting should therefore be looked upon as a continuing exercise, fully integrated with both short-range and long-range planning. By doing this, it is possible to ascertain the all-round level of expertise in the planning process and where any modifications need to be made.

6.4 Evaluating pre-planning forecasts and information

There are two circumstances that must be considered when monitoring the progress of plans, and also when evaluating the original process of planning. These are the volume and the suitability of the information and data gathered.

- Gathering the information on which to base the planning operation is rather like any other research: there is often a tendency to collect too many statistics, forecasts and other materials that will be likely to affect the planning. This has two effects. First, the plans may be woolly, imprecise and difficult to understand. In these cases, they are likely to contain too much detail and so the clarity of purpose gets lost. Second, because of the abundance of information, no clear course of action may present itself.
- It also occurs that too little information is gathered. This has the effect of reducing the planning process – and therefore, the overall direction of the firm – to guess work. Contingencies arise that could easily have been foreseen if only the planning process had been properly carried out.
- If the wrong information is gathered, the planning process is of no value at all. This comes about as the result of the wrong questions being asked, misunderstandings between planners and those responsible for organisational direction, and a lack of clarity as to what is truly required. When it is felt that this is happening, all those involved should ensure that whatever issues necessary are clarified before proceeding.
- Whatever information is gathered must be capable of use by those with planning responsibilities. In the past there has been a tendency to concentrate on volume rather than quality and value of information. Whatever is produced must be capable of summary in such a way that planners and managers can understand, so that it can be used in planning and decision-making processes.
- Planners therefore need to examine critically each forecast and other material, and to make sure that these are set in the context required. Any material that does not fit in this way must be discarded. Contradictions and variations must be evaluated so that decisions can be made as to what is really relevant. All planning processes must be able to differentiate between prejudice, opinion and fact, and to ensure that the balance is right in every set of circumstances. In particular, the source of opinions, however well informed, must be seriously evaluated before decisions are taken to proceed on those bases.

6.5 Levels of planning

All activities at every organisational level should be planned for, whatever the time span. The following types and levels of planning are normally identified.

(a) **Corporate planning:** concerned with securing the long-term viability, profitability, and development of the organisation. This is dealt with extensively in Chapter 7.

(b) **Strategic planning:** often called top-level planning and carried out by top management – the board of directors or other governing body. It considers the long-range objectives and policies of the organisation and is concerned with corporate results. Corporate and strategic planning act as the basis for all other managerial and operational planning activities. Though it is concerned mostly with the long range, it must be capable of being broken down into shorter-range sub-objectives, and short and medium-term activities.

(c) **Policy planning:** this concerns the 'how' – the principles and approaches by which the organisation and its undertakings are to be carried out. Policy planning sets standards of behaviour and performance, and is concerned with management style and approach. Policy planning is also concerned with social and ethical responsibilities, as well as the economic.

(d) **Tactical and operational planning:** this is carried out by senior executives, in consultation between themselves and with their departments, divisions and functions. This is overwhelmingly concerned with planning the deployment of resources to best advantage. It has therefore both short- and long-term concerns. Its attentions are devoted to the step-by-step attainment of the organisation's main objectives, or the segmentation of long-range plans, strategy and direction. It concerns relationships between functions and departments, as well as setting operational standards for each.

(e) **Activity planning:** the concern of departmental managers and supervisors. Its primary purpose is the short term, involving departmental operations and group and individual assignments. It also establishes performance controls. However, it must also have regard to the longer term, in that whatever is carried out on a day-to-day basis, must be capable of assimilation into the organisation's overall direction.

(f) **Functional balance:** this is both long-range and short-range. The reason for addressing this at the planning stage is to ensure that the correct and desired balance between primary and support activities is maintained, and that whatever administrative procedures are devised contributes to the overall business performance of the organisation, rather than acting as a drain on its resources.

(g) **Project planning:** this is concerned with ensuring that all resources necessary are available when project work is envisaged. Some organisations – e.g. building, civil engineering, information systems – have their business based almost entirely in project work; however, most organisations commission projects – e.g. the installation of new information systems, relocation, new production technology – during the course of their existence. It is usual in these cases for project teams and groups to be commissioned, and necessary resources gathered together to ensure that the particular matter in hand can be successful over whatever period of time is necessary. Project planning is therefore concerned with both the long range and the shorter range.

6.6 Planning relationships

The different levels and types of planning of necessity interact with each other. The following should be noted.

- Operational planning may impose restraints on tactical plans because of practical difficulties arising from time to time. The effect of a necessary alteration in an operational plan, because of the short term involved, is likely to be more of an inconvenience than a reason for abandoning a tactical plan. Operational plans are unlikely to have any effect on strategic planning, as they are relatively remote from each other. On the other hand, strategic planning will, although remote, have some effect on operational planning because the mode of operational activities will to some extent depend upon strategic plans.
- There is a closer relationship between operational and tactical planning because the former arises very directly out of the latter. A change of tactics may very well impose adjustments to operational plans. For example, a small change in the design of a product – a tactical decision to combat new competition – may well cause production plans at shop-floor level to be drastically revised. Unless, on the other hand, tactical planning has been very rigid, modifications in operational planning can often be absorbed at this level without difficulty.
- A similar situation exists between strategic and tactical planning. The strategic plan may remain constant despite the fact that the tactics employed to achieve it may have to be modified from time to time. In other words, tactics can change without alteration to the strategic plan becoming necessary. However, if the strategic plan alters, the tactical plans will almost certainly have to be changed to suit the new situation.
- Two other distinctions should be noted in connection with the relationship between strategic and tactical planning. First, strategic planning is concerned with the principal objectives that have been set for the organisation and with what to do to achieve these goals. Second, tactical planning accepts the objectives set by top management and concentrates on ways to bring the strategic plans to successful fruition. Strategic planning is concerned with ends: tactical planning is concerned with the means to achieve those ends.

6.7 The principles of planning

Whatever the planning period certain principles are involved, which can be set out as follows:

(a) The purpose of the plan must be determined. Planning cannot be done in a vacuum and the goals to be achieved must be clearly identified.

(b) Plans must be formulated on clearly defined data and information. Forecasts help in this direction but other sources must also be used, such as past records, performance experience and the like. The planners' own past experiences can be utilised, but in this connection it is vital to separate fact from opinion or prejudice. However, an excess of source material must be avoided if planning is not to become too complicated.

(c) Plans of the various sections of the organisation must be co-ordinated. The effects of one department's plans on those of others must be recognised and accommodated. In principle, this is relatively easy to achieve on a short-range basis through continuing consultations and communications. It is harder to achieve in the long term because of the elements of risk and factors outside the organisation's control.

(d) Standards to be achieved must be set. Performance must be monitored. Failure to attain predetermined standards is always detrimental to organisational and departmental, divisional and functional performance.

(e) Flexibility is essential so that modifications can be made.

(f) Communication and consultation at all stages in the planning process, and in all aspects, must always take place. Involvement and understanding by all concerned is essential if activities are to be successful.

(g) Plans must be achievable. Over-ambition must be avoided as this leads to discouragement and frustration when failure inevitably occurs. On the other hand, under-ambition provides no incentive and encourages inefficiency.

(h) Planning activities must be conducted in such a way so that when they are implemented, their progress can be measured. For this reason, they should be as specific and precise as possible, and also time and resource constrained.

6.8 Special considerations for long-range plans

In addition to the foregoing general principles, long-range planning has to concern itself with a number of other factors mainly impinging on management from outside the enterprise.

- These include recognised or conjectured trends in the political, social or economic climate; increasing concern for the environment, particularly where pressure groups are very active; general international and national trends in the markets in which the enterprise is engaged; changes in social habits; the availability of external investment; threats from take-over predators; and external competitive pressures.
- The high levels of expertise and past experience of planners is vital. So also is their ability to produce informed judgements based around the situation as they understand it. It is the duty of all planners to become as expert as possible in the vagaries and pressures that surround their particular industry, as well as the ways in which their organisation carries things out.
- Japanese and other Asian companies that have invested in the West – e.g. Nissan, Sony, Toshiba – have taken the view that, if they are to be successful in the West for a long period of time, hitherto accepted levels of investment are

simply not adequate. A substantial part of their long-range planning is therefore concerned with investment appraisal, together with a commitment to invest in high-quality staff, excellent production technology, and high levels of service as a prerequisite for the formation of long-range plans.

- Closer to home, companies that have invested successfully in new areas of activity have done so on the basis of meticulous long-range planning. For example, when Virgin went into the airline business, the company first hired those with expertise in all aspects of airline operation from different airlines. They then carried out a full appraisal of the airline market to see which were the niches in which they could operate profitably. Thirdly, they secured the long-term investment and backing necessary to ensure that their presence could be successfully established. Fourthly, 'measurement points' were established at each step of the way so that the company could measure its performance to date; account for any diversions or unforeseen circumstances; and to measure and assess the seriousness of specific issues that had arisen.

6.9   The importance of planning

Operational and short-range planning are important because they relate directly to the day-to-day activities of the organisation. No enterprise can function at all effectively if daily, weekly or monthly functioning is left just to chance. This type of planning is also mainly carried out at the lower levels of management and supervision, with the emphasis on the practical.

Long-range planning, both strategic and tactical, is also of vital importance, and is the only means of setting and keeping an organisation on course for the attainment of its principal objectives. The policies and objectives of the concern are laid down by its governing body: planning will bring out what resources will be required, will suggest the organisational structure needed to pursue these policies and objectives, and will be instrumental in promoting the controls necessary to carry out the plans formulated.

- Every aspect of the organisation should be subject to planning in order to make the utmost use of resources, to stimulate programmes for staff and management training, to promote sales and financial targets, to ensure a reasonable return on capital and investment, and generally to guide the enterprise in the attainment of its objectives.
- The development of well-considered plans enables management at all levels to take a hard look at itself and the organisation in which it operates. Management is required to examine its activities in the light of the past and the possibilities for the future, and to justify its decisions before they are implemented.

6.10   The responsibility for planning

- Operational and very short-term tactical planning is usually carried out by the manager or supervisor actually concerned with the activities involved. Thus, the office manager will formulate the plans necessary for providing office services over the short term, possibly subject to constraints such as limits on expenditure, staff recruitment and other matters under their direct control. The office supervisor will then take the responsibility of planning the operations over the day or the week.

- Long-range tactical planning will be carried out by the more senior executives in the areas such as marketing and production. In these cases, however, they will probably be aided by their immediate subordinates who will, in turn, have at their command reports and other information concerning operational capability. Forecasts in the areas concerned will also be taken into account, and these may be, in a large organisation, the output of a special department staffed by experts, such as operational research. In smaller organisations senior executives and their immediate staff will have the responsibility for gathering the necessary forecasts through perusing trade journals, government reports and the like, as indicated in 5.1 and 5.2 above.

- Long-range strategic planning will be done by the governing body with the assistance and advice of its senior executives. Forecasts from internal and external sources will be utilised as well as analyses of the past performance of the enterprise, and managerial experience.

- The establishment of planning departments may raise difficulties. Planners may take into consideration information and forecasts to which other executives have not had access. Executives who have the responsibility of operating the plans may not be aware of the precise information on which the planning was done, and particularly what was omitted from the planner's deliberations. Long-standing executives, used to doing things their own way, may feel resentment at having plans imposed on them by others. The planning may be carried out in such a way that its use and value is not immediately or readily perceived; this is a great criticism of think-tanks and other supposedly expert bodies. Planners may come up with proposals that are at variance with the preferred direction of the chief executive and senior managers. The rest of the staff may also not understand what is required of them, and why they are being asked to do particular things, or do them in a particular way.

    All of this may lead to disharmony and the detriment of the successful implementation of plans and direction. It is essential therefore that all those involved in planning, at whatever level, maintain close communication links with those whom their work is going to affect.

- Finally, as may happen with any department, those responsible for planning may be inclined to view their activity as an end in itself rather than as a service for the benefit of the organisation and its progress. Those responsible for planning should themselves have aims and objectives, capable of measurement and evaluation. The success or otherwise of what they propose should always be evaluated. Their activities must also be integrated with those of the rest of the organisation, rather than being viewed in isolation.

6.11 Monitoring

Monitoring the planning process needs consideration. Chapter 12 deals in detail with various aspects of control. However, it is useful to note the following which have specific connections with planning activities.

- The Gantt chart is relevant to short-term plans and is used to set out planned progress against actual achievement so that any deviations can be seen in good time and steps taken to correct them. An example of a Gantt chart is shown in Figure 12.1.
- Network analysis is also relevant, both to short-term and long-term planning. A number of techniques fall under this heading, and these can be grouped under: Critical Path Network (CPN); and Programme Evaluation Review Technique (PERT). Both techniques are concerned with defining the critical path or minimum timescale for given sets of activities. CPN is calculated on the assumption that completion time can be forecast precisely. PERT assumes that absolute accuracy is not possible, as explained in **24.2(d)** below.
- Techniques for risk forecasting and planning have greatly improved over recent years. Companies now have a much greater awareness of what can possibly go wrong when they go into particular areas of activity, or new markets – especially concerning the social, economic and political factors indicated above.
- Companies are much less inclined to take Return on Capital Employed (RoCE) as the only measures of success (i.e. the economic – see 2.1 above), and therefore planning techniques take into account a much broader range of factors, including the availability of labour markets, availability of people with particular skills or expertise, and availability of production processes.
- Percentage rates of return, and percentage shares of markets, are now very much more difficult to quantify, especially in the medium to long-term. Planning and forecasting techniques have therefore to take much more serious account of changing patterns and priorities in consumption; changing sizes and locations of customer bases; and likely and possible improvements made by competitors in their field.
- The final decision on the adoption and implementation of all proposed planning activities must lie with the chief executive. It is therefore essential that all chief executives understand the process, and have confidence in those who carry it out. They are ultimately responsible for the successful achievement of objectives and the long-term well-being of the organisation.
- The importance of planning cannot be over-estimated. In large measure, those responsible for planning decide the future of the organisation. The plans they draw up set its course in both the long and the short term, assess the opportunities and consequences that may arise, and establish the basis for short- and long-term successful activities.

QUESTIONS

1 What are the main components of long-range planning and to what extent should planning include judgement, experience and even intuition? (ICSA)

2 Do you think that the effectiveness of any public or private sector organisation can be improved by long-range planning? State your reasons. (ICSA)
3 Make a case for the establishment of a long-range planning unit in an organisation where the management feels that even its one-year plan is rarely on target. (IAM)
4 Your managing director has attended a conference at which a speaker said that long-term strategic planning was obsolete, and is naturally concerned about this comment.

   You are required to draft a report to your managing director stressing the benefits of long-term strategic planning and examining the case for its abolition. (CIMA)
5 Who has executive responsibility for long-term planning in a commercial enterprise? What may be the main obstacles to the development of long-term planning into a worth-while discipline with set procedures? (CIMA)
6 It is suggested that longer-term planning is currently inappropriate because of the rapid rate of environmental change and that there is an inherent rigidity in all planning which could sap initiative.
   (a) What is your view of this suggestion?
   (b) What may be done to reduce planning 'rigidity'? (CIMA)
7 Illustrate with examples, the essential differences between strategic, operational and contingency planning. (CIM)

▮ ▼ 7 Corporate and strategic planning

Chapter 6 looked at short- and long-range planning, the different types of planning, and the different levels of responsibility. While it is essential that each of these activities takes place, there is great potential for the fragmentation of planning activities; and this can result in organisational conflict, and divergence of interests in various parts of the enterprise.

It is therefore necessary to have a cohesive organisational and integrated approach overall. In recent years, many authorities on management, and professional institutions, as well as organisations, have come to recognise the great value of effective corporate strategy and planning.

7.1 A definition of corporate planning and strategy

Effective and successful corporate planning and strategy come about as the result of systematic and comprehensive processes of long-range planning taking account of the resources and capability of the organisation, and the opportunities in the environment within which it has to operate. As well as being composed of different activities, the corporate planning process must view the organisation as a total unit.

- Kenneth R. Andrews, a leading management academic, in *Business Policy* (Irwin, 1988) defined corporate strategy as 'the process by which the direction, policy, and activities in an organisation are woven together to secure the long-term viability of the particular organisation'.
- Securing the future of any organisation requires taking the long-term view. Corporate planning and strategy is also concerned with future possibilities and prospects in the broadest context – it must consider possible mergers, takeovers, acquisitions, withdrawals and divestments; as well as the extent, durability and viability of the markets in which it operates, and the resources that it has at its disposal. For this to be successful, strategy and corporate planning must frequently be monitored, reviewed and evaluated. It is also essential that strategy and planning can be compared with performance and results, so that changes, alterations and modifications can be made if necessary.

7.2 The obligations of corporate planning and strategy

The obligations imposed upon those responsible for preparing and implementing corporate strategy are extremely important. It requires a full and wide-ranging examination of the complete range of factors essential to survival and long-term prosperity. The balance of these factors varies from organisation to organisation, and within individual organisations from time to time. These factors always include the following.

(a) Identifying all the attainable long-term objectives required.
(b) Prioritising the long-term objectives.
(c) Evaluation of the internal resources of the organisation, including finance, marketing expertise, productive capacity, technology and staff.
(d) Appraising the external environment of the organisation within which it operates, including the economic environment, present and possible future government action, and legislation.
(e) The need to establish, as precisely as possible, the organisation's competitive and operational positions. There are a range of techniques available to do this effectively and these are outlined below.
(f) The need to establish formal monitoring, review and evaluation procedures.
(g) The need to recognise that, because they are long-range, corporate planning and strategy require constant updating and modification in pursuit of the chosen direction.
(h) The need to ensure that all activities, primary and support, are co-ordinated effectively.

7.3 Corporate and strategic activities

Strategy is concerned with the overall direction and long-term well-being of the organisation. In large and complex organisation, therefore, it is carried out by experts in analysis of each of the areas indicated, working in close conjunction with top management. The following factors have to be appraised.

(a) An appraisal of the existing internal situation of the enterprise. This involves an examination of the financial position; return on investment; the productive capacity; marketing effectiveness; product range, research and development; the expertise of the labour force; and investment, planning and appraisal.
(b) Reviewing the organisation's position in the market place. The organisation needs to know whether its position is strengthening or weakening, and the reason for this. It also needs to know whether the market is expanding, steady or contracting, and the reasons for this.
(c) Evaluation of present, future and potential competition.
(d) Assessment of the economic factors surrounding the organisation's activities.

(e) A review of factors outside the organisation's control – including over-whelmingly, government activity and political priorities; and also including shifts and changes in consumer demand and confidence and other such factors in the world at large.

(f) A review of the legal aspects of operating and organisation, including laws that are likely to be enacted that may influence industrial relations, credit operations, advertising, manufacturing, the environmental aspects of the firm's operations.

(g) A review of the effects of immediate and possible future governmental action, including taxation policy, VAT, licensing regulations, import and export regulations, and interest rates.

(h) A review of the effect of immediate and possible European Union action, along the lines indicated above, and including the creation of the Euro.

Information gathered on this basis is the starting-point for formulating strategy, and for corporate planning. Each area must be addressed, though the emphasis placed on each area will vary from organisation to organisation. Specific techniques can then be used to address particular issues, and to parcel up the range of organisation information available, so that a much greater understanding can be raised. These specific activities include SWOT; STEP; customer analysis; market analysis; and the 'five forces' approach.

7.4 SWOT

SWOT is the acronym for strengths, weaknesses, opportunities and threats. In this method, the information that is gathered is parcelled up under four headings – strengths, weaknesses, opportunities and threats. It may also be used as the basis for brainstorming and other creative activities.

(a) Strengths
In this area will be found all the advantageous aspects of the organisation. Examples would be exceptional customer goodwill and brand loyalty, highly efficient technical staff, adequate financial resources and an enthusiastic sales force. The strengths represent the foundations on which continued success can be built.

(b) Weaknesses
These must be honestly investigated and faced because they represent retarding influences on the success and growth of the organisation. Remedies must be sought to overcome them. Weaknesses occur in all areas of an enterprise, some examples of which could be obsolescent machinery, no provision for senior management succession, inadequate research and development facilities resulting in lack of new products to succeed current production models. What remedies to apply would depend upon the weaknesses revealed. In the given examples the organisation should consider carefully investment in new machinery, the promotion of management training schemes, and increased investment in research and development.

If finance is a strength then these remedies would not be difficult to implement: if a weakness this would have to be given attention first.

(c) Opportunities

Whereas strengths and weaknesses emanate chiefly (though not entirely) from inside the organisation, opportunities are usually external. They may come about fortuitously or by the application of some research. The important point is that they should be recognised and grasped firmly when they arise. Some examples of opportunities are a new market opening up that could be filled from existing resources, the opportunity to take over another company which would improve the organisation's capabilities, such as manufacturer taking over a retailing chain, or the opportunity to take on to the management team an expert in some appropriate field who would improve the organisation's performance.

Opportunities abound if they are sought and recognised. They are important for the organisation, and its management should be ready for them so that they are able to be taken when they occur, provided they coincide with the main objectives of the firm.

(d) Threats

Like opportunities, threats are most often from outside, and like opportunities must be recognised and steps taken to deal with them. Though the actual threats are mostly external, their disadvantageous repercussions on the organisation are chiefly due to weak or inept management and planning. Some examples of threats are changing technology, thrusting competition especially from overseas, economic and political uncertainty.

Having said that, there are important internal threats that must be dealt with. These include management complacency, inadequate financial management, low staff morale, short-termism, and lack of absolute (ethical) standards.

Complacency results from the assumption that things will always remain as they are, and this is the main reason for example, why Western companies have lost out to Japanese manufacturers in the car, motorcycle, electrical goods and computer industries.

Inadequate financial management results in insufficient financial resources being made available for research and development. The result of this is that products become obsolete, and the organisation gets overtaken by its competitors.

Low morale in the work-force is both damaging to the general well-being of the organisation, and destructive to productivity. It is largely brought about by unpopular personnel practices, adversarial management style, and an inability to deal with staff grievances before they become major crises.

Short-termism is related to investment levels, and comes about when organisations attach too much importance to the immediate appearance of financial prosperity, at the expense of investing for the long-term future. Resources are handed out in the form of dividends and bonuses, rather than being conserved for investment in production technology and facilities upgrades.

Lack of absolute standards means that people will assume that the organisation is dealing with them in a dishonest fashion. This may also extend to customers and consumers. The cause of this are short-termism, and self-centredness on the part of top managers, particular departments and divisions and other vested interests. This is also extremely damaging to work-force morale.

- The advantage of the SWOT approach to corporate planning is that it requires management to look very closely and analytically at every aspect of its operations so that objectives can be assessed as attainable, and a clear picture built up of the strategies that must be adopted to achieve them. Every strategy must also be examined with care so that the constraints under which operations have to be conducted will be recognised. Some of these constraints, which may cause certain strategies to be abandoned, will be external and some internal.
- Some external constraints may be outside management's control altogether: these include raw material price rises, government legislation and the economic climate. Others may be circumvented, examples being the substitution of an alternative material for one whose supply has ceased, or finding new outlets for products whose markets have ceased to exist for some reason.
- Internal constraints include the lack of specialist labour, bad industrial relations, faulty products owing to poor quality-control and lack of research and development support. Such constraints may require corporate strategies to be re-examined, and the planners and management will have to consider the alternatives of abandoning some strategies or of remedying the constraints.

7.5   Customer analysis

The purpose of conducting customer analysis is so that the organisation understands what makes customers and consumers use the organisation's products and services, and what makes them use the products and services of other organisations. The specific questions that have to be addressed are as follows.

(a) Asking the following questions: Who are our customers? Why do they use us? What do they expect from us? Do they get it? How often does an individual customer buy from us?
(b) Assessing the cost of a lost customer; and the value of a gained customer. This is closely allied to an assessment of what causes customers to take their business elsewhere.
(c) Assessment of the strength of brand reputation and product or service performance in the eyes of the customer.
(d) Assessment of the position of the product or service of the organisation in the priority order of the customers served.
(e) Assessment of the strengths and weaknesses of competitive and substitute products from the point of view of the customer.
(f) Assessment of the potential and likely effects on customers of such things as: price rises; price reductions; inability to purchase; repackaging, representation and new advertising campaigns; increases and reductions in product quality.

The outcome of all this is an understanding of the product or the service from the point of view of those who use it (as distinct from those who make and sell it).

7.6   Competitor analysis

In order to analyse competitors, it is first necessary to know who these are! After all, from the point of view of the customer, seeking an evening's entertainment, restaurants, pubs, cinemas, theatres, booksellers, news stands, and video hire shops are all in competition! So too – for some people – is a trip to the supermarket.

So this is a quite careful analysis. Having identified who the competitors really are, it is then necessary to pin down precisely:

(a)   what they do better than you;
(b)   what you do better than them;
(c)   what causes people to use them rather than you;
(d)   what causes people to use you rather than them;
(e)   where their organisational and operational strengths lie, including attention to technology, satisfaction, customer service, and reputation.

In many sectors it is possible to pin down 'like for like' competitors. It is always said that the first purchasers of a brand new model car are the other car manufacturers. Clearly, there are some differences – for example, Skoda and Rolls Royce are both car manufacturers, but they do not compete for the same customer. On the other hand, Ford, Vauxhall, Nissan, Toyota, Volkswagen and Rover clearly do compete more closely. These companies, when they carry out their competitor analyses, will ask the same questions as those indicated above, and also pay specific attention to the following:

(a)   reputation and reliability;
(b)   durability;

This process is addressed to each individual company in the sector. It is questioned from the point of view of its corporate strategy; business stragtegy; capabilities and assumptions.
    The result is a profile of each player against which the position of the organisation in question can be measured.

Figure 7.1   Illustrating competitor analysis
Source: Kenneth R. Andrews, *Business Policy* (Irwin, 1988)

(c) after-sales service;
(d) product lifespan;
(e) availability of new models.

7.7   Market analysis

Market analysis is concerned with determining how long the present state of the market is likely to continue; and identifying those factors which may give a clue to future trends in the market. It is concerned with the following.

(a) Patterns of customer and consumer behaviour.
(b) Specific changes in customer and consumer behaviour.
(c) The causes of changes in customer and consumer behaviour.
(d) The reputation of the organisation's products and services in the market place; and those factors that may cause this to change – both for the better and for the worse.
(e) Factors that may cause the market suddenly to change its behaviour – especially factors outside the organisation's control, such as government action.
(f) The size of the customer and consumer base – whether static, expanding or contracting.
(g) Other potential customer and consumer bases.

It should be noted that market analysis is straightforward to conduct, and it is possible to gain a great deal of information about customers, consumers and their behaviour very quickly. However, it is much harder to predict business performance from this – all products and services are capable of improvement, and they are also capable of overnight obsolescence in the face of some truly creative or innovative approach from a competitor. Conversely, many organisations have greatly underestimated demands for their products and services – especially in recent years with the demand for children's Christmas presents (e.g. Teenage Mutant Hero Turtles 1992, Teletubbies 1997).

7.8   'Five forces' analysis

'Five forces' analysis pins down five areas of concern, and the source of potential opportunities and threats, as follows.

(a) The market: the nature of competition; the extent to which the market is under- or over-provided; the nature of activities of the different players concerned.
(b) Suppliers: concentrating specifically on the availability of raw materials and components; the bargaining power of suppliers; the extent to which they are able to choose what to supply, and how much of the particular component or raw material.

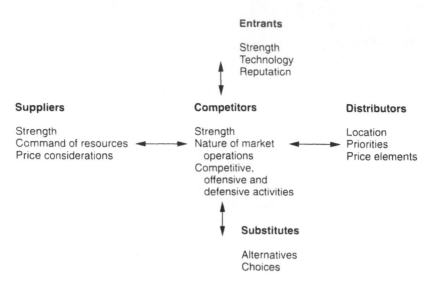

Figure 7.2   Illustrating 'five forces' analysis
Source: Michael E. Porter; *Competitive Strategy* (Free Press, 1980)

(c) Distributors: the extent to which distributors are dependent upon your product or service for their continued existence; their demand for your product or service.
(d) Potential entrants: the extent to which organisations operating in other sectors have production, technology and staff capacities to gain entry.
(e) Substitution: the extent to which the organisation's products are a matter of choice on the part of the buyer; the extent to which equivalent benefits can be gained from a product that is similar but not the same.

7.9   The corporate gap

Corporate gap analysis is carried out when activities are up and running. At any point, actual results of activities are compared with those required at the particular juncture by the corporate plan or strategy. These can then be projected into the future, when a) results expected from continuing the current course can be assessed and set against the planned results; and b) any revisions necessary to the plan can be carried out.

Where there is a discrepancy between planned, intended, forecast, and actual results, this is termed the corporate gap.

● The most frequently considered failure is that of net earnings or profit. This is termed the profit gap. This can also be applied to other aspects of strategy, such as sales production and marketing. The extent of the gap indicates the amount of effort that is required to achieve the long-term objectives. It also indicates shortcomings in the planning process; or where these have not occurred, factors outside the organisation's control. Strategies have therefore

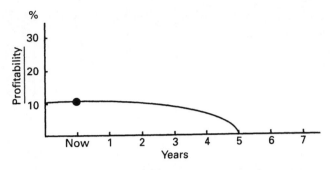

Forecast of profitability if current plans pursued

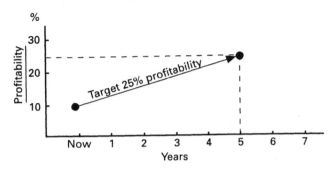

Target of 25% profitability in 5 years

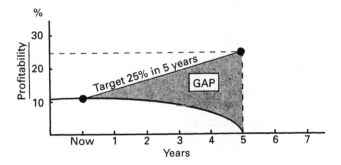

Target curve superimposed on current plan curve produces gap

Figure 7.3   Illustrating gap analysis

to be adjusted on this account. All the components going into the corporate planning activity that bear on these issues will have to be re-examined.

- It is also necessary to carry out gap analysis when actual takings, earnings and profits are far in excess of what was planned or anticipated. This may be due to a product suddenly taking off (e.g. the Turtles and Teletubbies examples above); or it may be due to seasonal factors (e.g. a sudden hot spell early or late in the year may lead to great increases in demand for ice cream and cold drinks that could not possibly have been predicted). It may also be that insufficient market, customer or opportunities analyses were carried out, and that the actual takings could have been predicted if this part of the job had been carried out correctly.

7.10 STEP

STEP (or PEST) analysis is concerned with the wider strategic situation, and with the organisation in its environment. It concerns the following.

(a) Social: social systems at the work-place; and the relationship between the organisation and its environment in terms of the social acceptability of its products and services; its marketing; and the regard with which it is held in the community.
(b) Technological: the organisation's technology and the uses to which it is put; and the technology that is potentially available to the organisation and others operating in the given sector.
(c) Economic: the financial structure, objectives and constraints at the place of work; levels of economic activity in the broader environment; and economic factors inside and outside the organisation's control.
(d) Political: the internal political systems of the organisation; and the external political factors that affect the markets and operations, including environmental aspects, waste and effluent disposal, legal constraints, and other political considerations.

Information raised in this way can then be further analysed and evaluated. It establishes in more detail the wider background against which particular activities are to take place. It raises wider issues or concerns that may, in turn, require more detailed analysis in the future. It may also indicate both opportunities and threats that may arise.

7.11 The keys to successful corporate planning

The advantages and benefits that organisations reap from effective planning and its careful implementation may be summed up as follows.

(a) It requires management to ensure that close analytical examination of the organisation is made.
(b) Provided the planning is carefully carried out and fully implemented, it provides the fuel for the continued progress of the organisation.
(c) Provided full consultation takes place, it ensures that everyone in the organisation is involved to a greater or lesser extent in shaping the future.
(d) It requires that adequate attention be paid to the long-term, as distinct from the short-term future.
(e) It requires that organisations take proper steps to ensure that they use, analyse and evaluate the information that is available to them.
(f) It concentrates attention on corporate goals, rather than allowing the organisation to drift along regardless.

(g) It ideally ensures a close relationship between corporate goals, and the objectives of those activities being carried out at departmental and work-group levels.

(h) It seeks to ensure the full participation and co-operation of everyone concerned.

It is sometimes held that corporate planning and strategy have deadening effects on commercial activity, and the exploitation of market opportunities as they arise or are discovered. It is also true that, if planning systems are allowed to operate in isolation from the rest of the organisation, they become either irrelevant, or else they restrict, rather than enhance, the progress of the organisation. All planning activities, and all aspects of organisation strategy, must be sufficiently capable of flexibility and modification, while at the same time ensuring that the organisation is not diverted from its chosen direction.

QUESTIONS

1 Define strategic planning. Explain the steps which should be taken in the development of a corporate plan (IComA)

2 Define the term 'profit gap' in the context of corporate planning, and discuss its relevance to the planning process. (ACCA)

3 Describe the different components of strategic planning at its corporate, tactical and operational levels, and show the relationship between these components. (ACCA)

4 It is felt by the many opponents of strategic planning that in instigating strategy, one is putting an organisation into a strait-jacket, and that there is a resulting loss of flexibility which renders impossible the exploiting of opportunities on a more free-wheeling basis. Evaluate this statement. (CIMA)

5 Define and explain the principal elements of a Corporate Plan. State the contributions to the plan to be expected from
(a) a senior functional manager;
(b) a Chief Executive.
(Answers should include examples from an organisation with which you are familiar.) (ICSA)

6 Discuss the criteria, financial and non-financial, which a business should use for the purpose of evaluating possible strategies. (CIMA)

7 (a) Indicate what an organisational SWOT analysis entails.
(b) Why should social responsibilities be taken into account when considering organisational objectives? (IAM)

■ ⌄ **8** Organisation (1)

Organisation can be defined as 'the framework of responsibilities, authority and duties through which all the resources of an enterprise are brought together and co-ordinated for the achievement of management objectives'.

It is a pattern of relationships, formally and informally established, which has as its purpose the creation of a structure through which the activities of personnel at all levels can be utilized in an orderly and controlled manner to the benefit of the enterprise as whole.

8.1　Responsibility, authority, duty and accountability

The terms responsibility, authority, duty and accountability are basic to discussion of any organisation and it would be useful at this point to give definitions of these terms used in the present context.

(a) Responsibility

Responsibility is the obligation to make sure that duties are properly, adequately and effectively carried out. It carries with it the prerogative to delegate authority and accountability. Responsibility is a key part of all effective management. It is given and accepted by those involved. Responsibility for departmental, divisional and functional activities rests with the manager or supervisor concerned. Ultimate responsibility for the effective functioning of the organisation rests with the chief executive.

(b) Authority

Authority exists whereby duties are assigned to subordinates; and authority is also given to those subordinates to ensure that those duties are carried out. The precise extent of authority must be clearly defined to the jobholder, who must act only within those limits. In such a way subordinates therefore become accountable for their actions, and for the quality and effectiveness of the particular tasks and duties that they carry out.

(c) Duty

This is the obligation to comply with orders and instructions given by those in authority within the limits enjoyed by that authority and within the sphere of activity designated to the staff member who is required to accept those instructions. Orders do not have to be explicit: there is also a duty to act on implicit instructions. For example, if a subordinate is required by the supervisor to produce 20 items of the company's product, then the subordinate has also the duty to ensure that those 20 items are of a sufficient quality, to ensure that they are acceptable to the organisation's customers. All organisations also have a 'duty of care' to their customers and staff.

(d) Accountability

Accountability reflects the acceptance of specific responsibilities for tasks, duties and actions. Thus, people are called to account for the quality and volume of their work; and managers and supervisors are called to account for the performance of their departments and divisions. Ultimately, the chief executive is called to account for the performance of the organisation as a whole.

8.2   Setting up an organisation

In many cases, the organisation pattern has simply grown to accommodate changing requirements and circumstances rather than having been planned. This is understandable where a concern has developed from small beginnings, or where a department has expanded to take care of greater volumes of work. However, this does not lead to the most effective form of organisation. Ideally, effective organisation structures are properly planned and should follow these guidelines.

(a) The various activities necessary to pursue and achieve the objectives of the enterprise must be determined. Normally this is by function, e.g. marketing, production, finance and so on. Customer, however, may also divide larger enterprises, up by product, by location or in any other way that is appropriate for effective working.
(b) These activities must be divided into logical sectional activities. Thus the marketing division may be split into home sales and overseas sales. These sections may then be subdivided into geographical areas, product types or any other suitable categories.
(c) Leaders must be appointed for each whole division and for each section of each division. The marketing division, therefore, will have a marketing manager, probably a senior executive, and there will be a home sales manager and also an overseas sales manager, both invested with the necessary authority to do what is necessary to pursue the marketing objectives of the undertaking, and both accountable to the marketing manager.
(d) Each section must now be staffed. The number of operating members of staff will be determined on the basis of the forecasts of the volume of work to be expected. Middle and junior managers and supervisors will then be employed, ideally on the basis of the principles of delegation and span of control discussed in 9.4 and 9.5 below.
(e) The necessary equipment for the efficient operation of each division and section must be determined and proper provision made.

(f) Effective procedures and communication systems must be designed and installed to ensure the proper co-ordination of all parts of the organisation.

(g) The extent and limits of responsibility, authority and duty of every member of the organisation must be clearly defined and made known to all concerned.

(h) The power to delegate authority must be given to all those who have managerial or supervisory responsibilities.

(i) Written procedures and staff handbooks should be prepared to cover all aspects of working. These should be made available to everyone involved, so that they know where they stand on any issue that may arise. These cover working routines, reporting relationships, and matters such as discipline and grievance.

In practice, it is very difficult to follow these guidelines. However, they should always be borne in mind as a point of reference when malfunctioning in the organisation becomes apparent; and should always be taken into account if reorganisation becomes necessary.

8.3 Forms of organisation

In considering the forms of organisation, it is usual to think in terms of distinct and traditional types. In practice, however, it is rare to find any one type in its 'pure' form. Most organisations operate with varying degrees of combination. Moreover, rigid, orderly and permanent organisation forms do not lend themselves to effective performance in the turbulent and global nature of today's business world.

The traditional patterns are: line organisation; functional on staff organisation; and line and staff organisation.

(a) Line organisation

This is the simplest form of organisation and one that is easiest to understand. The line represents a chain of command. Indeed, in some cases line organisation is also called military organisation. It is also known as scalar organisation or the scalar chain; and also vertical organisation. Line organisation indicates reporting relationships, chains of communication and command, and the relative status of job holders.

- The advantage of line organisations is that there is a clear line of responsibility and authority right through the management structure from the board of directors to the lowest level of supervision and below. Authority is derived by any level of supervision from the one immediately above, and this is clearly visible.

- In a similar fashion, each level of supervision is accountable to the one above. Again, this is easy to understand on the part of everyone involved.

- It also indicates clearly the functional duties and responsibilities that are present. It pinpoints precise areas of responsibility, authority and accountability.

- Line organisation has the following advantages and disadvantages.

Advantages

1 It is a well understood, accepted and traditional form of organisation in British firms.
2 It is simple and direct, and easy to visualise.
3 There is a direct chain of command.
4 Co-ordination of the activities of members of a department is simplified because of this directness of presentation.
5 Lines of delegation are easily and effectively presented.
6 It gives a clear indication of position, status and occupation of the different members of the organisation.
7 It gives a clear representation of organisational discipline.

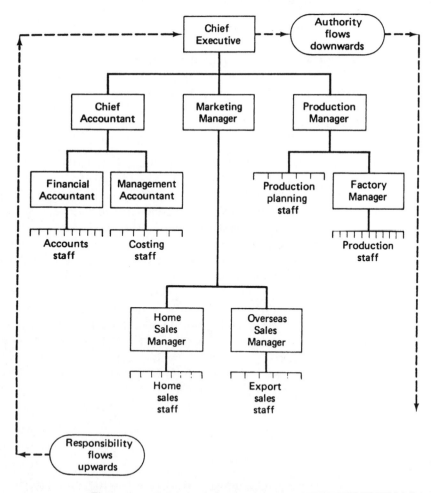

Figure 8.1   Specimen of a line organisation chart

Disadvantages

1 It gives the impression that everything is neatly parcelled up; and this is not the case in the overwhelming majority of present-day organisations.
2 It gives the impression of inflexibility; and again, this is not conducive to effective activities in today's business world.
3 It can lead to abdication of responsibility in grey areas – for example, when handling customer complaints it needs to be clear whether this is the responsibility of production, marketing, sales or public relations (or anyone else for that matter).
4 This form of organisation works best where there is a long-term steadiness in the scale of activities. It tends to be slow in responding to crises; and slow also in responding to sudden opportunities.
5 It tends to create an inward-looking mentality within functional departments, and as a consequence they become inward-looking, rather than seeking to contribute to the well-being of the organisation as a whole.

(b) Functional or staff organisation

In this type of organisation it is the function itself that determines the flow of authority and responsibility without reference to actual operating divisions. Each function of the undertaking is determined and an expert put in charge who will have direct control of that function wheresoever it occurs. The expert's authority will, therefore, override that of the line manager within whose department the function is being carried out and who is responsible for discipline and other matters.

● An example will make this position clear. If a production expert is appointed to act as functional executive responsible for the manufacture of a firm's products then they will have the authority to give instructions to anyone in any department where this function touches, without reference to the line manager concerned. Thus they can direct sales staff to promote certain items because they suit production schedules without consulting the sales manager; or insist that purchases of materials are made from specific suppliers despite the fact that the accountant is unhappy about the financial aspect of such purchases. This is because the production function is concerned both with the articles sold and the materials purchased, and because the sales manager and the accountant are line managers whose authority can be overridden by the functional executive. It will be obvious, however, that if the accountant and the sales manager were also functional executives then there would be a conflict of authority. In any event, in this situation line managers find their authority reduced, not only in relation to functional activity but also in relation to discipline and staff relationships. The staff themselves are left in doubt as to whose authority they should accept.

● Functional organisation has the following advantages and disadvantages.

Advantages

1 The undertaking benefits from the expertise of the functional specialists, who have direct authority in all aspects of their speciality wherever it occurs.

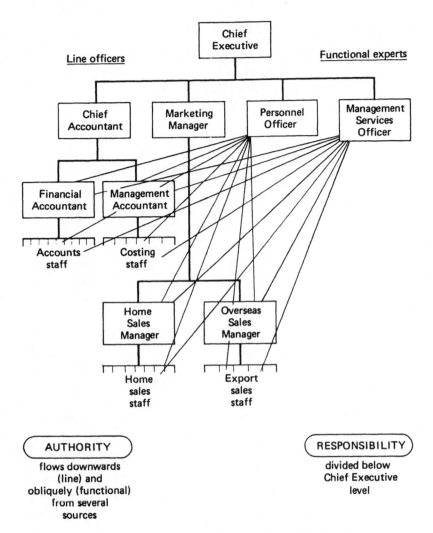

Figure 8.2 Specimen of a functional organisation chart

2 The functional experts are not involved in the day-to-day running of the organisation; this is done by line management. They are consequently free to concentrate exclusively on their function and its application.

3 The organisational structure is flexible and is able to respond to external or internal changes quickly, one of the functions of the specialist executives being to monitor what is happening in their spheres of interest outside and inside the enterprise.

4 Because the activities of the functional executives penetrate all sectors of the organisation they are excellently placed to assist in the effective co-ordination of the efforts of the various departments, to the benefit of the undertaking as a whole.

Disadvantages

1 There are no clear lines of authority in this form of organisation, which can make systematic control difficult, because the executive powers of the specialists cut right across departmental boundaries.
2 This, in turn, leads to difficulty in establishing responsibility when failure occurs, and also makes remedies to put things right more difficult to apply.
3 Functional experts command high salaries, and a large number are needed to operate the functional type of organisation satisfactorily. This can mean that this form of organisation can prove extremely expensive, sometimes too expensive to be economically practicable.
4 Workers can become confused by the many superiors who have direct authority over them.

(c) Line and staff organisation

Despite its drawbacks, functional organisation gives many benefits, as already explained in 8.3(b) above. In consequence it has been married to line organisation to produce a form that seeks to provide the best of both types, namely line and staff organisation.

- The availability of the services of functional experts is maintained in this form of organisation, but the specialists are required to act in an advisory capacity only and have no executive powers. These are the staff officers. The line organisation structure is maintained and line officers (line managers and line supervisors) retain responsibility for the day-to-day running of their departments: authority over departmental staffs is theirs alone. In this way the functional expertise is provided, but only as advice to line officers who then implement it if they see fit: the staff officers have no power to enforce compliance with their decisions. Line and staff organisation is illustrated in Figure 8.3.
- In practice, line and staff organisation is the pattern most commonly employed and the one that seems to be the most successful. Its advantages and disadvantages can be set out as follows:

Advantages

1 As in line organisation, the lines of responsibility and authority are clearly defined, and obvious to those they concern.
2 The departmental line officers retain total control of their departments.
3 Nevertheless, functional expertise and experience is available, thus bringing some of the benefits that accrue to pure functional organisation.
4 Similarly, co-ordination throughout the undertaking is facilitated because of the fact that the interests of the functional experts permeate throughout the various sections of the organisation, though on an advisory basis only.
5 Provided that the line officers maintain their own initiative within their own spheres of action, and do not lean too heavily upon the functional experts, decisions should be arrived at as quickly as they can be in purely line organisation.

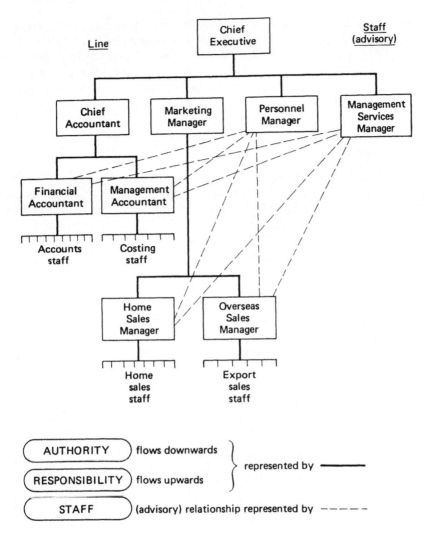

Line

Chief
Executive

Staff
(advisory)

Chief
Accountant

Marketing
Manager

Personnel
Manager

Management
Services
Manager

Financial
Accountant

Management
Accountant

Accounts
staff

Costing
staff

Home
Sales
Manager

Overseas
Sales
Manager

Home
sales
staff

Export
sales
staff

AUTHORITY	flows downwards	
RESPONSIBILITY	flows upwards	represented by ———
STAFF	(advisory) relationship represented by – – – – –	

Figure 8.3 Specimen of a line and staff organisation chart

Disadvantages

1 Inasmuch as the functional officers act only in an advisory capacity and have no executive authority, line officers are free to accept or reject their advice. In the latter case this means that the expensive expertise of the staff officers is being wasted, possibly to the detriment of the efficiency of the undertaking as a whole. Line officers are primarily concerned with their own departments and may not be able to appreciate fully the effects of decisions on the total organisation: the functional (or staff) officers on the other hand has an overall view of the enterprise.

2 There is a danger that staff officers may try to usurp the authority of line officers. This can come about through frustration at advice being rejected, particularly if this happens frequently, or because the staff officer has an over-

bearing personality. Whatever the reason, when this happens an unco-operative attitude is generated between the two types of officer. Further, where the line officers do not exert proper authority this may be seen to be a weakness by staff and their effectiveness and general discipline may suffer as a result.

3 Where clashes of opinion occur frequently between the staff and line officers this will be reflected in a lowering of the efficiency of the organisation.

4 As in pure functional organisation, line and staff organisation can be confusing to the workers, though this can be avoided if they are properly informed of the differing roles of the types of officer.

- Line and staff organisation works best when time and trouble is taken to ensure effective working relationships; and personal and professional confidence and understanding between those in authority, and those with expertise.
- Serious problems occur in this form of organisation when the views of the expert are overridden by someone with greater authority, for reasons other than those to do with the long-term success of the enterprise; and where interdepartmental conflicts arise.
- Further problems may also arise where both those with authority, and also those with expertise, feel that they have to lobby for their position with the chief executive and other top managers, in order to preserve their influence. This is extremely wasteful of organisation resources, and very damaging to staff morale.
- For this form of organisation to succeed, complementary roles for each aspect must be determined in advance.

8.4   Flexible organisation and work patterns

However effective in practice, the great and enduring problem with traditional forms of organisation has always been the cost of maintaining the establishment. In recent years, therefore, those concerned with the creation and management of organisations have sought alternative approaches. These approaches have, in turn, been concerned with reconciling the need for some form of permanence and order, with trying to find reductions in costs, while at the same time needing to ensure that they maintain their competitive position and operational effectiveness. The most common new formats are as follows.

(a) The Japanese model

Japanese companies working in the West have tried to create permanent organisations through offering high wages and excellent terms and conditions of employment to their staff. In return for this, those working in the companies have expected to be fully flexible – that is, to take on any duties that may be required of them (e.g. in exceptional circumstances, a production worker may be required to carry out cleaning duties, filing duties, or even take a turn on the switchboard). Staff are also obliged, as a condition of their employment, to undertake directed and prescribed staff training. The

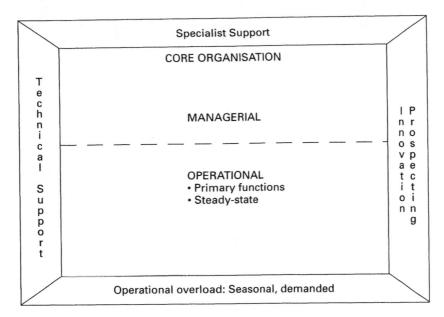

Figure 8.4 Specimen of core and peripheral organisation

company expects to be able to offer lifetime employment; and in return for this, staff are expected to undertake whatever activities are necessary. They may also be required to undertake extensive retraining if, for example, the company wishes to change the total direction of its business. As an example, Mitsubishi changed from manufacturing aircraft and ships, to cars, without any job losses; in order to do this, the workers had to be completely retrained.

(b) Core and peripheral organisation

This occurs where the organisation determines that it needs a core of permanent staff, responsible for the direction and effectiveness of the organisation, and for its core or primary activities; and that other activities can be carried out within the peripheral organisation – which may be engaged on a seasonal basis, on project work, on other job and finish type approaches, and so on.

(c) The shamrock organisation

This is akin to core and peripheral organisation, parcelling up activities under the heading of: the core or stalk – direction and key activities; seasonal activities; specialist activities; pioneering activities; and crises, emergencies and other short-term responses. Each area needs clarity of direction and its own core purpose; however, particular aspects may have very different patterns of employment –for example, some specialist services may be fully sub-contracted; while other activities may take place on a seasonal or part-time basis only.

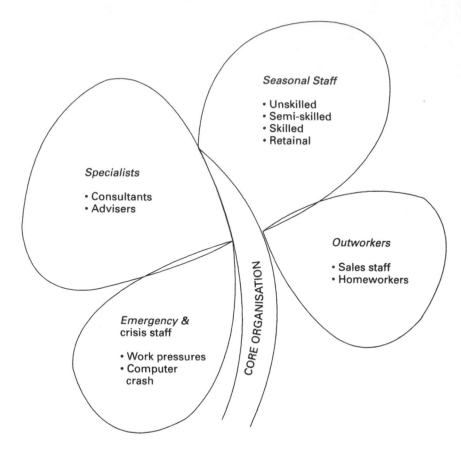

Figure 8.5 Specimen of a shamrock organisation chart

(d) Networks and federations

This is the ultimate extension of the core and peripheral approach. It exists where every activity is sub-contracted. Thus, for example, the accounts function would be carried out by a firm of accountants; personnel and human resource activities by employment consultants; marketing activities by marketing consultants; and primary work activities also by sub-contractors and agencies. This form of activity has always been common in the building and civil engineering industries in Britain, where both different activities in the projects, and also the labour itself, has been fully sub-contracted. Other organisations are now beginning to realise the benefits and possibilities of this approach.

(e) Work patterns

Alongside changing approaches to organisation have come changing approaches to work patterns. Organisations and their managers have come to realise that providing permanent work accommodation for staff is extremely

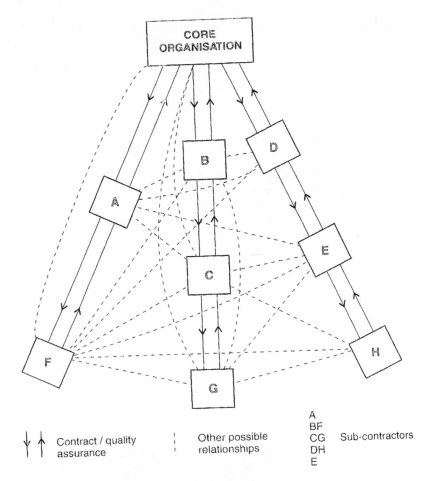

			A	
			BF	
			CG	Sub-contractors
			DH	
			E	

Contract / quality assurance   Other possible relationships

Figure 8.6 Specimen of a federated organisation

expensive – and this problem is exacerbated when staff are not always present (because for example, they are out and about meeting customers). In recent years there have, therefore, been great developments in the following.

1 Homeworking: in which people work from home, using their own private accommodation as a work facility.

2 Hot desking: in which individual offices and work spaces are not provided, but are claimed by staff on a first-come first-served basis.

3 Annual hours: in which staff are required to work a set number of hours per annum, and that this may be divided up according to peaks and troughs in work load.

4 Twilight and overnight shifts: formerly only found in factory work and public service work, this has now been greatly extended into, for example, banking and retail.

5 Short-term leasing: in which rather than establishing organisational offices, organisations rent business space and facilities by the hour (for example, at hotels and business centres).

6 Retainer systems: whereby staff are put on minimal wages whether or not there is any work for them to do; and these wages are enhanced when there is work for them to do.
7 Project work: in which activities are organised along the lines of project and job and finish, rather than as steady-state and enduring activities.

8.5   Committee organisation

Committees have traditionally been used to run charitable and other not-for-profit activities; and committees have always had great influence in the organisation and management of schools, hospitals and social services. However, the increasing complexity of modern industrial and commercial activity, and the greater participation of workers and consumer groups in certain areas of management decisions have led, in turn, to a greater use of committee organisation and an increase in the influence of those elected to serve on such committees.

Management by committee requires that committees be set up to deal with specific areas of activity. These will be serviced by members from all parts of the organisation, all vested interests, and where necessary, consumer groups and other local interest groups. Members of a committee may be either appointed or elected depending upon the circumstances of the case.

- The authority and function of a committee must be clearly defined as the outset. This clearly differs from committee to committee. Whatever is constituted, clear rules and guidelines must be drawn up; and it is increasingly usual for committee members to be made directly accountable for the performance of the organisation which they are overseeing. Those selected for committee membership are therefore increasingly required to bring specific expertise with them if they are to perform effectively in such a situation.
- For a full discussion of the role and function of committees see Chapter 15 below.

8.6   Informal organisation

Whatever the structure used, informality always exists to a greater or lesser extent in all organisations.

- The development over recent years of less rigid social structures in the world at large has had its impact on workers' attitudes. It has come to be realised that everybody seeks a satisfying life, and that part of this satisfaction lies in being a social, as well as operational, member of an organisation.
- There is always social as well as occupational or professional interaction in all work groups. It is neither productive nor possible to insist that people have no social contact other than for working reasons while at work.
- Where a community is closely knit, people from many different ranks and occupations within one organisation will meet as equals on a social basis anyway.

- The use of informal contact and meetings is, in any case, essential for the daily functioning of many areas of activity. Informal contact and clusters can be used to resolve interdepartmental grievances and disputes; industrial relations problems; and other aspects of organisation interrelationships. Informal contacts also exist in the shape of cluster groups; special interest groups; and more insidiously, in the presence of lobbies and vested interests.
- Problems arise with the informal organisation where it is allowed to supersede, rather than assist an enhance, the formal organisation. Chief executives and senior managers may encourage informal contacts, but must take great care to ensure that the boundaries of these are limited.
- Most insidiously and destructively of all, some managers take the view that it is better to 'divide and rule'. When this happens, people are actively encouraged to make informal contacts, to curry favour with the chief executive and senior managers, so that the formal organisation is actually subverted. In spite of its perceived popularity as a management technique, it never works, and is always ultimately destructive to the organisation as a whole.

8.7 Organisational styles

Other styles of organisation which should be addressed are as follows.

(a) Bureaucratic organisation. This occurs where formal procedures are rigidly adhered to and there is little or no provision for exceptions. It is found particularly in central and local government, and in the head offices of giant, multinational and domestic corporations, where everything is operated by rule books.

Some form of bureaucracy is always essential, because decisions and progress in all organisations have to be recorded. However, over-reliance in procedures and the rule book inevitably leads to slowness in decision-making and change; and it is only a short step from this to discouraging initiative. It is also the case that in line organisations where there are long chains of command, as well as bureaucratic procedures, communication and decision-making are certain to be ineffective.

(b) Contingency organisation. The organisation structure is fluid and determined by the current factors of the environment, technology, markets, enterprise, size and staff. The contingency approach is based on continued interreaction between the organisation and its environment.

(c) Matrix organisation. Matrix organisations occur when people are grouped under a functional heading, but expected to work anywhere in the organisation that requires the service of that function. Thus, for example, accountants may work within an accountancy division, but may be required to work at any other department – e.g. production, marketing, personnel – or location, if the organisation is complex or multi-sited. Those working in this form of organisation have, therefore, to be prepared for the complexities, and potential conflict inherent in having to report to at least two different managers.

(d) Just-in-Time organisation. Generally known as JiT, this system of organisation is mainly applicable to production and manufacturing industries and to retailers. The advantages of JiT are the minimising of stock levels, so freeing cash that would otherwise be locked up in stock, and the reduction of the need for storage areas, which are also expensive. The JiT approach is also increasingly being used by organisations keeping staff on retainers, and who can be then called in at very short notice if work is suddenly required.

QUESTIONS

1 Line and staff relationships are often thought to be a source of conflict. Taking account of the roles and responsibilities of line and staff positions, what factors may lead to conflict? How may such conflict be handled? (ICSA)

2 A company owns and operates 50 small hotels in its home country, 30 more in five other countries of the EEC, and six in Africa. The hotels are purpose-built to the company's design. Each one has about 25 rooms, a lounge area, and a restaurant in which simple standard food is served. The hotel manager has about ten staff.

You are required to draw an organisation chart (or charts) suitable for this company with notes as appropriate, showing clearly at which levels the important functions of the business are managed. (CIMA)

3 You are required
(a) to describe four advantages and four disadvantages of committees;
(b) to give two reasons for their increased use. (CIMA)

4 (a) Differentiate between the 'formal' and the 'informal' organisation structure of an enterprise.
(b) Discuss the advantages and disadvantages of an 'informal' organisational structure. (IAM)

5 Explain, with particular reference to the words underlined, the statement 'a manager who arranges or organises a *formal structure* determines how *authority* will be distributed in the total organisation'. (IAM)

6 Discuss the advantages and disadvantages of matrix organisation structures. How may we handle conflicts between the demands of a project, and the demands of the discipline or department within that structure? (ICSA)

7 Distinguish between 'bureaucratic' and 'contingency' concepts of organisation structure. (IAM)

8 Describe Just-In-Time systems, and their effect on organisation and management. (CIMA)

▪ ☑ 9 Organisation (2)

The smaller an organisation is, the more likely it is to be centralised with responsibility and authority for all activities resting with the chief executive. As organisations grow and diversify, however, it becomes necessary to consider how the organisation is to develop and whether it is possible to maintain this approach with a larger unit, or whether it should be split into parts, each with a measure of autonomy.

9.1 Centralisation

- This is the practice of having all responsibility and authority concentrated in one place so that major decisions are made by the central controlling body. In the worst cases, this means that little initiative is in the hands of those lower down the management ladder and growth and progress become difficult to achieve. It may also lead to a situation where all management decisions have to be approved by the chief executive before they can be put into operation. In many cases too, over-centralisation results in a bureaucratic organisation concentrating on procedural operation rather than business effectiveness.
- Centralisation tends to work best when common standards of practice are laid down for the organisation as a whole. Whatever the size, scale or complexity of the organisation everyone is given common standards of employment; common terms and conditions; common discipline and grievance practices; and common fundamental principles of treatment.
- The increasing complexity of modern organisations, in industry and commerce, and in the public sector, has led to the twin problems of achieving effective control of widespread activities so that policies are properly adhered to, and the necessity to adjust operations at local level to take into account the differing needs of those activities at the point where they take place. An example will make the position clear.
- A chain of retail shops may be centrally controlled and specific policies laid down as to the range and variety of goods to be stocked at each shop. This provides the organisation with the benefits of a restricted stockholding range (with the minimum amount of capital tied up in stock) and the ability to obtain very favourable terms from suppliers because of bulk purchasing. Managers of individual shops will, in these circumstances, be unable to

satisfy special local needs outside the stocking policy of head office – the centralised control: in such cases simple customer requests must be denied. A common occurrence, for instance, is the refusal of shops to split prepackaged goods so that a customer must buy, say, twenty-five screws in a packet when he needs only five. It is not only in small domestic items, however, that this happens. A similar attitude prevails in centrally controlled retail outlets selling expensive goods.

● The advantages and disadvantages of centralisation are as follows.

Advantages

1 It is possible to provide absolute control over the organisation and to ensure adherence to laid down policies.
2 It is administratively convenient in that the focal point for each function is readily discernible.
3 It is possible to have certain common standards throughout the organisation. Examples are indicated above, and specific organisations may also choose to broaden this approach to include customer relations, the granting of credit, and permission to spend organisational resources.
4 It is possible to engage highly qualified functional experts who can then work in relative autonomy ensuring that their particular area of expertise is adhered to with common standards throughout the organisation.

Disadvantages

1 Control can easily become autocratic and inflexible.
2 Managers and supervisors become frustrated because they are unable to use their discretion.
3 Bureaucratic control methods may be imposed resulting in a proliferation of forms and procedures and administrative overload.
4 It can lead to the proliferation of head office functions and overload, which quickly become extremely expensive to maintain; and in the worst cases, gain a life of their own so that the priority of the organisation is in adhering to head office procedures rather than business effectiveness.

9.2   Decentralisation

● Decentralisation (or departmentalisation as it is sometimes called) is, of course, the opposite of centralisation. It occurs where responsibility for various functions and operations is devolved from the centre and rests at the point where operations occur. If the example of the chain of retail stores is again referred to, decentralisation would mean that each shop would be responsible, under its manager, for all the operating functions required to carry on business, such as purchasing, the range of goods stocked and customer service. In this way each decentralised part of the enterprise can be geared to accommodate the specific needs of its operating environment, and can adapt itself to meet those needs without reference to central administration. Decentralisation, of course, does require the services of high-calibre managers who are able to anticipate and provide for local needs. It also poses considerable problems in overall control from top management, and in the integration of the activities of all the decentralised units into the overall strategies of the undertaking.

- The advantages and disadvantages of decentralisation can be set out as follows:

Advantages

1 It provides flexibility to meet changing needs at local level because that is where control resides.
2 It is rewarding to managers and staff because it enables them to exercise their own judgements and initiative and so promotes job satisfaction.
3 It provides good management experience to managers and supervisors. This promotes their personal development and thus their services become of greater value to the organisation.
4 Administrative paperwork may be reduced to a minimum at operating level, though more reporting to central control may be necessary.

Disadvantages

1 It is necessary to ensure that the same basic control systems and procedures are adequate and effective for each operating unit. Failure to do this may result in each section not following the same patterns of procedures; or not applying the same standards.
2 Decentralisation may result in more reporting and inspection, effectively a substitution of administrative and bureaucratic inefficiency.
3 Care has to be taken that localised buying does not lead to increases in the costs of components and raw materials.
4 It is possible that some decentralised sections and their managers and supervisors may start to consider themselves as autonomous 'kingdoms', without any relationship or responsibility to the organisation at large.
5 It is necessary to maintain regular meetings between the heads of decentralised units to that the commonality of purpose is maintained. The importance of this should never be under-estimated.

- In practice, most organisations combine a measure of centralisation with decentralisation and unit and managerial autonomy. In banking, for example, there has to be a commonality of interest rates and terms and conditions throughout the bank, together with branch level autonomy to deal effectively with the needs of individual customers. On the other hand, supermarkets are highly centralised in buying and pricing policies so that they can take advantage of their considerable buying power to affect manufacturers' prices, and so that they can predict with a fair level of certainty their own cost bases.

9.3   Divisionalisation

- Divisionalisation is the term used to describe the dividing up of activities of an organisation. This occurs for example, when a retail chain gives autonomy to its branches for purchasing, accounting and so on; and when a civil engineering company gives autonomy to its overseas offices for gaining contracts according to particular local rules. Divisionalised structures, however, still normally retain central reporting relationships, especially concerning the volume of work, and financial results.
- When an enterprise becomes very large, or when it grows by taking over other organisations, particularly if they operate in different spheres, then the need to divisionalise arises. This usually comes about because the undertaking has become too large to administer from one central control owing to a variety of reasons which include:

  (a) Difficulties in establishing and maintaining effective lines of communication because of sheer size.
  (b) Similar difficulties because the various activities of the enterprise are spread over a geographically wide area (this is especially relevant to multinational corporations).
  (c) Widely diverse activities with little or no relation to each other, an example being a company engaged in the manufacture of farm chemicals, pharmaceuticals and paint.

- Simply stated, divisionalisation involves carrying on diverse activities by means of subsidiary or associated independent organisations, central control being vested in a separate organisation. In industrial and commercial practice this is best exemplified by a holding company and its subsidiaries. Each subsidiary company has its own board of directors and managing director and has, virtually, a free hand in pursuing its objectives. It is, however, subject to the overriding authority of the holding company and its board, from whence the overall strategic planning of the group will derive.
- Co-ordination of the activities of the various divisions is achieved by the simple expedient of having the managing director, and maybe other directors, from each subsidiary company on the board of the controlling company. Further, it is also usual for there to be set up executive committees drawn from the boards of the group companies which will meet more frequently than the central board of directors and are thus able to resolve inter-group problems and difficulties without the necessity to call a meeting of the full board.
- The advantages and disadvantages of divisionalisation are very similar to those obtaining in decentralisation. However, it has further merit in that it provides opportunities to take advantage of large-scale working, and the member companies have the benefit of the backing of a powerful central management team.

9.4 Delegation

Since it is patently impossible for one chief executive, one local government official, or even one executive committee to carry out all the functions and duties necessary for an organisation to operate effectively, it is necessary to pass on authority to subordinates to pursue certain activities. This process is known as 'delegation': without it no undertaking larger than that manageable by one person doing every duty can exist. In fact, it is one of the major functions of effective management.

- The process of delegation relieves managers from involvement in the day-to-day detail of running their particular function, but at the same time does not absolve them from the responsibility of ensuring that the duties that have been delegated are correctly and efficiently performed. It does mean, however, that they can spend more time in a pursuit of this primary function of managing – pursuing objectives, making decisions and dealing with problems of policy.
- Just as managers find it necessary to delegate, so at every level of management and supervision delegation has to take place, either because of the need for specialist knowledge which the delegator does not possess or because of the amount of work they have to perform and which becomes physically impossible by virtue of its volume. In the first case, for example, the managing director may not have specialist production knowledge; thus is delegated the management of the production function to a production manager. Equally, the production manager's work-load may make it impossible to supervise personally each production shop so it is necessary to appoint a shop supervisor for each process – to delegate authority to the supervisor over the workers at operational level. Authority is thus passed on to the delegate in order to act on behalf of the delegator. Nevertheless, though authority is delegated, responsibility is not; it passes right back to the top, i.e. to the managing director, because the supervisors are accountable to their managers and they, in turn, are accountable to the managing director.
- Many people in positions of authority find it difficult to delegate; sometimes because they feel that their subordinates are not adequate; sometimes because they, themselves, feel insecure and they are reluctant to relinquish any power; and sometimes because they think they may become out of touch with the day-to-day events in their sphere of activity. Nevertheless, effective management relies on proper delegation and a competent manager or supervisor recognises this. It is not enough, however, for managers or supervisors to delegate aspects of their work and then to sit back and await results. Delegation must be planned properly and adequate monitoring must be put in to effect. A delegator must therefore:

  (a) Determine what tasks are most suitable for delegation, both from the point of view of his own overall work responsibilities and from the point of view of the organisational benefit.

(b) Select very carefully the subordinate to whom authority is to be delegated, from the aspect of the delegate's competence and in respect of his personal qualities.

(c) Specify very carefully the duties to be taken over, and the limits of the authority invested in the delegate.

(d) Ensure that the delegate is properly acquainted with (c) and provide guidance and training if and when necessary.

(e) Ensure that the authority delegated is fully commensurate with the responsibilities the delegate has to assume. It is not only usefulness but also patently unjust to require duties to be properly performed without at the same time giving sufficient authority to accomplish them.

(f) Allow delegates to carry out their duties with as little interference as possible, after having ascertained that they are competent to perform the tasks delegated. After all, the purpose of delegation is to free the delegator of the burden. Further, the responsibility undertaken should increase the competence, self-confidence and potential of the delegate.

(g) Despite (f), ensure that some form of checking is instituted to ascertain that the delegate is performing effectively. As has been pointed out, delegation does not absolve the delegator from responsibility for the work delegated. It has been said, with truth, that inspection is the corollary of delegation. What form the checking will take depends upon the status of the delegate. At the lower levels of supervision physical inspection is not only simplest, it is expected. However, nearer the top of the management ladder inspection may be more covert, and may take the form of reports and the like.

- It cannot be emphasised too strongly that the ability to delegate effectively is an essential attribute in a successful manager. Failure to do so results in a work overload, less than accurate decisions, and leads to stress. Failure to delegate also gives staff the impression that the manager does not trust them to work efficiently, which can result in resentment and a lowering of morale.

9.5 Span of control

Span of control refers to the number of subordinates who can effectively be supervised directly by one manager, supervisor or other person in authority.

- It used to be stated that the number six was the most effective span of control. This is, however, far too simplistic to fit into any set of circumstances without consideration of the particular situation. There are constraints of technology, location, the nature of work, reporting relationships and business demands which have also to be taken into account.

- The complexity of work-groups, the skills, knowledge and attributes present, and other relationships also affect the span of control. These are, in turn, affected by the organisation's own preferred method of establishing reporting relationships.

- What is also at issue is the amount of supervision that an organisation decides that it needs, and the approach or style to be determined by this supervision. If the supervision is adversarial or coercive, more supervisors and junior managers will be required than if the approach is more open. Other factors that need to be taken into account are as follows.

(a) The abilities of those being supervised: if they are competent and well trained, they will need less supervision than if the reverse is the case.

(b) The complexity of the work being done: if the work is complicated, queries may arise; if it is simple, less supervision may be required.

(c) The consistency of operations: if the work varies a good deal, then supervision will be required to indicate when the variations are to take place.

(d) The effectiveness of communications: and the extent to which these require interpretation.

(e) Visibility: a phrase much in vogue at present is 'Managing by Walking About' (MbWA), and the greater the ability of the supervisor to meet with staff regularly, the fewer the problems, and therefore the fewer the levels of supervision required.

(f) The ability of the supervisor: if technically knowledgeable and fully trained in the principles of supervision, and fully conversant with the work of the subordinates, staff will have greater confidence in their own ability.

(g) Labour turnover: where there is a constantly changing work-force, the need to keep training newcomers, and ensuring that they become productive as quickly as possible, means that spans of control will need to be smaller.

- Spans of management are normally at their narrowest at the top of the organisation, and widest at the bottom. Chief executives may have just four or five departmental or functional senior executives accountable to them; while on the shop floor, a foreman making a single component may be responsible for the supervision of twenty or more workers. In recent years, it has also become the practice (again, this is a lesson from Japan) to give individual workers direct responsibility for their particular aspects of the work. In this way, the need for supervision is reduced; and it must always be borne in mind that each level of supervision required is extremely expensive.

9.6   Organisational relationships

Every pattern of organisation gives rise to relationships between the people who comprise it, and these can be classified into four categories as follows:

(a) Direct
This type of relationship exists between the manager and the managed. It is the relationship that flows down the chain of command, as exists in line organisation. Referring to Figure 8.1 (p. 69) it will be seen that the marketing manager has a direct relationship with the home sales manager, and similarly the latter has a direct relationship with the sales representatives and, of

course, the reverse is the situation in both cases. Direct authority and accountability exists in this form of relationship, which is also known as the line or executive relationship.

(b) Indirect

This is a functional relationship and exists where advisory (or staff) officers are present in an organisation and where their expertise is available for use by the line officers. It is shown clearly in the line-and-staff organisation chart at Figure 8.3 (p. 73). Here it will be seen that the management services manager (a staff appointment) has an indirect relationship with the financial accountant (a line officer). The management services manager can guide and advise the accountant but cannot give direct orders in the operation of the accounting system.

(c) Representative (or staff)

This relationship must not be confused with the advisory function of a staff officer in a line-and-staff organisation. It is unfortunate that the same term, 'staff', is so frequently employed when reference is made to the representative relationship. This form of relationship exists between an executive and a personal assistant. It is an especially difficult one for the assistants concerned because they have no delegated authority to make decisions for the executive, yet because of the close association with the chief, other members of staff are inclined to assume that they have this power. It is a frequent source of misunderstanding and possible resentment. A refusal to act or make a decision is often seen as an unco-operative attitude, despite the fact that the personal assistant has no authority. Being the assistant to the managing director is not the same as being the assistant managing director, though to third parties the two positions are often confused.

(d) Lateral

Lateral relationships exist between executive supervisors and staff at the same levels of responsibility and authority in different departments. They exist for purposes of co-operation and co-ordination and no organisation could function effectively without them.

(e) Organisational

All staff, whatever their rank, status or occupation, have a direct responsibility to their organisation. They therefore have a direct relationship with it. They are responsible for making their own contribution to its well-being; and have, therefore, implicit duties and responsibilities to its reputation, enhancement, and general well-being. Conversely, the organisation (impersonally) has responsibilities to ensure the continued well-being of each individual member of staff. This applies especially in the payment of wages; standards of treatment and behaviour; and matters concerning health and safety. This last is often called 'a duty of care' (see also above, p. 67).

(f) Human relations

Everyone, whatever their rank or status in an organisation, is entitled to a basic humanity of treatment. This clearly varies between situations – for example, people in military organisations accept treatment very different to those in emergency services, retail supermarkets, or the corner-shop. However, humanity as well as operational effectiveness must always exist.

(g) Informal relationships

Informal relationships – friendships as well as interdepartmental co-operation and meeting groups – are always certain to grow up in an organisation of any size at all. At their best, these work in the best interests of the organisation, as well as contributing to its basic humanity.

It should be noted from the above that both occupational and human relationships within organisations have the potential for great complexity. One of the key tasks of managers and supervisors, at all levels, is to understand this complexity and be able to engage in effective work alongside it.

9.7 Simplifying management levels

As organisations grew, there was historically a tendency to increase the number of levels of management with the stated purpose of ensuring adequate supervision of staff. This has been found to be extremely expensive, as well as a hindrance to effective communication and decision-making, and this has given rise to consideration of new methods and approaches of management.

- As a consequence, many large businesses have started to question the need for such proliferation and have begun to reduce the number of levels of middle and senior management; and also to engage in different approaches to supervision.
- Savings in overhead costs also result when the number of management levels is reduced. Savings in the administrative burden and overhead carried also accrue when levels of supervision are reduced.
- If the reduction of levels of management is to be effective, however, managers at all levels, and supervisors, need to be highly trained and expert in the principles and practices of management, as well as being fully conversant with the particular functional aspect for which they are responsible. For the inevitable consequence is that, as levels and hierarchies of management are reduced, spans of control become wider. There is also a clear implication here for the delegating of much greater autonomy to individual workers, and those responsible for delivering the products and services of the organisation in question.

QUESTIONS

   1 'Effective delegation is often preached but rarely practised.' Outline the essential actions a manager should take if delegation is to be effective. (ICSA)

   2 In what ways will the extent of decentralisation in an organisation create impetus for greater accountability of individual departmental managers to the top management team? (ISCA)

3   Henry has for some time been in charge of a department which was producing satisfactory results before he took over. However, recently, several of his staff have asked whether jobs in other similar departments are available. There have also been a number of unexpected mistakes, and information has not been transmitted properly.

You are Henry's manager. As a result of your concern you have been keeping an eye on the situation. You have found that Henry comes in early every day, stays late, takes large amounts of work home with him, and is showing definite signs of strain.

In the meantime his staff appear bored and uninterested. You are required to describe

(a) possible causes of this situation;

(b) what you would do to determine the true cause;

(c) with reasons, the changes you propose. (CIMA)

4   'Responsibility' and 'Accountability' are terms often misused in relation to delegation. Define each and clarify your answer with examples. (IAM)

5   Some business organisations are highly centralised with power concentrated in head office. Discuss the possible advantages and drawbacks of this type of organisation structure. (IComA)

6   In recent years many organisations have adopted 'flatter' organisation structures reducing the number of levels of management. Discuss the possible benefits and dangers of this policy. (IComA)

7   Some administrative activities lend themselves to centralisation whereas others are less easily organised in that way. Select an activity with which you are familiar, and state the problems associated with making it central to a large organisation. (IAM)

8   Line and staff relationships are found in many organisations. Briefly differentiate between these two relationships, and discuss how, in a large manufacturing organisation, they could create inter-personal problems, and suggest how such problems might be overcome. (IM)

▚ 10 Command or direction

In all human enterprise, in whatever sphere it exists, wherever a group of people are concerned with achieving specific objectives, there arises the need to have someone with ultimate responsibility; in other words, a leader or commander to whom authority is given to direct the group's activities and to assume accountability and responsibility for the resources allocated in accordance with the wishes of the organisation as a whole.

The word 'command' suggests a rather military arrangement that demands unquestioning adherence to orders or instructions from the top. While this may have been the case in the past, this is not so in modern industrial, commercial and public service society. Those in 'command' of modern organisations concern themselves much more with the overall direction of the enterprise, taking strategic decisions which are then implemented by individual managers working in their own particular ways. People at all organisational levels have much greater access to organisation information; they have a much greater understanding of their own value and contribution. Willing acceptance of command, direction and authority is based on mutual understanding, and mutuality of interest, rather than blind obedience to orders.

10.1 Chain of command

In all organisations, command and direction start at the top. Through the process of delegation, they travel down through the management structure to find the level at which action is required. Each level, therefore, has a narrower sphere of influence than the one above it and a narrower field of accountability; spans of authority also narrow in the same way. On a line organisation chart this is shown very clearly, as illustrated in Figure 8.1 (Page 69).

At each level, managers and supervisors will be concerned with how to implement their particular part of the purpose, when to implement it, and how it is to be judged for effectiveness and success.

10.2 'The law of the situation'

In small organisations, the chain of command is obvious, clear and simple. In more complex and diverse organisations, chains of command become much less obvious and more convoluted.

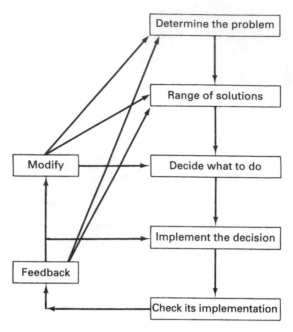

Figure 10.1   Basic steps in command, direction and decision-making

- It is also true that functional departments have become very much more specialised and expert. As a consequence, directions from top management will be concerned with what they want out of the functional department; how this is to be achieved is left very much in the hands of the experts.
- Standard practices, however, can be established so that, whatever the matter in hand, staff can adhere to these. They are developed out of the need to meet circumstances as they arise, to maintain flexibility, to respond to opportunities, while at the same time ensuring that everything is standardised as far as possible.
- Whenever it does become necessary to issue direct instructions – orders – it is necessary that these are fully explained, so that those involved can understand the reasons why departure from standardisation is necessary.

Mary Parker Follett, a management academic and accepted authority on the use of power and influence in industry, expressed this concept as 'the law of the situation'. This is supported by the present-day assertion that, rather than exercising authority or power, managers should be sufficiently professional and expert in creating effective and successful operating and reporting relationships.

10.3   Unity of command

No organisation can function effectively unless, ultimately, there is only one person in overall charge who is responsible for the success or failure of the enterprise. This person is the chief executive, as we have already seen.

However, this does not mean that they are required to act entirely on their own. It does mean that the top management of an organisation must speak with one voice. The differences between them must be reconciled before directions are issued; and where serious differences persist, it may be necessary to replace the source of those differences.

This is also true lower down the management ladder. No supervisor should ever express adverse opinions about instructions that have to be implemented. It is also true that confusion is caused when staff are required to accept direction from more than one supervisor or manager.

10.4   Difficulties in achieving effective direction

When unity of command or direction does not exist, confusion occurs. It also leads to a serious loss of confidence on the part of the staff, who are uncertain or unsure of where they stand; and when this confusion is allowed to persist, they lose confidence in the capabilities of their manager.

- Unity of command must therefore always be maintained. If mistakes are known to have been made, those in authority should admit to these and remedy them. In many organisations, large amounts of resources are wasted in trying to cover up the fact that mistakes have been made.
- Managers and supervisors should always be supported by their superior; and in turn, managers and supervisors should always support their subordinates. Again, when mistakes have been made, these should be remedied quickly – but in private.
- Dilution of command and direction can also occur where there is overlap between the functions of different departments. A simple example is where both the sales and production departments have direct access to customers. Unless there is a commonality of direction in dealings with customers in both departments, it is very easy for customers to be sold different things at different times – and again, this leads to loss of confidence.
- This, in turn, has to be reconciled with the fact that functional and expert departments and individuals are hired because of their expertise – and that they may not have direct line or managerial authority over particular situations. This problem was referred to in Chapter 8 above. In such situations, managers need to reconcile the preferred direction, with the input of the expert.
- In all situations, a unity of purpose and direction can only be achieved if there is mutual respect and understanding; full understanding of the overall direction of the organisation, and of the contribution of each department to it; and

a basis of mutual trust, respect and value between all members of staff whatever their position.

10.5 Decision-making

Inherent in the activity of command is the need to make decisions and it can be said with truth that, fundamentally, all management is concerned with decision-making. Also inherent in the activity of command is the need to delegate authority and functions, and so the power to make certain decisions has also to be delegated. It is necessary, therefore, to examine the process of decision-making from the point of view of the levels at which it operates.

There is no consensus of opinion among writers on management as to the categories into which decision-making should be divided, but a useful classification as shown by practical experience could be as follows:

(a) Long-range decisions that will affect the prospects of the organisation for a very long time. These are almost certainly the province of top management, who are charged with the responsibility of the continued survival and prosperity of the enterprise. Such decisions include major capital investment, determining the sources of finance for such investment, product and market choice, and similar long-term problems. Such decisions embrace a considerable amount of uncertainty and take a long time for the results of their implementation to be known. They are essentially strategic.

(b) Medium-term decisions that are less far-reaching, involving problems such as minor capital investment, product modification, tactical market planning and similar decisions that are needed to keep the enterprise on course in the implementation of top-level planning and objectives.

(c) Operational decisions that have immediate results and are, or should be, taken at the lower levels of supervision. Such decisions include, for example, replenishment of stocks, routes for deliveries, credit control in normal circumstances and so on. All decisions can be reduced to a sequence of activities as shown in Figure 10.1. It will be seen that inherent in the implementation of a decision is the need to have feedbacks as to its effectiveness so that modifications to the instructions can be issued where necessary to ensure the ultimate success of the decision.

10.6 Steps to effective decision-making

Many managers and their subordinate supervisors shirk the responsibility of making decisions, and give many reasons such as not having sufficient knowledge of all the facts, difficulty in finding competent operating staff, lack of time for proper consideration and so on. Very often the real reason is lack of courage or lack of self-confidence; but even not making a decision is a decision to refrain from action. Other managers and supervisors rush into decisions without due regard for circumstances or resultant effects, sometimes with disastrous results, and sometimes with unexpected success.

Neither of these attitudes, of course, is the right one, and decision-making can be made easier and more effective by taking the following, considered, steps:

1 Define as accurately as possible the problem to be solved. This entails going into detail about every aspect of the problem and making sure no relevant facts are omitted, however remote they may appear to be at first sight.
2 Ascertain the relevance of this problem to other areas that might be affected by any decision taken.
3 Analyse the problem into its component parts so that each can be considered fully.
4 Review the resources available to solve the problem, or those that can be provided if necessary.
5 Determine as many possible solutions as can be reasonably considered given the circumstances as stated.
6 Test the most attractive solutions on the basis of their probable success and their impact on the rest of the organisation.
7 Determine the solution that promises to be the most effective.
8 Implement the decision and monitor its effectiveness.

It is obvious that not all these steps will be necessary at operational level, but they may be thought essential for long-term and medium-term decision-making.

10.7 Programmed and non-programmed decision-making

It is also common to divide decision-making into programmed and non-programmed, and it is considered good management practice to have as many decisions as possible in the first category.

- Programmed decisions are simply those that are taken automatically in any given set of circumstances. They are thus those normally taken at the lower levels of supervision. An example is that of stock replenishment. If it is a rule that the stock of a certain product should not fall below one hundred units, then the decision by the storekeeper to replenish the stock when this level is being reached is programmed one. The amount to be ordered will also be programmed by the setting of a maximum stockholding figure, the reorder amount being the difference between maximum and existing stock. This decision is now commonly made by computer, where an automatic reorder request is produced: a perfect example of programmed decision-making.
- Non-programmed decisions require the exercise of managerial judgement, and the higher up the management hierarchy the decisions are required to be made the greater the exercise of judgement that is required. A decision to invest large sums of money in new buildings and plant requires judgement of a very high order and is done at the level of top management.

- However, judgement at all levels is required where the decision is not automatic. Taking the case of stock replenishment again as an example, should the firm be offered a quantity of the product at a very attractive price, but this would mean departing from the laid-down stockholding level, a judgement would have to be made as to the wisdom of departing from the normal holding. This requires a decision of a non-programmed kind even though it may be taken at a low level of management. It involves assessing the risks of having stock left on hand, of tying up working capital which, perhaps, could be better used in other ways, of taking up storage space and other associated problems.

10.8 Where decisions are made

Each level of management and supervision is responsible for taking decisions within its own environment.

- The extent to which such decisions are matters of judgement and experience depends upon the level at which they are taken and the extent of initiative allowed at each level by top management.
- Whatever the decision made, and wherever it is made, the key to its effectiveness lies in its implementation. Many of the factors upon which decisions are made emanate from front-line activities. Items such as production levels, machine utilisation, sales targets and the like, are operational factors which have to be taken into account.
- Many organisations now recognise this, and have regular consultations with employees before taking significant decisions that will affect working conditions, job content, pay, and work security. This is approved by many as a step towards industrial democracy and certainly entails the involvement of all staff in the making of important decisions. It is also increasingly a statutory requirement as membership of the European Union begins to take effect.
- Similarly, in the upper reaches of organisations, decisions have to be implemented by senior and top management. Again, this is only possible if those concerned fully understand the need for the chosen direction.

10.9 Aids to top-level decision-making

Long-term decisions especially, are fraught with the problems of uncertainty, and errors can have the most far-reaching repercussions.

- Many organisations now go to great lengths to try and assess the risk inherent in particular decisions. They have extensive databases, and employ expert analysts, in order to try and gauge the effects of the range of possible outcomes in advance of decisions being taken. Approaches to the assessment of risk normally try to present the potential outcome of decisions in terms of best, medium and worst scenarios; and risk assessment information databases include factors outside, as well as inside, the organisation's control.

- In the management of risk, all organisations try to have 'early warning systems' available. Again, this is based on having complete and high quality information concerning the state of markets, products and services; and also taking active and positive steps towards assessing the state of the work-force, the effectiveness of production processes, and so on.
- To try to take some of the risk out of decisions, management now also make use of sophisticated mathematical and statistical techniques, some of which are touched on in Chapter 24. It is essential to remember, however, that these are only tools to aid managers and do not usurp their responsibility to exercise their own judgement and evaluation of situations.
- At the point of implementation, many organisations and their managers engage in a final brief review or 'wait a minute'. At the point of implementation, the main factors are reconsidered and re-evaluated, just to make sure that everything necessary is in accordance with what is to be done. Any last minute hitches can therefore be picked up; and it is also a useful check on whether everyone is in accord.
- As stated in Chapter 5, all organisations depend on high quality information for long-term and enduring success. This is especially true of decision-making; all decisions, whether long-range or short-range, should be based on as full a picture as possible, and this can only be achieved if information is available.
- Most decisions have to be taken by particular deadlines. Again, therefore, there is a balance to be struck between the volume and quality of information required and the deadline by which it is necessary. The longer the deadline, the greater the ability to gather information; however, in practice, this is not always possible. If a decision is required in a short time, it has to be taken on the basis of the information that is available at that time.
- All organisations also need the facility for taking crisis and emergency decisions. This means ensuring that all managers and supervisors have guidelines to work to when they are effected by crises and emergencies. For crises and emergencies should never become excuses for guesswork; there must always be available a rational for the management of such situations.
- All of these factors are only aids to decision-making. They will never make the right decisions for managers. They assist managers in forming their judgements, and provide the information and basis on which to back these judgements. All decisions must therefore remain within the judgement of managers, whatever tools they use in particular circumstances.

10.10 Rationality of decisions

It is clear from the preceding section that all decisions, therefore, have some measure of subjectivity; complete objectivity is only possible in a small proportion of programmed circumstances. There are nearly always, also, elements of uncertainty. Moreover, some decisions are arrived at through personal prejudice, personal influence, political manoeuvring between parties involved in decision-making, and other expedient and self-seeking factors. These should always be examined when major decisions are being taken. For, if given the opportunity, both managers and their staff will present their case to their own best advantage, and this is not always in the wider interests of the organisation at large.

10.11 Decisions by committee

Committee organisation has been dealt with in **8.5** above. Where the main function of a committee is to make decisions, its constitution and rules should be drawn up to ensure that this can take place. The following are essential.

(a) The chairman should have a clear remit, brief, agenda, and guidelines to which to work.
(b) There should be formal procedures for the conduct of discussions leading to decisions. Clear time frames must be allocated to each point.
(c) A formal method agreeing decisions, or coming to a consensus, must be a part of the rules. The most usual method is by voting, though there is a risk inherent in this in that a narrow majority may carry a point of view to which there is substantial opposition.
(d) In the management of decision-making committees, care should be taken that no decisions are arrived at through the influence of a clique.
(e) Where critical decisions are being taken, these should be taken in consultation with all committee members, whether or not they are able to be present at meetings.
(f) Committees should never be used as the means of delaying firm decisions unless this is the deliberate intention.

This applies to all decision-making groups. In other circumstances, however, procedures may be less formal and a more relaxed attitude prevail. Nevertheless, these principles must still be followed.

QUESTIONS

1 The process of management may be defined as comprising planning, organising, directing and controlling. Describe each of these activities, illustrating your answer using examples with which you are familiar. (ACCA)
2 What are the essential differences between the approach to decision-making at the strategic level and at the operations level? Demonstrate these differences by reference to a typical example of a decision at each level. (CIMA)
3 The term 'unity of command' means that each subordinate should be accountable to only one superior. Describe two situations where this principle might reasonably be violated by a company. (CIM)
4 'In business, from the factory floor to the boardroom, decision making by consent is replacing traditional autocracy.' Discuss. (CIM)
5 Can decision-making be an entirely rational process? In what ways is decision-making limited by inadequate information and by the style of management in an organisation? (ICSA)
6 How could group decision-making be made more effective? (IAM)

░ ▼ ▌▌ Co-ordination

Co-ordination is the integration and synchronisation of the various activities of an organisation in order that all its functions can work harmoniously towards its common objectives. In effect it can be described as 'organisation in time' because timing is of the essence if co-ordination is to be effectively achieved. An example will make this clear.

- If a manufacturer decides to launch a new product it will entail the provision of finance to provide materials and equipment for its manufacture and marketing. It will have to be put into production and it will need a marketing, and selling campaign to bring it to the attention of potential customers. Each of these activities will have to be co-ordinated – that is, timed – so that funds are available to finance the initiation of the project or it will not be able to start, the marketing effort must be put in hand early enough to create consumer interest ready for the sale of the products directly they start coming off the production line, and manufacture must be timed so that units of production are available to meet orders as soon as they come in. A failure in the timing of any one of these activities will mean a failure to achieve maximum results from the product.
- Lack of finance at the right time may delay the start of production or of the marketing campaign. Failure to time the marketing effort correctly will result either in stocks of manufactured goods awaiting customers' orders, so locking up working capital and storage space, or in lack of goods available for delivery to customers so that goodwill suffers. Failure to harmonise productive effort with selling effort will lead to goods being in stock unnecessarily, or to disappointed customers.
- Co-ordination of the activities of all the functions of an enterprise, therefore, is clearly of the utmost importance to the success of that enterprise because all functions are interdependent. The failure of one section of the organisation to meet its required objectives can jeopardise the success of the other functions that rely upon it, as the example indicates. Further, co-ordination is a continuing requirement which needs constant attention if it is not to fail at some point with detrimental consequences for the organisation. Failure to purchase materials at the right time may delay production; delayed production may result in non-delivery to customers on the promised or contract dates; non-delivery according to customer requirements may mean loss of goodwill and actual loss of customers which, in turn, means loss of revenue.

11.1 Planning for co-ordination

Co-ordination does not happen by itself. It has to be planned and the very act of planning emphasises the need for it to function properly.

- Co-ordination is much easier to achieve if the means to do so are recognised and worked out at the beginning of a project rather than after it has been progressing for some time. This is true whether the project is the establishment of a whole organisation or if it relates only to a small procedure involving only two or three functions. In a major project such as the installation of a computer or the building of a large factory a plan of action must be formulated at the very beginning which sets out details of all the necessary operations, with the dates and working times required, so that the various activities can be scheduled to fit in with each other. This schedule shows the completion date towards which all the activities are geared and is, in fact, a schedule of co-ordination.
- On a very much smaller scale the posting of an urgent parcel to a customer also requires the co-ordination of the efforts of the sales clerk, warehouse and post room, and this must be planned with no less care than the large project, otherwise the post will be missed.
- In order to achieve the goal set it is usually necessary to plan backwards from the completion time. In the example of the parcel, for instance, if the mail is collected at 5 p.m. then all activities must be planned and co-ordinated from that time backwards, so indicating how much time can be allocated to each of the required operations. Similarly, in a major project with a fixed completion date this date is the starting-point from which to plan so that the time allowance for each activity can be determined.
- Where certain activities have rigid time requirements other more flexible activities must be adjusted to suit the total time limitation. Critical path analysis is very useful in these circumstances to provide a clear picture of the situation (see 24.2 (d) below) to determine those activity periods that are critical and those where times can be adjusted, by one means or another, to ensure effective maintenance of the schedule to meet the completion date.
- In a continuous activity there must be review points set so that it can be seen whether co-ordination has been effective or whether there has been some slipping away from the required plan. Without such review points for examination of progress co-ordination can break down completely, with one or more sections of the organisation becoming entirely out of step with the remainder. An example might be the loss of co-ordination between manufacture and sales resulting in over-production and stocks accumulating. Monthly reviews of the situation would do much to bring both into line. It could even be held that the annual profit and loss account and balance sheet of a company are means of monitoring the proper co-ordination of all of its functions, with over-stocking, poor cash flow and other indicators bringing evidence of the effectiveness or otherwise of the co-ordinating effort.

11.2 Ways to assist co-ordination

Co-ordination depends to a very large extent on the existence of goodwill between the various sectors of the organisation, so it is important that management takes steps to promote good relations between departmental managers and staff.

- It is not unknown for some managements to foster a competitive spirit between one section and another with the idea of generating an aggressive enthusiasm for their department's activities and showing themselves to be superior to the other departments. While this may be successful initially, it is usually very soon results in bad feeling between the various sections, a disregard for the needs of other departments and, ultimately, to an imbalance in the organisation's activities and a breakdown in co-ordination. If the sales department is set to sell more than production can make, the enterprise as a whole must ultimately suffer.
- The objectives and plans of the organisation must be clearly set out and understood by both managers and their staff, and each sector's role must be fully appreciated. In this way the need to co-ordinate one with another will be made obvious and the risks of failure reduced.
- The responsibilities, authority and duties of all must be clearly defined, particularly in relation to the lines of demarcation. Effective co-ordination relies heavily on everyone's being aware of precisely what is required and expected of him or her. Haziness on this point results in overlap and consequent personal irritation, or in indeterminate areas of responsibility neglected by all. In either case co-ordination will suffer.
- Specific procedures should be laid down where possible to deal with routine and non-routine activities. With routine matters set procedures result in automatic co-ordination. Non-routine matters and emergencies may or may not be able to be dealt with in this way. However, if policies are formulated and well-known in regard to such eventualities co-ordination will be assured without specific executive intervention. While senior executives may be ultimately responsible for co-ordinating the organisation's activities – some would even argue that the chief executive has this responsibility – their intervention should be called for only in matters of the utmost importance.
- It is contended, with some justification, that management and staff training programmes can assist in promoting effective co-ordination. This is because such programmes tend to bring about a common approach to problems and a standardised reaction to them. Thus, in any situation one manager can be reasonably sure what another manager will do. This common approach is a decided help in promoting co-ordination, precisely in unexpected circumstances.

11.3 Practical steps in co-ordination

Effective co-ordination is extremely difficult to achieve, and it is a key management task. While the suggestions set out in **11.1** and **11.2** above point the way, they need to be turned into practical terms if they are to be of any use or value. The principal steps that need to be taken are as follows.

(a) Strategy, direction, objectives and policies for the organisation as a whole must be clearly defined and known throughout the concern. Communication is best carried out through writing specific policy documents and handbooks, and the use of in-house journals, memoranda, briefing sheets and the like; and these should always be supported by face-to-face presentations.

(b) Departmental and divisional objectives and policies should be dealt with in the same way.

(c) The scope and duties of each job, and set of tasks, must be properly defined. It is usual to write job descriptions for each member of staff.

(d) There must be clearly defined procedures for each activity. Some form of monitoring is necessary to check adherence to this. Co-ordination is likely to fail without some form of control mechanism. An example of this is the activity of progress-chasing in factories, where the progress of work is checked at various points during its journey through the various stages of the production process, especially concerning quality, volume and time.

(e) All staff need to know how their activities fit into the whole effort of the organisation. This is best achieved by some form of induction when staff are engaged. Formal and informal meetings of staff should be arranged from time to time to keep them up-to-date. Management meetings and cluster groups should also take place regularly.

(f) All forms of communication must be effective, open and honest. Lines of formal communication must be laid down, and the style, quality, value and volume of information that is to flow through these must be clearly directed. Informal communication should support this; in particular, it should be noted that organisational grapevines flourish when there is a lack of good quality information in the formal systems.

(g) All meetings play a large part in ensuring good co-ordination. Specific, formally constituted, meetings should have regularised agenda to which to work; while *ad hoc* meetings called for specific purposes should take steps to make sure that these are fully addressed. There also needs to be clear organisational provision for the calling of emergency and crisis meetings.

(h) Committees, cluster groups, project groups, work improvement groups, quality improvement groups and the like are also useful in promoting effective co-ordination. These activities break down barriers between departments, divisions and functions. They enable mutual confidence and trust to be engendered; and a greater understanding of the pressures and constraints in different areas of the organisation.

However, organisations that depend heavily on these forms of committee and group working have to be aware that, to be effective, the approach contributes to the well-being and effectiveness of the organisation as a whole. There is a danger that the group and committee working becomes a substitute for real activity. The use, value and output of all such groups have therefore to be monitored.

(i) Co-ordination is also improved through general face-to-face contact. Written memoranda, orders and instructions tend to make communication formal and impersonal; and this can be detrimental to organisational effectiveness. Reference was made in Chapter 9 to 'Management by Walking About' (MbWA), and the great benefit of this is that people get to know and recognise each other on a human, as well as operational, level. This greatly assist co-ordination of efforts.

(j) Verbal communication should however always be supported in writing, to ensure that everybody involved understands what has been decided or arrived at. Any misunderstandings are then down on paper and may be remedied.

(k) Co-ordination is a key management activity, and therefore a key responsibility of top management. Top management should never seek to play one department off against another; neither should they favour one department at the expense of others. It is the combined and co-ordinated efforts of all that contribute to organisation effectiveness and maximise its chances of a long-term future.

Co-ordination is, therefore, clearly a key management task and activity, and these steps provide a useful guide to achieve this for both departmental and corporate activities.

11.4 Co-ordination and co-operation

Whatever principles and rules are laid down for co-ordination, they will not be effective unless co-operation exists between members of the organisation.

- Steps set out in **11.3** above are guidelines for successful co-ordination. Properly carried out, they foster confidence and mutuality of understanding and concern. This is a key to stimulating a sense of co-operation among all those concerned.

- Co-operation is a personal and professional attitude. It comes about through the evolution of good management and staff relations, personal and professional involvement, and inter-departmental confidence and support.

- Co-operation is also greatly reinforced if everyone concerned is known to be fair, open, honest and above-board in their dealings with each other. It is ruined where this is not the case.

- The greater the sense of wholehearted co-operation throughout the organisation, the easier it is to achieve co-ordination. Where co-operation does not exist, there may nevertheless be inter-departmental acquiescence – a recognition that at least everybody has their own job to do and they are doing it to the best of their capabilities. However, where full co-operation does not exist, it is much more usual for there to be conflict and mistrust. This is one of the greatest destructive forces to all organisations. In any case, where there is not full co-operation, the most carefully laid approach to co-ordination will be less than successful.

QUESTIONS

1 What practical steps may be taken to ensure that the activities of the various functional departments within an organisation are effectively co-ordinated? (ICSA)

2 Discuss the relationship between co-ordination and co-operation, and show how the latter affects the former.

3 Discuss the possible consequences of using inter-group competition as a means of increasing performance. (IAM)

4 How might co-ordination within an organisation be improved in a practical manner? (IAM)

5 Define co-ordination. Describe the various ways in which co-ordination may be achieved within a business. IComA)

6 Outline the need for the marketing department to co-ordinate its activities with other management functions. (CIM)

7 Explain how the necessary co-ordination between the marketing and production functions can be achieved, using an organisation of your choice as an illustration. (CIM)

■ ✓ **12** Control

Planning, both at management level and at operational level, looks to the future and lays down what has to be achieved. Control checks whether the plans are being realised and puts into effect corrective measures where deviation or short-fall is occurring. Without effective controls an enterprise will be at the mercy of all the internal and external forces that can disrupt its efficiency and will be unaware of, and therefore unable to combat, such forces.

In the past it was common to review the position of an enterprise only once a year, at the time of the annual accounts. Between one year's end and another there was little information prepared to indicate the performance of the concern, and little specific control was able to be applied simply because of this lack of information. The only real controls were those imposed at shop-floor level and at staff level, particularly in regard to sales representatives, and then only because operation would have been difficult without them.

Nowadays, however, control is exercised over every aspect of an organisation's functions, and this includes management performance. Effective control is a key management task. It ensures that efforts produced at all levels are commensurate with those required to ensure the long-term future, effectiveness and success of the organisation.

12.1   Setting standards

Effective control is based on standards with which actual performance can be compared. If there are no standards, then there can be no effective measure of attainment. These standards fall into five categories: quantity; quality; time; complaint; and value.

(a) Standards for quantity
Standards for quantity include those for sales, production, machine utilisation, output per worker and many others. They are also likely to include figures for the growth of the enterprise, drives for greater efficiency and effectiveness, improvements in cost bases, and so on.

Standards for quantity need to be co-ordinated – for example, a standard can be set for each month's sales, but these must be commensurate with the possible level of production.

Standards for quantity are often set on data derived from past perform-ance, and on forecasts of future possibilities. Standards for quantity should also be set bearing in mind potential output, and maximum output, as well as that which is actually required. If production machinery, for example, is working below its capacity, then there may be scope for a sales effort to seek new markets and new outlets for the production, so that the return on investment in production plant and machinery is improved.

(b) Standards for quality

All aspects of a concern's activities need to be controlled and monitored for quality. In many cases, this is very difficult. Errors and faults can be measured and taken as percentages of the total output produced, which can then be compared with what is deemed to be acceptable. However, error levels may fluctuate, and not all of this may be inside the control of management – they may for example, be dependent upon the quality of components and raw materials available, or packaging machinery.

Quality is also much more difficult to measure in 'human activities' – for example, customer goodwill and relations; the effectiveness of management style; and some functional and expert activities such as design, accounting, and lecturing.

(c) Standards for time

Timescales must be set for each activity. There must be reasonable and capable of achievement – if they are too easy, this is a waste of organisational resources, whereas if they are too difficult, nobody will pay any attention to them and they lose all credibility.

Similarly, imprecise time factors are also to be avoided. Phrases such as 'as a matter of urgency' or 'as soon as possible', should never be used; it is much better to say that 'something should be done by Friday', 'something should be done by the 31st', and so on.

(d) Complaints

Both internal and external complaints should give rise to management attention. Such areas as customer complaints, lack of courtesy by telephone operators, speed or slowness in replying to letters should also be of concern as they have a profound effect on goodwill and on customer relations. The nature and number of complaints received, and the points that they address, should be the subject of monitoring with a view to taking corrective action.

Similarly, internal complaints – poor or deteriorating relations between departments, divisions and functions – should also be the subject of management investigation and concern.

All complaints, whether internal or external, should be addressed early; the particular matter should be put right, and steps taken to ensure that it cannot happen again.

(e) Value

The place of value in control mechanisms is concerned with identifying where value is added; and where value is lost. Internally, this concerns the contribution of support functions; monitoring of costs and charges; attention to resource utilisation; and the relationship between primary and support functions. Externally, it is concerned with some of the reasons why customers choose to use the products and services of the organisation in question – matters concerning perceptions of quality; product appearance; service promptness and reliability; design factors; and branding and brand strength. Remedial action is necessary whenever it can be shown that one or more of these is beginning to give cause for concern.

12.2 Monitoring, review and evaluation

When standards have been set, some mechanism must be devised and installed for each activity whereby to check performance and compare it with the standard. Monitoring performance is a vital part of control because it is not realistic to expect to be able to control an activity if it is not constantly monitored. It is, for example, not possible to control the output of an assembly shop on a factory floor if the number of units completed are not counted. Inspection of the completed units is also necessary to control the maintenance of quality standards and time factors; regular inspection also indicates the potential or likelihood of customer complaints, and where value is being added or lost. How the monitoring, review and evaluation is to be carried out depends otherwise entirely on the activity to be controlled.

- Monitoring, review and evaluation activities should be carried out at all levels and this concerns all activities, both primary and support. It should be the subject of:
  (a) Constant informal review as the result of enduring effective inter-departmental and inter-group relations; and a key feature of day-to-day management at all levels.
  (b) Regular reports and reporting relationships, checking progress and remedying faults when they arise.
  (c) Addressing wider concerns such as staff relations and staff morale; clear indicators of problems here are rises in the number of accidents, rises in absenteeism, and rises in the number of leavers.

- At the very top of the organisation, the chief executive will be gauged principally by the results shown by the annual accounts and reports, and corrective action is often a matter for the whole directoral body. Chief executives also have especial concerns for media relations; dealing with difficult issues (e.g. environmental problems); and other concerns when the organisation is brought into the public eye.

12.3 Regulating mechanisms

Given that standards must be set and adhered to, regulating mechanisms must be established. As suggested in 12.2 above, these will depend upon the type and level of activity that has to be checked. Some examples are as follows.

(a) Policies and plans

To ensure that these are adhered to, there should be written policy manuals and regular reporting relationships so that progress in all areas can be monitored. Reports should emanate from the operating departments or divisions to top management and regular meetings with senior executives should be scheduled to examine and deliberate on the results. Action can then be taken to regulate deviations. This is a key feature of policy implementation and needs to be dealt with at all levels.

(b) Effectiveness of delegation

The extent and limits of delegated authority and the duties of managers and supervisors at all levels should be set out clearly in organisation and procedure manuals. Internal management and procedure audits should take place in the same fashion as internal accounting audits and other reports prepared for consideration by senior executives responsible for their subordinate's activities.

(c) Operational effectiveness

Much monitoring and regulation of the performance of workers should be carried out on-the-spot by supervisors and foremen. This professional and personal control is most immediate and effective where small groups of people are involved; though this is now becoming more prevalent in large organisations also. Traditionally, larger groups have required such methods as job cards, progress slips, time cards and time sheets, and other forms of documentation. To a great extent, this still persists; though it is recognised as being extremely expensive to regulate, and very divisive. Similarly, many progress-chasing and quality-control activities have been handed over to work-groups to become their direct responsibility. Thus, if there are customer complaints, these can be addressed directly to the work-group that produced the product or delivered the service.

(d) Quality and quantity controls

Inspection by supervisors is necessary to control quality standards. Some organisations also have progress chasers and quality control inspectors, though these are again extremely expensive to maintain.

It is usual to have some form of visual presentation of what is expected and what is achieved, so that the two can be compared. A commonly used activity is the Gantt chart (see Figure 12.1). This format can be used for most activities. The example given is for an assembly shop.

(e) Expenditure control

Both capital and revenue expenditure can be regulated by budgetary control which sets limits to permissible expenditure on all activities. At departmental level, there will be budgets covering sales expenditure, expenditure on production, administration and so on, and these budgets will be incorporated in the organisation's total planned expenditure.

Assembly Shop Output Control					
Four weeks commencing 18 May 1833					
Operator		Week 1	Week 2	Week 3	Week 4
E. ALING	Standard	400	400	400	400
	Actual	320	400	200	420
	%	80%	100%	50%	105%
R. EADING	Standard	450	450	450	450
	Actual	450	450	338	450
	%	100%	100%	75%	100%
S. TOKE	Standard	300	300	300	300
	Actual	285	300	210	300
	%	95%	100%	70%	100%
Key:	———	Standard output to be achieved			
	– – – –	Actual output produced			
	%	Percentage of actual to standard			

Figure 12.1   Specimen Gantt chart

(f) Reporting

Most monitoring of activities is done by reporting in one form or another. Reports need to be believed in and valued, and presented at the proper time. They also need to be in a form acceptable and usable to those who receive them. Some reports may be required daily or weekly; others less frequently (e.g. once a month; once a quarter).

(g) The use of work improvement groups

One of the key features of control is to see where improvements can be made. Many organisations now use work improvement groups and quality circles, and other project groups, to work on problems and issues where deficiencies have been identified. This may involve, for example, the need to speed up customer responses, production times, or the operation of administrative and support processes. It may also involve attention to one specific area of activity which always gives rise to customer complaints. Or it may involve simplifying a reporting relationship, or enlarging the area of authority and accountability of those who deal directly with customers, so that complaints are more quickly resolved.

The contribution of such groups is that those directly involved with the problem work on it, and produce solutions that they know are practicable. For it to work effectively, organisations must have complete confidence in the staff involved. They must also be committed to implementing what is proposed, or of giving sound reasons why what is proposed cannot be implemented. Moreover, when it is carried out properly, it is also extremely useful in enhancing staff morale and commitment.

12.4   Problems of measurement

It has been established that proper control cannot be instituted and maintained unless standards have been set as, unless this is done, there is no basis for comparison. However, though the bases for some standards are easy to measure, others can prove very difficult. Some examples will illustrate this.

- If the output of a secretarial service is to be the subject of control with output standards specified, it is not particularly difficult to measure the work-rate of those involved. Their work can be inspected over a period of three to four weeks, or even longer. Targets can then be established in conjunction with the supervisor, who should know what is a good level of output in the particular circumstance. Complaints can also easily be tracked to their source and dealt with.
- The setting of standards for sales orders presents a very much more difficult problem simply because their work is more varied. Every customer's requirements are special to that customer and there is no way of forecasting the number or length of the telephone conversations the proper fulfilment of their function is likely to demand of the staff. It is, therefore, necessary for both the staff and their supervisors to establish where particular problems and anomalies occur; vagaries in dealings with specific customers; and a normal basis for steady-state activities.
- Efforts to set measures of performance for managers is fraught with imponderables. Particularly, this is so where the managers are dealing with long-range plans that provide no performance indicators in the short-term. It is therefore necessary to break managerial activities down into shorter-term or stepping-stone activities, and to use these as the basis for both daily performance, and also as progress towards the longer-term objectives. It requires proper supervision by experts who know and understand the vagaries of managerial performance; and this should be conducted on continuing face-to-face bases, together with regular written statements used as punctuation marks along the way.

12.5   Budgetary control

The most common form of financial regulation is budgetary control and this is now more or less universally applied. In practice, each department, division and function is required to forecast its future expenditure. The period given is usually a year, though this does vary. It will be divided up into the various elements that make up its costs. The actual period will depend upon what type of industry or activity is being budgeted for; where there are violent fluctuations in work-load, seasonal factors, entries into new markets, and exits from existing activities.

- Budgets will be prepared for production, distribution, purchasing, personnel, administration and capital expenditure. They will also be prepared for sales which represents the main source of daily and cash income; and cash flow which represents the estimated income and payments for the period. Capital expenditure budgets are determined by top management in pursuit of the organisation's overall aims and objectives.
- When budgeting, it is useful to assess the fixed costs of each department, division and function. In practice, because these are fixed, however, very little can be done about them in the short-term. Varying fixed costs is a major corporate activity in itself! The emphasis of budgetary control should always be on variable costs, whereby the use of resources goes up and down with the volume of activities. Any deviation in actual resource usage can then be assessed and accounted for.

    Budgeting activities should also be concerned with marginal costs – the costs incurred by taking on one extra activity or series of activities – so that the true costs of engaging in this can be assessed.
- An administration budget is shown in Figure 12.2.

Administration Budget for the year 1988			
Prepared by E. Dean		Date 1.1.88	
Expense	Annual	Per Month of Four Weeks	Remarks
	£	£	
Salaries	26,500	2,038	
Motor car expenses	4,330	333	
Light and heat	1,500	115	
Rent	7,800	600	
		120	
General insurance			
Stationery	1,300	100	
Sundries	650	50	
Audit fee	260	20	
Totals	£ 71,500	£ 5,500	

Figure 12.2 Specimen of a fixed budget

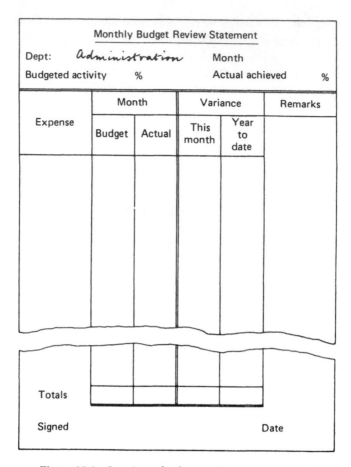

Monthly Budget Review Statement

Dept: *Administration*   Month

Budgeted activity   %   Actual achieved   %

Expense	Month		Variance		Remarks
	Budget	Actual	This month	Year to date	
Totals					

Signed   Date

Figure 12.3   Specimen budget review statement form

This is a simple statement of the budget allocation. The preparation of such a budget is, however, only the first step in controlling expenditure. It is necessary to introduce the means to ensure compliance. This is done by requiring regular budget review statements, and holding regular meetings and discussions concerning budgets. It is then easy to see whether the department concerned is overspending or underspending, and exactly where and why the variances occur. These variances, especially where increased expenditure is indicated, must then be examined to discover why they have occurred so that corrective action can be taken without delay where necessary to bring the activity back into line (see Figure 12.3).

- Some large organisations, especially in public services, have tried to introduce 'internal markets' to assist in monitoring their spending. The chief problem with this is the basis on which costs and charges are apportioned. Very often they bear little or no relationship to the actual expenditure incurred. The creation of a system of internal invoices is also extremely expensive and resource-consuming. It is also necessary not to lose sight of why the internal market has been created – and to remember at all times that this can only be used to control variable and marginal costs. In the past, for example, the National Health Service has seen fit to close hospital wards on the basis that it was cheaper to have them closed than open!

12.6   The flexible budget

Flexible budgets occur where the various elements making up the budget are shown not only at 100 per cent for total budgeted activities, but also at varying levels of activity other than 100 per cent. Thus, flexible budgets might show permitted or expected expenditure at 70 per cent, 80 per cent, 90 per cent and 110 per cent of activity. However, it is not sufficient simply to apply these proportions to all the items because certain expenditures do not vary in direct relation to activity volume.

- It is first necessary to identify fixed and variable costs. Fixed costs are those that are obtained whatever the level of activity and include such items as rent, rates, overheads and staff salaries. Variable costs are those that vary in direct proportion to the level of activity such as materials, power consumption, supply and distribution levels. Reference was also made above to marginal costs – and these are costs incurred as the result of taking on an extra item or series of activities; it is important to be able to identify the marginal cost because at some point it will be necessary to take on new administration staff, and even premises, and this would represent a significant increase in the fixed cost base.
- The technique of flexible budgetary control therefore involves planning the sales target, stating this as 100 per cent activity and then preparing individual budgets and a master budget at this level and at the other levels as percentages of the target. In working out the proportionate levels account will be taken of fixed costs, which will be common to each activity level; variable costs, which will be precisely proportionate; and semi-variable costs, which will be the subject of assessment for each level (see Figure 12.4).
- A favourite device for illustrating the effects of variable levels of activity in a flexible budget is the break-even chart (see Figure 12.5), which emphasises the point at which the operation becomes profitable. In this chart the semi-variable cost is often not shown as such but is incorporated in the other two categories for simplicity of presentation.

12.7   Advantages of budgetary control

While budgetary control, contrary to some expectations, does not provide total regulation of expenditure, it does have many advantages:

(a) The expenditure limits set do impose a brake on extravagance and unthinking financial commitments: they ensure that serious consideration is given before expenditure is indulged in instead of afterwards. Attention is drawn to undue expenditure needs at an early stage and reasons sought for them.

Monthly Administration Budget						Financial Year 19ΞΞ	

Type		Activity below normal			Normal		Activity above normal	
		70%	80%	90%	Month	%	110%	120%
		£	£	£	£		£	£
	Sales volume	28,532	32,608	36,684	40,760	100%	44,836	48,912
F	Salaries	2,038	2,038	2,038	2,038	5.00%	2,038	2,038
V	Car expenses	234	267	301	333	0.82%	368	401
F	Light and heat	115	115	115	115	1.47%	115	115
V	Stationery	71	82	92	100	0.25%	112	122
V	Sundries	36	41	46	50	0.12%	56	61
F	Audit fee	20	20	20	20	0.05%	20	20
	Totals	4,240	4,543	4,852	5,096	12.5%	5,189	5,377

Prepared by *R. Bourne*   Date 31.12.19ΞΞ

F = a fixed expense   V = a variable expense

Figure 12.4   Specimen of a flexible budget

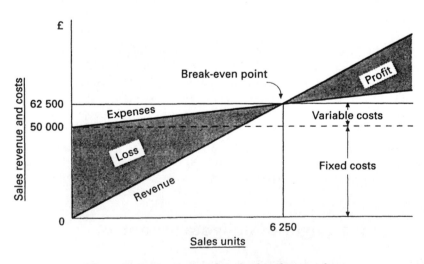

Figure 12.5   Specimen of a sales break-even chart

(b) The preparation of budgets requires all concerned to examine very closely the working of their departments. Forecasts have to be made and targets set. These actions tend to impose restraints on unrealistic ambitions and emphasise the need for practical and attainable goals.

(c) As all budgets are interdependent, budgetary control has a positive effect on co-ordination. Related departments must work together in order that their budgets may be compatible and correlate with each other.

(d) The requirement to prepare periodical budget review statements, and the holding of regular budgetary control review meetings ensure constant monitoring of budget performances.

(e) Such monitoring has two effects. The first is that managers and others responsible for budgets are disposed to try to ensure that the budget figures are adhered to as far as possible; the second is that non-compliance with budgeted performance is brought to management's attention at an early stage so that any necessary remedial action can be taken with the minimum of delay.

(f) Similarly, this monitoring may also reveal that the original budgets have been unrealistic and that the figures may have to be adjusted in the light of internal or external conditions coming about subsequent to budget formulation.

(g) Because managers are responsible for their own budget figures they have an incentive to keep within the limits set, and to ensure that their staff comply with the constraints put upon the department.

Formula for break-even point:

$$B/E = F\left(\frac{S}{S-V}\right)$$

Where B/E = break-even point

F = Fixed costs

S = Selling price per unit

V = Variable costs per unit

In the chart illustrated above

F = £50 000

S = £10

V = £2

Thus

$$B/E = £50\,000\left(\frac{10}{10-2}\right)$$

$$= £62\,500 = 6250 \text{ Sales units.}$$

Thus

Variable costs at break-even point

= 6 250 £ = £12 500.

12.8 Disadvantages of budgetary control

Despite the undoubted advantages of budgetary control it does have some disadvantages, which will now be examined:

(a) A budget is a monitoring aid, it is not a regulator. Some managers are inclined to treat it as the latter and abrogate their responsibilities as managers. If expenditure is necessary outside the scope of the budget to ensure efficient operation in a specific instance, this additional cost must be argued for, not accepted as barred.

(b) In many cases budgets are looked upon as indicators of expenditure that should be incurred. Where the budgeted figures will not be attained it is not unknown for unnecessary expenditure to be incurred because a budget surplus is available and 'must be used up'. This occurs most frequently where annual budgets are based on previous years' budget figures instead of realistic new forecasts being formulated. The oft-repeated comment is that 'our budget will be cut next year if we do not spend all of this year's'.

(c) Where budgetary control is so fine that separate budgets are prepared for sectionalised needs it is often the case that any surplus from one budget will not be passed over to a budget likely to be in deficit, even though for practical reasons this may be highly desirable. This does not benefit the organisation as a whole. An example would be where a secretarial department has a budget for stationery and another for photocopying materials. Nothing is gained in practical terms if a surplus on the stationery budget cannot be transferred to make good a deficit in the budget for photocopying materials, though this attitude does often obtain. Experience shows it to be particularly prevalent in connection with small items of capital expenditure.

(d) In times of fluctuating prices budgeting presents especial difficulties, and when high rates of inflation occur budgets become out of date very quickly. The remedies are frequent reviews of the bases for the budgeted figures and the installation of flexible budgets which can, within limits, accommodate price changes.

(e) The calculation and implementation of budgets and budgetary control does, of necessity, impose an extra burden on departmental and functional managers over and above their routine responsibilities, even where there is a budget officer or department.

(f) As there is inevitably a finite financial resource to be shared throughout the organisation, friction at best, and antagonism at worst, can be generated between departments seeking a proportion of this resource.

(g) It is also the case that budgeting tends to be driven by the annual cycle. All organisations have to produce annual reports and accounts, and this tends to be the driving force for budgeting. In managerial terms of course, activities do not begin and end at the start and finish of each year; activities are continuous, and for some project-based activities (e.g. civil engineering) projects may last for anything up to ten years. Nevertheless, costings for activities may become seriously distorted if there is a rigid adherence to the principle of the annual cycle.

(h) There are also problems at the margins when budgets are established. For example, if a department has a budget of £200,000 for a particular activity, and the activity will in fact cost £205,000, a decision has to be taken whether or not it should go ahead. Similarly, at the micro level, a manager might be given authority to spend up to £20 per item, and problems arise when permission has to be sought to spend resources on something that costs £22.

The point is that all budgeting activities need to contribute positively to managerial and organisational activity. Serious problems arise when they become the driving force of the activity, and the quality and volume of activity is governed by budget constraints. It is also a problem in public services where mangers are expected to come in under budget so that this money can then be clawed back (and most insidiously of all, some managers are given salary incentives to make sure that this happens). The purpose is to ensure that resources that have been decided essential for given activities can be monitored and evaluated so that expenditure is seen to be effective.

12.9   Control decisions

As far as possible, control decisions should never be made automatically. The ideal situation is where the necessary control is easily carried out through human interaction. The only controls that should be automatic are those concerning heating and lighting levels where the equipment is switched off and on by thermostats which sense the ambient temperature. There will be reasons for variances in performance, and these should always be the subject of human intervention, however brief and routine. They can always be followed up with written reports in support of what has been found.

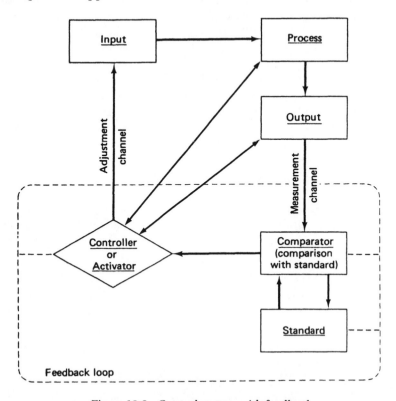

Figure 12.6   Control system with feedback

Where judgement is needed in the control process it will depend, to a very large extent, on feedback in order that appropriate steps may be taken to correct a situation that is not proceeding to plan. It is essential, therefore, that a proper system of communication for management information be established so that necessary reports can flow to the manager or supervisor responsible with a minimum of delay. Such a system of control is illustrated in Figure 12.6.

12.10   Principles of control

For control to be truly effective, it must be governed by firm principles.

(a) The method of control must be suitable for the activity it seeks to regulate and should be the minimum required to achieve the desired results. Over-elaborate controls often lead to the system being ignored or distorted.

(b) Accuracy should be commensurate with control requirements. Absolute accuracy is often quite unnecessary; on the other hand, it must ensure adherence to the principles of quantity, quality, value, time, and redress for complaints.

(c) Control activities will stick to the principles indicated, though the ways in which these are carried out will clearly vary between organisations and sectors. Controls that suit a shipbuilder will not be satisfactory for a hospital.

(d) Feedback information must be available to the controller in time for corrective action to be taken before matters have gone too far wrong.

(e) Maintenance of organisational and operational standards must be a key performance target; and action to remedy this when it falls short of organisational requirements must be taken quickly.

(f) Exceptions, quirks and anomalies should always be examined. These can occur as the result of freak conditions; or they may be symptomatic of something more serious. However, it is necessary for organisations not to create undue administrative control mechanisms in order to try and prevent something that may happen only very infrequently. Moreover, it is simply not possible to predict the full range of human situations that may occur at a place of work.

(g) Finally, areas of accountability and authority should be clearly defined so that there is no doubt where ultimate responsibility lies for controlling all of the various activities.

QUESTIONS

1 'The management function of control is the measurement and correction of the activities of subordinates in order to make sure that the objectives of the organisation are achieved. Control is a necessary management function at all levels in the management hierarchy' (Henri Fayol).
   Discuss. (ICSA)

2 Why should 'Control' be one of the key factors in the management of organisations? (IAM)

3 Why is quality control important in manufacturing industry? Discuss the methods by means of which quality can be monitored. (IComA)

4 Draw a diagram of a control system, clearly indicating the major component parts. What impact does the human factor have on the effective operation of such a control system? (IAM)

5 Budgeting is a major task of all organisations.
   (a) Summarise the main features of a budget.
   (b) Identify the typical problems faced in budgeting. (IAM)

6 Explain the essential contribution of budgets as a key component of the annual marketing plan. (CIM)

7 Budgets are sometimes seen as plans for co-operation, and sometimes seen as restrictions to be defeated. What factors would you expect to lead to one view rather than the other? (ACCA)

▓ⱱ 13 Motivation

Motivating the staff of an organisation towards the attainment of its objectives is a key question for all managers. Despite much research and study, no set of rules satisfactory for every situation can be offered simply because the behaviour of human beings cannot be predicted without absolute certainty. Nevertheless, it is the duty of managers to endeavour to attain the organisation's objectives and this can only be done with the willing co-operation of the people involved. It is, therefore, absolutely essential that staff at all levels be motivated to co-operate in the organisation's interests and to work as effectively as possible. This applied equally to managers and supervisors and everyone else.

13.1   Motivation and incentives

It used to be thought that enhanced financial reward was sufficient to motivate a worker to maximum effort. However, this is to confuse the two terms 'motivation' and 'incentive'.

- Intrinsically they are not the same in as much as motivation springs from within – it is, essentially, an attitude of mind that may be encouraged by external factors but is fundamentally firmly related to self-discipline. Further, it can remain even when the external influences that engendered it have ceased to exist. Often it is entirely self-generated because it arises through innate character attributes and remains unaltered by external factors.
- Incentive, on the other hand, belongs to those forces that are applied from the outside and is a positive external influence to encourage improved performance. This being so, the effects of incentives cease as soon as those particular influences are withdrawn. An example would be that of sales representatives. Normally the majority of these are paid on the basis of a basic salary and commission on sales. The commission is an incentive and in very many cases if the rate of commission is reduced then the sales representatives' efforts are likewise reduced. Only if there were personal financial commitments to be met with required greater selling effort because of the reduced commission would a particular sales representative work as hard or harder than before in order to maintain his income level. This, in itself, however, is an incentive. When the financial commitment had been satisfied (perhaps a hire-purchase agreement discharged) then it would be very likely that the selling effort would be reduced.

- However, continuing this example, very many people who take up the career of selling are motivated by the challenge it presents and a reduction in the rate of commission will not permanently affect their selling effort though it may do so initially because of a sense of pique or resentment. These sales representatives are urged on by an inner drive – that is, motivation – and not by an external factor – that is, incentive. It follows, therefore, that people at work, even managers, may be encouraged to greater effort by an increase in financial reward, be it earned by effort in the case of commission or bonus payments or by a straight increase in the contents of the pay packet. However, this will usually have an effect only while the incentive is applied (where extra earnings are added by way of commission or bonus) and in the case of a rise in pay only in the initial period after the increase is awarded. In fact, in the latter case there is some experience to indicate that after a given point an increase in pay without the stimulus of additional work or responsibility may even result in a diminution of effort.

13.2   The social sciences and motivation

If additional financial rewards are incentives and not truly motivational, there must be other means of motivating staff to perform at their best. There are many theories advanced by industrial psychologists and sociologists, some of which are outlined later in this chapter. However, the results of research projects carried out by different practitioners have not always agreed and universal conclusions should not be drawn from the work of one or other of these researchers. Often the samples are too small, or the time too short, for generalisations to be made. Further, the precise conditions from one research project to another are not truly comparable. These observations must not be taken to denigrate the work in this field that has been done and is being done: rather, they are made to sound a caution against accepting such findings uncritically.

13.3   Principles of motivation

If extra money does not motivate, what does? As mentioned in **13.2** above, no hard-and-fast rules can be laid down about this. However, there are some factors that are practised with success in many organisations and these are based on operational experience as well as formal research. They centre around the following aspects of work and, to some extent, also indicate why people work in the jobs that they do. Above all, managers need to be aware of the fact that people do not work for money only – once a satisfactory income has been achieved, pay becomes a secondary consideration even though it may be given emphasis at different times. Reasons for working are different for different individuals as are the factors that motivate them.

(a) Security

A job spells security and is a common positive reason for working. It is also true that people become familiar with their surroundings and may prefer to continue in one job with one organisation than seek alternatives elsewhere. Working in central and local government services used to be considered extremely secure and this used to cause people to remain within these areas. Japanese industrial companies working in the West also now try to ensure a form of job security, through great attention to training and development programmes.

(b) Status

To be employed gives status in the worker's own social environment. Also, both socially and at work, some jobs are looked upon as having greater status than others and many people are motivated to achieve such a status. A skilled tool-maker for example, is deemed to have a higher status than a cleaner.

(c) Use of skills and intelligence

People are proud of their skills and work to employ them to the best advantage. Dull, repetitive work is not calculated to motivate anyone to give the best possible performance. Work that demands imagination or the use of initiative is more likely to do this.

(d) Goals and aspirations

Everyone has goals and aspirations. Some people fulfil these through work, others elsewhere. In general, however, everyone at work responds to the opportunities to progress, develop and enhance their range of skills, qualities and experience. Failure to offer these as widely as possible leads to demotivation; moreover, dull, boring and repetitive work is now known to be both physically and mentally debilitating.

(e) External aspirations

To some people, job titles are important as a mark of social standing. A part of work motivation clearly comes from within the individual; to some people, the wider social knowledge that they are a chief executive, head teacher, manager, and so on, is a key feature of motivation. Others concentrate on earning sufficient money to be able to have a new car, take longer holidays, send their children to private schools, and so on. Again, it must be noted that everyone has external aspirations of some form or another.

(f) A congenial work environment

Everyone is much more motivated when they know that they are going into a positive environment, than when they are going into a negative environment. Bad and adversarial managerial styles are always demotivating; and any steps taken to remedy these always have a positive effect on the staff involved.

(g) Type of industry or occupation

Many people are motivated by the fact that they work in a particular sector, or carry out a particular occupation. It is a serious problem for personal and social morale when, for example, an organisation closes down, because of the feelings of rejection and failure left on the part of the staff.

(h) Respect and value
Everyone, whatever their occupation, requires to be treated with respect and value. If people are paid badly, or know that they are being exploited, then they suffer loss of self-respect and self-value, as well as the respect and value of others.

(i) Achievement
Everyone should be rewarded for their achievements, whether financially or otherwise. People deserve recognition for what they have done. Again, it is extremely demoralising when the manager takes praise for the successes of the staff, but blames the staff when things go wrong.

(j) Engendering commitment
It is becoming increasingly recognised that motivation is a function of commitment. If organisations require commitment from their staff, then they should be committed to their staff. They need to take whatever actions are necessary in order to ensure that this commitment is present; and that the maintenance of this commitment is a part of long-term policy and objectives.

The reasons for people working at all are therefore many and various. Everyone will have a different combination of attitudes and motivations. The basic principles, however, are those indicated above. A recognition that these reasons do exist should assist managers to motivate their staff at all levels to give of their best efforts.

13.4 Practical motivation

If financial incentives are not effective as true motivators what steps can managers take to create positive motivation in their work-people? It has been pointed out that different workers respond differently to any particular stimulus and it is certainly true that some motivating factors have only a temporary effect. Nevertheless there are a number of factors that are generally accepted as being of value in achieving some measure of success in encouraging positive attitudes. These include:

(a) Atmosphere
An atmosphere of co-operation and trust must be generated between management and staff. Perhaps it would be better described as mutual respect. The old autocratic style of management is now resented by most workers, and managers no longer respected just because they are managers. Such a management style is indicative of a lack of respect for their subordinates by those in authority, and such a situation does not generate respect in the workers for their managers or supervisors.

Without relinquishing authority a manager must have concern for his staff and their needs, and must nowadays actively seek their co-operation in making decisions which affect them as individuals. In other words, there must be generated an atmosphere of participation, co-operation and mutual respect. One certain sign as to whether this has been achieved is when the workers, when discussing their employers, refer to 'we' rather than 'they'.

(b) Recognition

Human beings have a need to be esteemed and the manager who realises this and actively recognises his subordinates as people rather than working units is likely to be successful in motivating them positively. Some senior executives, particularly, are aware of this as evidenced by the chairman of a substantial company who invariably made it his business to ask after the families of his staff, at all levels, whenever he made a visit to the works or branch offices, remembering personal details from the previous visit.

Recognition of the efforts of workers is also necessary. All employees like to feel that their efforts are appreciated, particularly if some improvement in performance or some contribution outside the work requirements of the job has been achieved. Words of praise or encouragement raise the morale of staff, but they must be justified. Mere flattery without a sound basis will have the opposite effect to that intended.

(c) Status

Really linked with recognition, to many workers status within their organisation is important to them. To some it must be overt but to others tacit recognition of status is enough. Status must, however, carry with it commensurate responsibility and authority. Just naming a worker 'X supervisor' or 'Y manager' without commensurate responsibility or authority, in other words bestowing an empty title, very soon turns sour. Not only does the worker personally become dissatisfied, the respect of other workers may be lost and this mutual respect between members of a work-force is of extreme importance.

On the other hand, where someone has been carrying out the duties of a supervisor or manager without the formal title, to bestow the title is not an empty gesture, but is an acknowledgement of status.

(d) Involvement

Much has been written concerning worker participation, and it means different things to different people. In almost all cases, however, it is taken to involve formal recognition of what is stated to be the workers' right to participate in making decisions that affect their working conditions, even to the extent of making such participation a legal requirement.

People always respond better when they feel fully involved in a situation. They are therefore committed to it. The basis of this involvement and commitment is trust, integrity, communication and information. People work much better when they know why they need to work in particular ways; and what the consequences of working or not working are. Ideally, therefore, it is necessary to draw everyone into contributing to planning and decision-making. This should be supported by informal discussions between managers and subordinates on matters concerning work practices, welfare and the host of other problems affecting daily activities. This is a key contributor to building morale and trust. It is also an early warning system for problems; an early indicator of dissatisfaction; and it is much easier to put these matters right early before they become serious, than later when a crises has occurred.

(e) Work satisfaction

Satisfaction with work is dependent upon the rewards that are available. Some of these rewards are clearly financial. However, as indicated above, these are not the only rewards for which people work. People also expect development, variety, enhancement, and the opportunity to progress – whatever their chosen field. Work satisfaction is, therefore, a function of the extent to which these factors can be satisfied in terms that the individual requires. People therefore need to understand what is available to them as the result of working in a particular occupation or organisation; and by the same token, what is not available to them. Increasingly, it is being recognised that organisations should demonstrate the limitations of working at a particular place, so that when staff are ready they can move on with the blessing of their employers to something else that they would like to do. And if they do wish to stay at the organisation, then in order that their commitment remains secure, they must be offered opportunities when they arise.

13.5   Group motivation

The issues surrounding group motivation are largely the same as those relating to the motivation of individual workers. There are, however, additional factors that must be taken into account.

(a)   The contribution of everyone to the group must be valued equally. To give some people enhanced rewards at the expense of others within the group is extremely damaging to morale. Everyone should be subject to the same standards of discipline, attendance, output and control. This will clearly vary if there are widely differing occupations within the group (e.g. surgeon, administrator, secretary); nevertheless, the fundamental principles must be the same.

(b)   Rewards to the group, other than salary, should be the same. Opportunities should be offered on an even basis. People must be treated equally and fairly at all times. If there are bonuses accruing to the particular group, they should be shared out so that everyone is treated fairly, rather than giving someone additional rewards at, again, the expense of others.

(c)   Work must be allocated fairly between members of the group. The group should receive the acclaim for successes; and must take responsibility as a whole when things go wrong.

(d) The group's manager or supervisor must set targets that are reasonable and achievable.

(e) The achievements of the group as a whole must be recognised by management and appreciation for these achievements made known to the group.

(f) No individual in the group should be consistently singled out for special treatment as this causes resentment and a diminution of motivation. That is not to say that an occasional word of praise for an individual should not be given for an outstanding contribution to the group effort.

By paying attention to these factors the manager or supervisor of a working group can do much to promote positive motivation in the group and earn the respect of the staff.

None of these practical suggestions for motivating staff will work effectively unless they are applied honestly and sincerely, and without bias or prejudice. Any hint of insincerity or deception by management will quickly disillusion staff at any level and any hope of positive motivation will vanish.

So far this chapter has been devoted to the more practical aspects of motivation. There have been many studies made on the theory of motivation, however, and the contributions of some of the most quoted authorities on this subject will now be briefly examined.

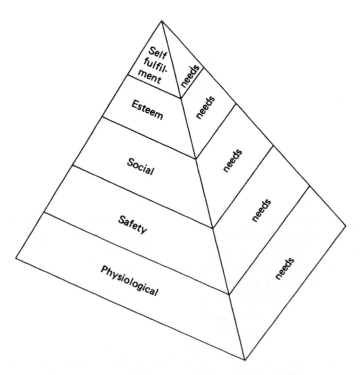

Figure 13.1 Maslow's hierarchy of basic needs

13.6   A. H. Maslow

Maslow propounded the theory that people are motivated by five basic needs, which he called ' the hierarchy of basic needs'. The primary need is that of physical survival and at the highest level it is that of self-fulfilment. These needs can be likened to a pyramid which has the primary needs as a base and which are universal, rising in steps to the highest need, which is the least well felt. This progression is represented in Figure 13.1.

(a) **Physiological needs,** as Maslow called them, are those that are basic to continued existence. These include the necessity to satisfy hunger, to be clothed and to have basic shelter from the elements. These are primary needs and predominate in motivating an urge to work. Not until these needs are satisfied to an acceptable level, so argued Maslow and his adherents, will a person aspire to the next step in the pyramid, which he called 'safety needs'.

(b) **Safety needs** are those connected with protection. Being assured of adequate sustenance and shelter, an individual will then look for a measure of security, of protection against lowering of living standards, of his job and of the fundamental physiological elements of life. Anything that threatens the orderly organisation of life, either in the world at large or in the work-place, will be looked upon also as a threat to the individual's safety. When such threats are removed then the individual will feel safe, and will be motivated by the next needs in the pyramid, social needs.

(c) **Social needs** are those which motivate a person to enter actively into the social environment in which he or she is placed, both at work and in society at large. Such needs, at the primary level, are encompassed in love and affection, family circle and social groupings such as the club, the religious group and so on. At work they are concerned with working-groupings, social and welfare activities and, perhaps, trade union activities. The average individual has a deep-rooted need to belong to social groupings and to be accepted by his or her peers. Freed from the necessity to pursue the satisfaction of physiological and safety needs, the individual is now motivated to pursue those social needs, the gratification of which leads to the pursuit of what Maslow called the esteem needs.

(d) **Esteem needs** are those which follow from self-satisfaction arising out of achievement and the respect of others. Sometimes referred to as 'ego needs', they involve self-respect, self-discipline and a feeling of adequacy and confidence. The status flowing from the esteem of others is an important factor here. Almost everyone needs and seeks the approbation of others and gains stature from it. Only the strength of the motivation in this direction limits this need. Failure to achieve esteem within the social- or work-group often leads to a sense of inferiority and a lowering of morale.

(e) **Self-fulfilment needs,** which Maslow called 'self-actualisation', are at the top of the pyramid of needs and become active when the previous four have been satisfied. This area of need is the one that motivates a person to seek and find the activity which satisfies a deep, often previously unconscious, urge and is very frequently associated with creativity or with the drive to exercise ultimate power. So artists, writers, actors, chief executives and politicians can all be said to be attempting to satisfy this need for self-fulfilment.

It will be apparent from general observation that this hierarchy of needs is not immutable. In fact Maslow himself called attention to the fact that in some people the stages are reversed, or some are ignored. The most common examples are those of the struggling artist, composer or actor, each of whom will forgo the satisfaction of many needs in pursuit of self-fulfilment or public acclaim. Many a successful industrialist has given up the esteem of society and the satisfaction of basic social needs to pursue the goal of industrial power. Some workers, however, are not driven by such high passions and are able to feel satisfied with less than total achievement. In some, ambition is almost non-existent to the extent that an income, reasonable security and shelter are all they ask. However, the drive for self-fulfilment is present in most people in some form or other, even if it is not workplace ambition.

13.7   D. M. McGregor

D. M. McGregor is probably most quoted in connection with his propositions (or theories) *X* and *Y*. These can be stated as follows:

(a) Theory X asserts that the average human being:
1   is inherently lazy and works as little as possible;
2   has no ambition and prefers to be led rather than take responsibility;
3   is self-centred, dislikes change and is unconcerned with the needs of the organisation;
4   is gullible and not particularly intelligent or discriminating.

Because of these traits managers have to persuade, coerce, reward or punish workers in order to achieve organisational goals: people cannot be trusted to work effectively without active and constant supervision.

Traditional management subscribes to theory *X* in the main and many traditional management practices can be attributed to this belief. McGregor, however, accepted Maslow's concept of the five basic needs, which led him to formulate his theory *Y*.

(b) Theory Y states, among other things, that people are not the selfish, indolent creatures that theory *X* suggests but, in fact, that:
1   they are naturally inclined to expend effort in working and playing – they are not passive nor are they unconcerned or resistant to organisational needs: this attitude is engendered by their experience of working in organisations that do not recognise their potential;
2   they are not without the urge to assume responsibility and have the capacity of self-discipline and self-direction provided they are properly motivated by management. Such motivation will not, however, be based only on the principles of punishment and reward: management must

recognise the human need for self-satisfaction and the other needs propounded by Maslow;

3 management, therefore, has the task and duty to harness these innate
attributes to enable the work-force to contribute willingly to the achievement of organisational objectives.

13.8   F. Herzberg

F. Herzberg's chief contribution to motivation theory was to suggest two distinct
categories of factors relating to people's attitude to work, which he named the
hygiene or maintenance factors and the motivating factors.

(a) **Hygiene or maintenance factors,** Herzberg found, do little to promote
job satisfaction, but their absence or presence at any unacceptable level
leads to dissatisfaction, which caused him to term them 'dissatisfiers'. He
likened them to hygiene in medical matters or maintenance in mechanical
areas, which prevent unwanted results arising but do not promote good
results of themselves: for example, good hygiene can prevent illness but
cannot, unaided, cure a patient.

He suggested that these hygiene factors are:

1 organisational policies and practices; organisational rules and related
factors;
2 style of supervision and management controls;
3 scale of pay and related benefits such as sick pay, retirement pensions
and security;
4 interpersonal and social relationships within the working environment:
status within the organisation;
5 working conditions, working environment, equipment and general work
arrangements.

These factors, relate to the conditions under which the worker operates
rather than to the actual work itself. Because of this, any improvement in a
hygiene factor will have only a temporary effect. Experience indicates that,
for example, improved lighting may remove dissatisfaction in this area for a
short time after the improvement takes place, but familiarity soon causes the
improvement to be forgotten and in consequence its positive effect also
declines. In fact, further demands may be made subsequently for even better
lighting.

This phenomenon of temporary effect is common to all the hygiene
factors. Improvements will stop complaints for a short time, but are unlikely
to have a permanent effect.

(b) **Motivating factors,** unlike the hygiene factors, have a positive and longer-
lasting effect on worker performance and also, unlike the hygiene factors,
they relate directly to the work itself. These motivating factors include:

1 achievement: this is the satisfaction derived from work well done;
2 recognition of achievement: the worker needs to have his efforts recognised by his superiors, which adds to his self-esteem;

3 the work itself: this needs to be challenging and rewarding; it is in this area that much industrial organisation falls down in motivating the work-force, since much work is repetitive and monotonous;

4 responsibility: increased responsibility should motivate a worker to greater efforts, especially where it is associated with intrinsically reward-ing work;

5 self-satisfaction: actual or promised promotion is a very positive motivator and staff development plays an important role in ensuring satisfaction.

These satisfiers, as Herzberg calls them, motivate staff in a positive fashion to produce better work, greater co-operation in aiming for organisational goals and higher morale. Though longer-lasting in their effects than the hygiene factors, nevertheless it is a fact that, generally speaking, familiarity also plays a part in these factors to make them less effective as time goes on.

13.9 W. G. Ouchi

W. G. Ouchi's contribution to management thinking is known as theory Z. In this theory management places very great importance on the participation of the work-force in operational decision-making, involving them in the operation of the affairs of the organisation, and ensuring that their commitment to the organisation is encouraged and rewarded. Management needs, therefore, to encourage a high level of consensus and trust among its work-force throughout the enterprise. To embrace this theory management requires to change its think-ing in terms of the theories previously discussed and to concentrate on achiev-ing a consensus of values throughout the organisation.

Successful management under theory Z requires:

(a) a high degree of co-operation between members of working groups, depart-ments and other sections of the organisation; this is because a consensus for decision-making depends upon good interpersonal relationships between associated workers;

(b) minimising status differences so that informal relationships between man-agers and those managed can be built up;

(c) the creation of trust between workers themselves and between workers and their supervisors and managers; this assumes the integrity of each individ-ual concerned and his commitment to the goals of the organisation; it also assumes the worker's ability to work with the very minimum of supervision – this trust is essential if decision-making by consensus is to be achieved and be successful;

(d) that there will be free communication throughout the organisation of infor-mation on operational factors, on environmental issues and on all the other matters of concern to the work-force to enable it to make informed and intelligent judgements when contributing to the group decisions;

(e) that despite the involvement of employees in the decision-making process individual managers are still responsible for these decisions in the final analysis;

(f) that a policy of long-term employment coupled with a clearly defined career structure will be pursued, to retain the services of valued staff, to reinforce and to reward commitment to the enterprise.

Unlike theories X and Y, theory Z is based on the premise of total staff involvement, together with management, in the running of an enterprise.

It will be observed that many of these factors, particularly the motivating factors, have been found to be common in all the researches discussed. It should also be mentioned that the research that Herzberg undertook was concerned principally with accountants and engineers, not with workers on the shop-floor or in clerical occupations. His specific findings in certain areas should, therefore, be applied with caution to those below supervisory or management level.

A discussion of motivation could not be complete without mentioning the Hawthorne Experiment.

13.10 The Hawthorne Experiments

These experiments were carried out by Elton Mayo, a psychologist and Professor of Industrial Research at the Harvard Graduate School of Business, at the Hawthorne Works of the Western Electric Company, between the years 1924 and 1932. The main findings, which broke new ground at the time, led to an entirely new outlook on motivation psychology and resulted in a changed approach both in research and in practice. Research that took place over so many years cannot be summarised effectively in a work of this nature, but the main findings can be given:

(a) social factors are of great importance at work; both the behaviour and motivation of individual workers are affected by group relationships;
(b) it was discovered that an informal organisation of work-groups exists alongside the formal organisation and that these informal group patterns contribute as much to work satisfaction and worker motivation as does the physical environment, more so in some cases;
(c) job satisfaction and social satisfaction are important to the worker;
(d) work-groups are inclined to set their own standards of behaviour and their own levels of output, often in disregard of organisational requirements; any member of a work-group who fails to conform is subject to sanctions applied by the group;
(e) the need for adequate communication between workers and management was established, as was the need for satisfactory social relations.

Perhaps the greatest contribution that the Hawthorne experiment made to industrial psychology and the study of motivation was the realisation of the need for full understanding of the human factor in industrial relations and work, and the significant impact work-group behaviour has on individual worker performance.

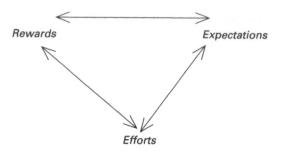

Figure 13.2   Expectancy theory: a simplified model

13.11   Expectancy theories of motivation

This approach to motivation draws the relationship between efforts put into particular activities by individuals and the nature of their expectations of the rewards that they perceive that they will get from these efforts. The expectancy approach to motivation draws a relationship between:

(a) the expectations that people have in work situations;
(b) the efforts that they put in to meet these expectations;
(c) the rewards offered for successful efforts (see Figure 13.2).

The expectancy approach relates to the ways in which the individual sees or perceives the environment. It relates to their view of work, expectations, aspirations, ambitions, and desired outcomes, and the extent to which these can be satisfied at the work-place or carrying out the particular occupation. For example, the individual may have no particular regard for the job that they are currently doing but will nevertheless work productively and effectively at it and be committed to it because it is a stepping-stone, in their view, to greater things – and these are the expectations that they have of it. It constitutes the basis of their current efforts and the quality of these efforts. This is compounded by other factors – the actual capacities and aptitudes of the individual concerned on the one hand, and the nature of the work environment on the other. It is limited by the expectations and perceptions that the organisation has on the part of the person who is actually carrying it out. It is limited also, by the capability of the organisation to meet those expectations.

There is also a distinction to be drawn between the effort put into performance and the effectiveness of that effort – hard work conscientiously carried out does not always produce productive effort; the effort has to be directed and targeted.

There also has to be a match between the rewards expected and those that are actually offered – a reward is simply a value judgement placed on something, offered in return for effort, and if this is not valued by the receiver it has no effect on motivation.

When rewards are not forthcoming, therefore, demotivation occurs. When rewards are available for little effort, a lack of mutual respect occurs – if something comes too easily, people do not value it. If people have been given unreasonable expectations, they will see all their efforts have been put in for no good reason, and again will become demoralised.

13.12 General observations on motivation

The main issue for managers is to understand the great complexity of the subject. It is impossible to produce a set of rules that will apply to everybody. What motivates one person may have no effect at all on another. Workers in a group react differently from the individual. The group is likely to establish its own norms and values, and the pressure to conform and be accepted by the group may constitute a high level of motivation in the individual.

In consequence, the theories propounded in this Chapter must be viewed with caution. It is possible to identify a set of principles from which to work; however, if, in certain situations, these are found not to work, or not to work fully, then it is necessary to review both the overall attitude of the organisation, and what is genuinely being offered to the staff. Above all, it must be recognised that no genuine, positive, enduring motivation or high level of morale can be contemplated unless the organisation is fundamentally honest in its dealings with its staff.

QUESTIONS

1 Compare and contrast two recent theories of motivation in terms of their utility to management. (IPM)
2 By reference to three motivation theories, explain the role of social factors in motivation. (CIMA)
3 (i) What do you understand by 'employee commitment'?
   (ii) How can the fundamental human needs for power, achievement and affiliation be harnessed to develop employee commitment to an enterprise and its goals? (IAM)
4 Explain the role of the system of remuneration in the motivation of the workforce. What other motivating factors should be considered by management? (IComA)
5 How can supervisors effectively motivate:
   (a) an individual at work?
   (b) their own working group? (CIMA)
6 How can senior managers set out to encourage innovation and entrepreneurial attitudes in their own organisations? (ICSA)
7 (a) Briefly discuss the principles of job enrichment.
   (b) How could job enrichment be practically applied to administrative staff? (IAM)

■ ⊻ 14 Communication in the organisation

Effective communication is a vital tool of management because without it all attempts to carry on the activities of an organisation must fail. Without communication nothing can happen. No instructions can be given, no orders taken, no contact made with superiors or subordinates and no information provided or received. Only by communicating effectively can any activity of any kind be planned, organised and carried through. The only exception to this is the individual working entirely alone with no contact at all with any other person. Further, the communication carried on must be understandable and acceptable to both parties.

- Communication has been defined in many ways, and there is no simple, all-embracing definition. It could, however, be said to be the transmission and reception of a message or idea from one party to another in such a fashion that it is mutually understandable. The key words here are 'mutually understandable', because unless both parties to a communication are of one mind as to what communication means there is no communication at all. This definition also implies that the sender of the communication is quite clear about what the message is intended to convey. Much communication is 'non-communication' simply because the transmitter's mind is imprecise on the subject of the communication. It follows, therefore, that unless management can make itself properly understood throughout the undertaking then the proper functioning of the organisation will be impaired.
- It is usual to think of communication in an organisation as being vertical or horizontal. Vertical communication is that which flows downwards from the top and upwards from the bottom of the organisation, and horizontal communication is that which flows across and between departments at more or less the same management level.

14.1 Vertical communication

- In the past, when the authoritarian approach to management was the prevalent one, vertical communication was predominantly, if not entirely, downward. Decisions were made at the top levels of management and instructions were passed down the line until they reached the level at which action has to be taken. Any upward communication came about through necessity; for example, responses to questions put from above. The attitude was that management managed and their subordinates did as they were told; there was no right of question or to information. Instructions were issued to be carried out, not explained.

- Times have changed, however, and workers at all levels, including junior and middle managers, are not content blindly to accept edicts from above. They are aware that many management decisions and instructions, particularly the more significant ones, may have an effect on their livelihoods or on their working conditions, and they therefore demand the right to be heard before such decisions are put into effect. There has developed, therefore, the concept of two-way vertical communication which is almost universally accepted by modern management. Hence an organisation must provide a formal channel for the upward flow of communication as well as the traditional channel for a downward flow. In fact, if there is a failure to provide a means of communication from the operating level upwards management may well find itself making important decisions that will be thwarted by the work-force simply because of non-consultation. Many unofficial 'lightning strikes' can be traced to this cause.

- An important result of the acceptance of the need for two-way vertical communication is the increased burden that has fallen on middle managers and on supervisors. In addition to their traditional task of receiving and interpreting communications coming from the top and passing them on in an understandable form to their subordinates, they have the additional and onerous task of doing the same thing in reverse. If these upwards communications are handled reluctantly or are dealt with tactlessly or without understanding the effect on the would-be communicators can be unfortunate. Management–worker relations can be soured and morale damaged. Fortunately, at the lower end of the communication chain there is usually personal contact between manager and managed, or supervisor and supervised, and so, given goodwill on both sides, misunderstandings can be prevented or resolved.

- However, good staff relations are in greater danger further up the management scale. Inevitably the upwards flow lines will come together on some senior executive's desk and at this level the person concerned is unlikely to have the advantage of personal contact with the originators of the communications. Unless, therefore, the middle managers and supervisors have been whole-hearted and effective in relaying these communications there is the danger of misinterpretation and a consequent breach in good management–worker relations. In addition, of course, a senior executive is burdened with an ever-increasing flow of information which leaves little time for detailed study of any individual communication. In consequence such an executive has to rely to a large extent on the ability of subordinate managers for proper interpretation of the communications received.

14.2   Quasi-vertical communication

- Vertical communication within an organisation used to be confined to that organisation. However, nowadays there is another channel which runs parallel to the official internal one but which is strictly speaking external to it, and could be called the 'quasi-vertical' communication channel. This has been brought about by the increasing influence of trade unions, staff associations and the professional bodies, and is most marked in large undertakings where workers and functional staff are well-organised. The trade unions and staff associations exist for the purpose of protecting and improving their members' pay and conditions of work, and the professional bodies are concerned with professional ethics and practice.
- It has become customary for trade unions, and to a lesser extent staff associations, to speak for and negotiate on behalf of their members direct with the higher levels of management. In doing this they by-pass middle managers and supervisory staff and so superimpose their own line of communication over that of the formal internal vertical flow. Similarly, the professional bodies established standards of professional practice which they require their members to comply with, entirely without consultation with individual managements. By virtue of the strength of these outside bodies, particularly the trade unions, this quasi-vertical upward flow often carries a weight of authority far superior to the established formal internal upward flow. At times its weight equals that of the downward flow from top management.
- One of the results of this condition is that some of the authority over their subordinates is taken out of the hands of the middle managers and supervisors and usurped by internal union representatives such as shop stewards.

14.3   Horizontal communication

The need for effective co-operation and co-ordination between the various sections of an organisation demands a high level of communication between them, and is satisfied by the establishment of an effective horizontal communications network.

- This system operates through internal communication channels such as the internal telephone, memoranda or face-to-face consultation. It takes place between staff of about equivalent status in the different departments, for instance between the factory manager and cost accountant, or sales representative and sales account clerk. There is no authority flowing along the lines of horizontal communication, and it is tactless for the manager of one department to communicate direct with a subordinate in another department.
- Where requests, orders and instructions have to flow horizontally any implied authority to have them carried out is contained in the established procedures covering the operation and is not a delegation of authority to the giver over the receiver. Thus, in a procedure in which a sales representative

demands information about a customer's account from a sales account clerk, this request has within it the authority for the sales representative to make this demand, but any authority over the sales account clerk's actions is in the power of the latter's supervisor and not in the power of the sales representative.

14.4   Difficulties in vertical communication

- The most common failures in communications occur in the vertical flow. This is especially so of the flow upward. Proper provision must be made for the flow of information both ways and the appropriate methods must be pressed into service and known by all concerned. Further, some method must be established, where necessary, within these lines of communication to obtain feedback, to ensure that communications are known to be received and understood. The provision of practical systems is a matter for the communications expert; the concern of this section of this chapter is how difficulties arise.
- In all probability the commonest cause of problems in vertical communication is that of lengthy chains of command. This is particularly prevalent in large organisations where a large number of management and supervisory levels exist. Two problems arise: first, because of the number of levels concerned the communication takes a long time to reach its ultimate receiver; and, second, some distortion tends to occur at each stage so that at the end of the chain the message can be quite direct from the original. This is a particular danger where the communication is verbal at any point in the transmission. While written communication can avoid misquoting, this is often too expensive or too difficult, particularly where speed is necessary.
- Geographical location also causes vertical communication problems, particularly upward. Where the decision-making centres of an organisation are divorced from the operating centres, as happens in concerns with many depots or branches, delays and frustrations can occur in the communications network. A particular example of this is where either the transmitter or the recipient is constantly on the move. Such circumstances obtain in communicating with travelling sales representatives, in keeping up communication with a working group that changes sites frequently and whose movements are dictated by work conditions (a street-lighting gang is a good example here), and many others.
- Management style has a decided influence on the effectiveness of vertical communication. If it is authoritarian then there is likely to be a reluctance willingly to accept communications coming down the line and such instructions may be grudgingly complied with. There will certainly be an unwillingness to attempt any significant upwards communication. Unco-operative attitudes may have already developed at the lower levels of the chain, producing a grudging response to communications from management. This is often symptomatic of poor industrial relations which have caused workers to set up obstructive emotional barriers to the acceptance of management communications.

This authoritarian attitude may also obtain at middle management and junior management levels, though where this occurs it is often a reflection of attitudes higher up. Such managers may see no reason to inform subordinates of many aspects of the organisation's affairs even though these have a bearing on their working conditions. Often such communications come to a stop at a particular manager's desk instead of being passed on. This lack of sensitivity on the part of such managers gives rise to resentment by the people lower down the chain and makes normal communication in either direction that much more difficult. It must be admitted, however, that sometimes communication stops at a certain level simply because the manager concerned is overburdened and neglects this aspect of his duties in favour of what he considers to be more pressing matters. Horizontal communication has higher priority because without it the organisation would slow down unacceptably or stop altogether. Vertical communication is rarely so urgent and thus is likely to be neglected at times of pressure. Naturally, such an overburdened manager should examine the possibilities of delegating some of the overload, perhaps even the communication task.

- The problems so far discussed have been concerned principally with downwards communication. Difficulties also, of course, obtain in the upward flow often because there is simply no provision made for it despite the fact that it is accepted as being highly desirable. Where upward flow is lacking management cannot be properly aware of the attitudes and feelings of their subordinates and are thus unlikely to be able to couch their communications in such forms as will encourage their work-people to accept them willingly and to implement their decisions ungrudgingly. The effectiveness of all communications depends to a large extent upon the willingness of the receiver to participate.

- Merely providing the means for upward vertical communication will not, however, ensure an effective flow in that direction. Such a flow is normally channelled through the line hierarchy and an unco-operative foreman or supervisor, or a manager with no real commitment to communication from work-people upwards, may cause distortion of the communication or stop it altogether. Such attitudes by those in authority eventually discourage lower-level workers from even attempting to communicate, to the eventual detriment to the well-being of the organisation.

- Misunderstanding through different uses of language also affect the effectiveness of vertical communication. The language of the boardroom is not that of the burger bar or the factory floor, and this may lead to lack of understanding.

14.5   Difficulties in horizontal communication

- Because of the common interest in dealing with internal matters it might be thought that horizontal communication would be free from too many difficulties. This is not so, however. The effectiveness of horizontal communication relies very largely on the attitudes of the departments to one another. Where this is good, communication will be good, but where there is an atmosphere of non-co-operation, for whatever reason, then communication can be poor. As effective communication between all sections of an organisation is necessary for its proper functioning, the non-co-operation of even one can lead to loss of efficiency.

- There may be, for example, specific demarcation lines between departments and the crossing of these lines can cause resentment and a non-co-operative attitude. An example will clarify this. It is not uncommon for customers to discuss their accounts with a sales representative, and the representative may take up the customer's queries with the accounts department on the customer's behalf. However, the accounts department may take great exception to this action and may point out to the sales representative in no uncertain terms that accounts are their prerogative and should not be discussed by members of the sales force. Such an occurrence may sour relations between the two sections of the organisation, especially if repeated, and cause difficulties in regard to future communications.

It should be pointed out in connection with this example, that in many organisations the sales force does play a part in the collection of customers' debts and the accounts department sometimes seeks the assistance of sales representatives in connection with particularly difficult customers. However, this collaboration is by no means universal.

- So-called 'empire-building' is another example of a cause of interference in free horizontal communication. Where the head of a department is determined to increase the department's importance, and the head's own position in consequence, there may be a reluctance for that department to pass on information to other departments unless it is specifically requested, thus indicating how important that department and its head are to the running of the organisation. Such practices lead to severe difficulties in co-ordination and co-operation and slow down the work of the organisation as a whole.

- Finally, horizontal communication also suffers from the two problems of distortion and language. Distortion is a particular danger because so much inter-departmental communication is by internal telephone or verbally face-to-face, and messages passed from mouth to mouth are subject to unconscious alteration. In this respect horizontal communication suffers in the same way as vertical communication. The language problem arises principally where a line department and a specialist department are trying to communicate. The specialists are prone to use their own particular jargon, much of which is not really comprehensible to the line staff, who are lay people in that respect. For example, the computer department may tell the accounts department that last year's accounts records have been dumped. The accounts department may immediately imagine that the records have been destroyed whereas the computer people simply mean that the records have been taken out of the current computer files and stored elsewhere.

14.6   The mechanism of communication

To improve communication and make it as effective as possible it is necessary to understand its basic mechanism.

- Essentially, communication requires a source (the sender or transmitter), a signal or code, a channel which is the means of transmitting the communication, and a receiver. In the ideal situation action will result, which may mean anything from simple understanding by the receiver to some actual activity performed at the receiving end. In addition, it is advisable if some form of feedback is available so that the transmitter can see that the communication has been received, understood and has produced some reaction. If there is no feedback future action by the sender which is dependent upon the correct receipt of the communication may be hampered. A simple example will clarify this. If a company writes to a job applicant offering employment, with a specific starting date, unless the company receives an acknowledgement and acceptance by the applicant agreeing the starting date, the company will be quite unable to plan the day's activities which depend on the arrival of the applicant to take up the post.
- The mechanism of an effective communication system is best illustrated in a diagram, as in Future 14.1. It will be seen from this diagram that Stage 4 indicates decoding by the receiver; in other words understanding. This is the area where most breakdown in communication take place, and may remain undiscovered without some form of feedback.

14.7   Reasons for breakdowns in communication

In order to achieve effective communication throughout an organisation it is necessary to understand the obstacles that occur to prevent it. In doing this it becomes possible to reduce or avoid these barriers and so lessen the risk of breakdown.

(a) Physical obstacles
These have been dealt with in 14.4 above and relate to all forms of communication. Thus long lines of communication and moving locations increase the practical difficulties of communicating efficiently. So do defects in mechanical and electronic apparatus, including faulty telephone connections, breakdowns in fax machines and so on. Inefficient, reduced or entire lack of service may be included under this heading. These breakdowns include poor postal services, electrical power failure affecting word processors and similar apparatus, and the simple absence of a competent telephone switchboard operator. Such physical problems suggest their own solutions, examples being a thorough overhaul of the lines of communication, proper maintenance of mechanical and electronic equipment and not being totally reliant on electric typewriters or word processors. No organisation should have only one skilled telephone operator; a standby should always be trained and available in emergencies.

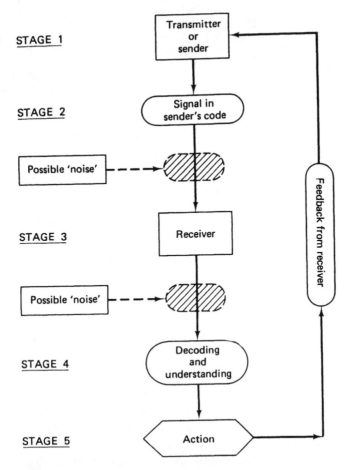

Figure 14.1 A diagram of the mechanics of communication

Other physical obstacles include background noise such as noisy machinery and equipment, traffic and aircraft flying overhead, which interfere with telephone and face-to-face conversations.

(b) Coding difficulties

The most common communication code is language. Care should therefore be taken to ensure that the language used in any communication is within the understanding of the intended receiver and will be interpreted as the sender intends. Different words mean different things to different people. Common words such as 'capital' and 'profit' have quite different meanings to accountants, economists, politicians and to those with particular political views. Where there is any doubt at all that the message may be misinterpreted, unintentionally or intentionally, then the communication should be worded so that this does not happen.

(c) Difficulties with a psychological basis

Much misunderstanding is caused by the communicator's failure to appreciate the receiver's background and attitudes.

- A person's understanding is conditioned by the social, educational and work-environment in which he or she has been raised. If a worker has been conditioned by family distrust of employers generally, or has been subjected to constant anti-employer propaganda, then management's attempt to communicate will be beset by the difficulty of obtaining an unbiased hearing. Any communication from management, however well-intentioned, will automatically be treated with suspicion. More unfortunate, in cases where management/worker relations are at a very low ebb the workers may see every communication as an attempt to deny them fairness even though, in fact, management is being absolutely honest. Of course, the reverse can be the case and managers can also be guilty of an adverse attitude to their workers, with the same unfortunate results in communication.

- Managers also sometimes forget that sometimes work-people on the shop-floor have not had the benefit of an education that enables them to think in abstract terms and so all communications, to be properly understood, must be in concrete terms. Neither have they been taught to think a long time into the future; their interests lie in the present. Communications which try to put into effect plans that will not bear fruit for some considerable time are not likely to capture the interest of the work-force in the same way that they might capture that of junior or middle managers, and especially that of senior managers.

- Even between one level of management and another there may be difficulties of attitude and prejudice. This is particularly so where a junior manager or a supervisor has developed a certain resentment against a superior. This may have come about because of a need, at some time in the past, for a reprimand which the junior manager felt to be unjust, or because suggestions made by the junior manager were completely ignored or were the subject of tactless remarks. Some middle and senior managers can be guilty of an autocratic or arrogant attitude which generates animosity in their subordinates whether managerial or in the work-force, and this can have a very deleterious effect on the way their communications are received and acted upon.

(d) Overload difficulties

Where, as is often the case, managers become subject to an excess of communication – and this is particularly true of middle managers – then an arbitrary system of priorities may be applied which may not help to ensure an effective communication system. In such circumstances telephone messages may take precedence over written communications simply because the telephone is more immediate and seems to be more urgent than a letter or a memorandum, both of which demand more time than a telephone call. Equally, face-to-face verbal communication may rank in priority not in accordance with its relative importance to the organisation, but rather to the importance of the person being addressed.

Where this problem of overload exists the managers concerned should urgently delegate those duties that do not require their personal attention, including those appertaining to communication, in order to ensure that no blockage in the communication flow occurs.

14.8 Formal communication

It is important that there should be an effective formal communication system. With external communication this poses few problems. The methods used for external communication, the letter and the telephone, are firmly established and few significant decisions have to be made as to when to use the one instead of the other. This will normally be dictated by the circumstances of each case. Similarly, fax and other electronic email communication devices are now firmly established and in current and effective use.

With internal communication, however, the picture is a little different. Where a tight organisation pattern obtains with few levels of management, particularly if it is line organisation, the communication network may be very clearly defined. However, few organisations fall into this category and so some rules must be formulated.

- An important first step is to establish who may, formally, communicate with whom. This is important in order to avoid bad relations building up between different people within the organisation. The question of demarcation lines has already been referred to in 14.5 above. Thus it is essential to lay down specific rules on the subject. May, for example, a stores controller communicate direct with a buying clerk or must he go through his own manager, who will go through the chief buyer? In what circumstances is direct contact allowable? Again, may a sales representative communicate direct with the production department or must this communication go through the sales office?
- The second step is the even more important one of determining who may communicate orders and instructions to whom. May, for example, the credit controller give instructions direct to a sales representative on a matter to do with a customer's account or should this be done only through the sales office? Much uncertainty and umbrage may be saved if firm and certain rules are established on this matter throughout the organisation.

The actual means of internal communication will vary according to circumstances. Normally memoranda and the internal telephone will carry most of the load with, possibly, the email and fax being used where external depots and branches are involved. Personal contact also plays a large part in formal internal communication, both person-to-person and the holding of formal meetings. The methods used for purely staff matters, however, should be examined a little more fully.

14.9 Formal staff communication

Where matters of personnel policy are concerned various means are employed.

(a) Staff meetings
These can be simple meetings called by management to provide staff with information and to evoke discussion or may be joint consultative meetings which are formally set up with proper constitutions and comprise members from management (mostly appointed) and worker-members (mostly elected), or may be meetings falling between these two extremes. Joint consultative meetings, in particular, may be concerned with any aspect of working conditions and practices from productivity and pay through to welfare and safety. They work to a properly drawn up agenda and accurate minutes are kept.

(b) Notice boards
These are one-way communication, in effect a way of purveying information on decisions already taken or announcing the holding of meetings or other appropriate subjects. They are not a channel for discussion and are often ignored by a large proportion of employees. One particular golden rule in regard to notices is that they should be short and to the point, as well as being in appropriate language. A second golden rule is to date each notice and take it down immediately the business to which it refers has been completed. A board of out-of-date notices does more than anything to discredit this form of communication.

(c) Staff journal or magazine
This is an attempt both to encourage a corporate feeling in the workers and to provide a channel of active communication. By publicising the undertaking's successes and future plans it generates staff goodwill and a pride in belonging; by announcing promotions and various social and welfare improvements it helps to generate positive motivation in the work-people; by including articles, letters and various personal matters such as engagements and weddings it provides a voice for the work-force at all levels.

(d) Staff handbook
Not to be confused with the staff magazine (or house journal) this handbook provides new members of staff with all the information they should know about the organisation and their jobs. It also sets out both the legal and domestic rules concerning conditions of employment, pay, holiday benefits and similar matters. All employees, whatever their status, should be in possession of a staff handbook, and if it is produced in loose-leaf form it can easily be up-dated as conditions change.

14.10 Informal communication

Any management ignores at its peril the channels of informal communication that exist within its organisation. They are principally concerned with the organisation's internal affairs but there are some channels of informal communication which exist externally. Where formal lines of communication are firmly established and positive, informal communication is not present to a significant degree, but it does abound where the organisation does not provide adequate formal channels.

(a) The grape vine

Sometimes known as the jungle telegraph, this is a network of channels for rumour and gossip. It is most active horizontally but can also exist vertically.

- As it is essentially verbal it is very much prone to distortion by its very nature, but the messages it carries are also embellished at various stages with exaggeration. Because of this, even if the information at the start is substantially correct it may be far from the truth before very long.
- Such a method is, of course, an attractive vehicle for malcontents to use to spread rumours and falsehoods that can damage the organisation. In fact it is true that the grape vine usually carries more bad news than good. There is normally little possibility of checking the veracity of the information being carried and the false gossip can have a disturbing effect upon workers.
- The grape vine can be truly effective only where workers are not kept fully informed of management's intentions and decisions; thus the best counter to the subversive activities of those who use the grape vine to the disadvantage of the undertaking is to ensure that all employees are aware of management plans. Undoubtedly the greatest difficulty concerning gossip and rumour is that it is normally impossible to trace the source. The answer lies in building up complete faith in the management by providing fully adequate formal lines of communication and releasing information at the earliest possible moment through these lines. Thus rumours are less likely to be believed, and trust in management will be maintained.

(b) The canteen lunch

Where an organisation provides canteen facilities then much informal communication takes place over the meal tables. Remembering that such meals are also a channel for the grape vine, an astute manager or supervisor can acquire much information as to the way work-people are thinking, and as to their attitudes or grievances.

Similar to the canteen lunch is the working lunch, where suggestions and plans may be discussed without any formal record being kept or any firm commitment entered into. Such working lunches can be used for both external and internal communication.

(c) Social occasions

Any type of social gathering can be a vehicle for informal communication, both external and internal, from rounds of golf to a reception dinner, from membership of a church to a visit to the local public house. Many of these occasions are engineered deliberately for information-gathering purposes, but in many cases information is passed on quite unwittingly and its importance quite unrealised by the giver.

Communication is a vital tool in the successful management of an enterprise and its use should not be left to chance. Proper efforts must be made by every management to utilise it to the full.

QUESTIONS

1 (a) Describe the principles of the communication process indicating the objectives to be achieved.
   (b) What are the factors which can lead to failure in the communication process? (IAM)

2 Describe in some detail *three* important psychological barriers which can act as obstacles to good communication. Illustrate your descriptions from your own experience or reading. (IAM)

3 Outline the important characteristics of internal communication systems within an organisation. What is the significance for management of the concept of 'information overload', with special reference to internal management information flows? (ACCA)

4 What actions can management take to stimulate the upward flow of communication within an organisation? (ICSA)

5 What are the minimum functions fulfilled by an organisation's 'house journal'? (IComA)

6 The management of business organisations often ascribe the cause of problems experienced to 'communication breakdown' or 'communication failure'. Examine a case of communication failure, in an organisation familiar to you, identifying its causes and suggesting means by which such problems may be prevented from recurring. (CIM)

7 What are some of the difficulties experienced in organisations as far as vertical communication is concerned? (IComA)

▪ ▼ 15 Communication and people

If a key purpose of management is to 'get things done through people' (see Chapter 1) then all managers, and all those who aspire to be managers at whatever level, must be effective communicators. Lack of communication, or inadequate communication, always leads to problems.

It is also true that some organisations, and their senior managers, do not encourage communication. The worst of these restricts communication, operating a 'need to know' policy. This, too, is detrimental to morale, and can be extremely divisive. It is also true that in many such situations, serious organisational and operational problems have arisen because some people did not know what others were doing.

People today have much greater access to information, and a much wider variety of sources, than ever before. So it is certain that they will get an indication of what is proposed, even if organisation communication systems are not good. And a lack of true, proper and credible information always leads to a proliferation of the grape vine (see Chapter 14). Within organisations, the only genuine matters of concern should be trade secrets, commercial and operational confidentiality, and matters concerning the personal or professional performance of an individual.

Openness of information also tends towards a much greater mutual confidence in the organisation, and its management. It also makes much more effective the conduct of the matters that are now discussed in this Chapter, in which everyone who aspires to any level of management should be proficient.

15.1 Meetings

Meetings are 'the gathering together of two or more persons in order to discuss matters of common concern'. This definition covers all types of meeting – formal, informal, statutory, and *ad hoc*. It also explains the principal purpose for holding a meeting: to have discussion about a matter or number of matters, and if necessary, to come to a decision about action that needs to be taken.

15.2 Categories of meeting

The following categories should be noted.

(a) Statutory meetings

Many organisational meetings are required by law. this includes the Annual General Meeting (AGM), in which shareholders are given information about the progress of their company over the previous financial year, are asked to elect or re-elect members of the board of directors, and to declare any rate of dividend. Shareholders of companies may also call Emergency General Meetings or Extraordinary General Meetings (EGMs) in order to address some form of organisational crisis.

Under the aegis of the European Union, statutory mechanisms for the participation and consultation of staff are likely to be required for many organisations in the near future.

(b) Organisation constitutional meetings

These arise as the result of bodies formally constituted in staff handbooks, e.g. joint negotiating committees, joint consultative committees, staff meetings and the like.

(c) The meeting to solve problems

Some meetings are called to discuss problems and seek solutions. Normally, this involves everybody directly concerned together with any other experts present, available or required who may be able to bring their own expertise and judgement to bear.

(d) The meeting to inform

Some meetings are called to inform those involved of a decision already made and possibly to attain their consent. This may arise as the result of a crisis or emergency, in which case the organisation's top management, and others involved, have to promulgate their views to everyone else.

(e) The meeting to persuade

Meetings to persuade occur in order that a member may put a proposal which he then seeks to persuade the meeting to adopt. The role of the persuader is that of advocate and the aim is to sell his idea.

At both meetings to inform and meetings to persuade it may, or may not be, necessary to gain the formal approval or consent of the meeting.

(f) The consultative meeting

Consultative meetings cover a wide variety of matters. In large organisations, they are used most often in industrial relations and staff management situations, especially where trade unions are involved. In such situations, it is increasingly usual for the organisation to take upon itself the responsibility of defining the agenda, remit and boundaries of authority of the meeting.

(g) The negotiating meeting

Negotiating meetings exist in two situations. The first is informal industrial relations and staff management situations, especially concerning the annual pay round and variations in terms and conditions of employment, and again, there will be rules, boundaries and limitations placed on what the meeting may discuss.

The second occurs in situations where the organisation is negotiating or tendering for work from an outside body. Again, the organisation will vest in those involved the authority necessary to conduct the meeting to a successful and effective conclusion.

(h) The *ad hoc* meeting

These are convened informally for a variety of purposes. They are concerned with managing everything from crises and emergencies, to inter-departmental misunderstandings, to rectifying customer complaints, and so on; the potential for *ad hoc* meetings is virtually limitless.

15.3 Making a meeting effective

To be of any value a meeting must be fully effective. If it is not fully effective it has been a waste of the time of several people. If these are salaried officers of a company, a considerable expense may have been suffered as well. In order to avoid failure or only partial success there are certain steps that can be taken by the leader and convener of a meeting:

1 The objectives of the meeting must be made quite clear to those invited. The topics to be dealt with must be given in precise terms so far as this is possible so that members are quite prepared for proper discussion.
2 Members must be given adequate notice of the meeting, and a prepared agenda should be provided.
3 The accommodation chosen for the meeting must be suitable; it must not be cramped for the number expected, it must be comfortable and as free from noise as possible, and efforts must be made to avoid interruptions. Such items as writing materials and drinking water should be provided.
4 The time of the meeting must be convenient for all concerned, and its probable duration specified.
5 Leaders of meetings must be adequately prepared. They should have in advance all the information and material they know they will need to deal with the proposals to be put, and they should anticipate possible questions and arguments so that they can meet them with confidence.
6 They should be acquainted with the kind of people who are to take part in the meeting and try to gauge their likely attitudes so that they are prepared for their response and likely participation. Of course, in the case of very many meetings, the members will already be known to each other through previous acquaintance.

If these six points are given proper attention, then the meeting should start off in the right way and there is every chance that it will be successful and effective.

15.4   The conduct of a meeting

The conduct of the meeting is equally important, and this is the responsibility of the leader of the meeting. The following points need attention.

1 The meeting must always begin on time and end on time. If those involved know that the meeting will not begin on time, then they will not arrive on time.
2 The leader or chairman's authority over the meeting must be absolute.
3 It is up to the leader or the chairman to set the tone of the meeting, and to ensure that business is conducted in a brisk, positive and complete manner.
4 if there is any doubt over the purpose of the meeting, this must be clarified at the outset by the leader or chairman.
5 The chairman is there to ensure that members make useful and positive contributions.
6 Discussions should be kept to the point.
7 Useful discussion can take place only in a positive atmosphere. If bad feeling does arise, it needs to be dealt with, either briefly at the meeting, or at more length elsewhere.
8 It is necessary to recognise at the outset that different agenda items may take different lengths of time to resolve, and the meeting should be structured in order to do this.
9 Sufficient time must be made available to ensure that all agenda items are dealt with in a useful and constructive manner. These should be prioritised so that the most substantial issues are dealt with first.

A survey carried out by the Industrial Society in 1992 found that managers can spend as much as 30 per cent of their working week in meetings. Clearly, therefore, this is a very expensive activity; it is necessary to get the best possible return on this expense. In an effort to do this, some organisations insist that their meetings take place standing up, without refreshments, because they believe that if they do this, people are much more inclined to stick to the point, and that meetings will be shorter.

15.5   The chairman of a meeting

All formal meetings must have a chairman (nowadays often called 'chair' or 'chairperson'), properly appointed, whose responsibility is the conduct of the business. In some cases, where the chairman has not been properly appointed, courts have ruled that meetings have not been properly constituted, and this has led to all the business conducted at such a meeting being invalid.

Otherwise, it is usual for someone to accept responsibility for the conduct and outcome of the meeting, and that those involved will elect someone from among themselves to accept this responsibility.

The duties and responsibilities of a chairman are as follows:

1 Be satisfied that their own appointment is valid.

2 Ensure that the meeting is properly convened, validly constituted, and that those present have the right to attend.

3 Make sure that a quorum is present.

4 Ensure either that the minutes of the last meeting have been circulated and read, or that they are read at the current meeting. This having been done, the agreement of the members present is necessary that the minutes are a true record of the last meeting and then sign them.

5 See that items are taken in agenda order. This does not, of course, prevent the meeting altering the order if it so wishes provided the majority of members agree.

6 Give those who wish equal opportunity to speak on any subject on the agenda as it arises. In doing this, the chairman should try to encourage shy members to voice their views, at the same time curbing those who are verbose.

7 In the case of dispute, act fairly and impartially.

8 Reject matters that may be introduced that are outside the agenda or not within the jurisdiction of the meeting. The last item on practically all agendas is 'any other business'. This should not be permitted to be taken as an excuse to bring up matters quite outside the business of the current meeting.

9 Maintain proper order during the proceedings and break up any unruly disputes between members. Most rules allow the chairman in such cases to adjourn the meeting for a short while for tempers to cool.

10 Insist that all motions, amendments and remarks are addressed to the chairman. No direct communication between different members of the meeting should be allowed and offenders should be asked to put their remarks 'through the chair'. By this means the meeting as a whole is kept in the discussion and also some of the heat is kept out of arguments.

11 Put motions and amendments to the vote of the meeting and pronounce the results.

12 See that voting is carried out in strict accordance with the regulations of the meeting. Where there is no formal vote, as often happens at informal meetings, the chairman will pronounce the 'sense' of the meeting.

13 In the event of equal voting, and where the regulations allow, use their casting vote. Contrary to popular belief, a chairman does not have a casting vote as a right. This has to be given by the regulations. Where such a vote is allowed and is used the chairman must exercise the utmost discretion. It is, in fact, usual for the chairman to vote in such a way as to retain the status quo.

14 After each discussion, summarise the sense of the arguments for the benefit of the meeting.

15 If another meeting is to be held obtain the agreement of the members as to its date and time. This is, of course, not necessary where a series of meetings is planned to be held on specific dates.

16 Declare the meeting closed at the end of the business, or if a valid quorum has ceased to exist through the departure of one or more members. The chairman has the prerogative to close the meeting, though the members may also request this.

17 Make sure that adequate notes are taken during the meeting so that proper minutes may be written up. These notes may be taken by the chairman, but are more often made by the secretary, who will be responsible for actually writing the minutes.

In addition to the points mentioned above, the chairman also has power to have disorderly members expelled from the meeting and to adjourn the meeting if it is impossible to restore and maintain proper order.

15.6 The regulation of meetings

Many formal meetings are governed by specific regulations as to procedure. These rules are designed to provide a procedural framework for the meetings concerned and are particularly helpful to members who may not be familiar with the conventions governing the conduct of meetings. These regulations help to avoid misunderstandings, provide specific rules for most circumstances that may be met during a meeting, and generally assist in ensuring that the event will run smoothly and effectively.

Regulations are usually formulated for the benefit of the particular meetings for which they are designed. However, there are some rules that are common to most situations.

1 **The quorum**
   The quorum shall consist of ... members, entitled to attend and to vote.
   No meeting shall be considered as valid unless a quorum is present continuously throughout the whole of the duration of the meeting. If at any time a quorum is not present, or maintained, then the meeting shall stand adjourned on instructions from the chairman.

2 **Notice of the meeting**
   Seven clear days' notice must be given in writing to each and every member entitled to attend at a meeting whether or not such member is entitled to vote.

3 **Order of business**
   An agenda must be prepared and circulated with the notice of the meeting to every member entitled to attend.
   The business before the meeting shall be dealt with in the order set out on the agenda unless it be altered by agreement of the members. Such agreement shall be signified by a simple majority on a vote by a show of hands.
   No business not included on the agenda shall be considered by the meeting but by agreement with the members such business may be carried forward for the agenda of a future meeting.

4 **Chairman's ruling**
   The chairman's ruling on any matter shall be final. However, should any ruling be challenged by not less than 25 per cent of those present and enti-

tled to vote then the ruling shall be put to the vote on a show of hands. The decision shall be by a simple majority.

5 Speeches

Members shall at all times address the meeting through the chair. No member may speak on any motion more than once, except with the permission of the chairman. Nevertheless, any member who has spoken on the original motion may also speak on any amendment.

Speeches must be addressed strictly to the content of the motion or amendment before the meeting, and shall be immediately terminated if so directed by the chairman.

6 Motions and amendments

All motions must be in writing and must be submitted to the secretary of the meeting not less than fourteen days before the date on which the meeting is to be held.

Amendments to motions before the meeting shall be put in writing and handed to the chairman, who will read them out to the members. All motions and amendments shall have a proposer and a seconder. The chairman may act in neither capacity.

Amendments must be put to the vote before the motions they seek to qualify. If an amendment is carried, the amended motion shall be put to the meeting as the substantive motion. If an amendment fails then the original motion must be voted upon without further discussion.

The chairman shall not allow any amendment that is merely a negation of the original motion.

A motion, having been carried, shall not be the subject of further discussion at the same meeting.

7 Voting

Voting shall be by show of hands and the chairman's decision on the result shall be final, subject to standing order 4 above.

A motion shall be deemed to have succeeded if it obtains a simple majority of the votes of those present and entitled to vote. There shall be no right of proxy.

In the event of a tie in voting the chairman may, use a casting vote. Should the chairman decline to use the casting vote in the event of a tie then the motion shall be deemed to have failed.

Any member entitled to vote may abstain if they so wish.

8 Unruly behaviour

If any member acts in an unruly manner, uses unseemly language or interrupts a speaker without permission of the chairman, or if they refuse to obey the chairman when called to order, then they shall be required to leave the meeting. Neither shall they be allowed to return unless and until they give to the meeting an acceptable apology. Should this expulsion reduce the number of members to below the required quorum, the meeting must stand adjourned notwithstanding an apology.

9   The adjournment

The chairman may adjourn the meeting as and when necessary. Similarly, any member may move the adjournment, when the motion must be seconded and put to the meeting. However, if at the time the motion for the adjournment is put a previous motion is being discussed, no member who has already spoken on the latter motion may move the adjournment.

Note: Many organisations and their committees now substitute the words 'chair', 'governor', or even 'leader', for 'chairman'. The original still persists in many cases, however.

All meetings require the presence and acceptance of these elements. However brief or *ad hoc*, a meeting should always be conducted in an orderly fashion. In this way, everybody is clear about: who should attend; who is in charge; what the purpose of the meeting is; and what is to happen as the result.

15.7   Committee meetings

All organisations have committees. Some of these are required by law – e.g. safety committees. Others choose to have committees as the most effective way of dealing with day-to-day business, or as a means of formalising communications. Boards of management appoint specialist committees to deal with various matters for information, guidance and advice. What-ever the constitution of the committee, the following should always be noted.

(a) **Committee membership:** so that everyone with a legitimate interest or expertise is represented.

(b) **A committee's authority:** so that it has the power, authority and account-ability to carry out the duties for which it was constituted.

(c) **Standing or continuous committees:** with a regular, enduring or perma-nent remit or one particular aspect of the organisation (e.g. public bodies normally have a finance committee).

(d) **Sub-committees:** formed to deal with one aspect of the wider remit of a committee.

(e) *Ad hoc* **committees:** appointed to investigate a particular matter in hand. This is normally to a particular timescale, and to provide information, a report, or a direction for action at the behest of higher authority.

(f) **Specialist groups and think-tanks:** these used to be called brainstorm-ing or creative committees and their purpose was to produce a wealth of expert information on a particular topic. It is usual now to find their activities more orderly and directed, though the wider creative imagina-tive remit still exists in marketing departments, and advertising and other consultancies.

15.8 Other factors in the management of meetings

(a) Notice of meetings

All formal meetings require specified notice to be given to all those who are entitled to attend. Failure to do this may lead to the possibility of the business conducted at the meeting being declared invalid. Notice that has to be given should be laid down in the rules or standing orders governing the meeting or committee and such regulations must be rigidly observed.

For informal meetings, it is usual to set upon an agreed date and time at which everyone can attend. Formal meetings, and committees with published standing orders, may require meetings to be conducted with prescribed frequency and regularity.

(b) The agenda of the meeting

Every formal meeting must have a guide so that its business is carried forward positively and in an orderly manner. Every meeting should have a guide, even if this is only accepted by agreement by those present.

Tradition has given the agenda an accepted format. This starts in most cases with apologies for absence. This is followed by minutes of the last meeting and then matters arising. Then follow the main items to be considered. The agenda finishes with two standard items, any other business and date of the next meeting.

NOTICE OF MEETING

A meeting of the Safety Committee will be held on
14th May, 20 . . , at 3.30 pm in the Committee Room

4th May, 20 . .

AGENDA

1. Apologies for absence.
2. Minutes of meeting held on 12th February, 20 . .
3. Matters arising.
4. Provision of fire extinguishers in Paint Store.
5. Recruitment of Safety Officer.
6. Any other business.
7. Date of next meeting.

Figure 15.1 A specimen of combined notice of meeting and agenda

It is usual for the notice of a meeting and its agenda to be combined and a specimen is given in Figure 15.1.

(c) Methods of voting

Voting procedures for formal meetings need to be formally constituted and written down so that everyone can understand them.

Minutes of the meeting of the Safety Committee held on 14th May, . . , at 3.30 pm in the Committee Room.

Present: A. Dorritson (Chairman)
 B. Sideley
 F. Bothamstone
 S. Sydnie

In Attendance (Secretary)

322. Apologies for absence were received from Messrs A. Anville and B. Burdock.

323. The minutes of the meeting held on 12th February, 20 . . , having been previously circulated, were taken as read. They were signed by the Chairman as a correct record of that meeting.

324. Matters Arising
A tender has been accepted for the installation of sprinkler valves in the General Office and work is due to start on 1st June.

325 Fire Extinguishers for Paint Store
It was agreed that an additional four fire extinguishers should be purchased and installed in the Paint Store. Mr Sydnie was instructed to obtain tenders from three suppliers for consideration at the next meeting.

326. Recruitment of Safety Officer
It was agreed that a Safety Officer should be recruited as soon as possible. Mr Dorritson will instruct the Personnel Department to draw up a suitable job specification with a view to advertising this post.

327. Any Other Business
The low level of lighting on the stairway in the old building was brought up by Mr. Sideley. Mr Sydnie promised to look into this matter and report at the next meeting.

328. The next meeting will be on 30th July at 3.30 pm.

CHAIRMAN

Figure 15.2 Specimen minutes

(d) Minutes of the meeting

Minutes have a conventional format. They are headed with the title of the meeting concerned, its venue and the date and time it was held.

When minutes are written up, the agenda of the meeting is used as a guide.

Rather than reporting discussion, it is usual to summarise the main points; some meetings simply report the points for action or future activity. A specimen of a common form of minutes is given in Figure 15.2. This is based on the specimen agenda shown in Figure 15.1.

(e) Advantages and disadvantages of committee meetings and work

The main advantages are:

1 It regularises and formalises key and enduring aspects of organisational activities.
2 It gives the opportunity for experts and those with a legitimate interest in the matter to come together for a stated purpose.
3 It indicates a consensus on the required outcome of a particular discussion.

The main disadvantages are:

1 It is time-consuming; and it may be expensive and resource-consuming if the committee is not seen to make the required progress.
2 It interferes with the daily activities of all those affected.
3 Large meetings inevitably become cumbersome and slow to make progress.
4 Some committees become talking shops, leading to very little action being proposed or decisions taken.
5 Committees may become introverted or inward-looking, and the relevance of their discussions be lost to the organisation.
6 Committees may become dominated by lobbies or vested interests, advancing points of view that serve these interests rather than those of the organisation as a whole.

15.9 Interviews

All managers and supervisors should be effective interviewers. The extent and nature of the interviews that they carry out will vary according to their position in the organisation, their authority and responsibility, an the extent of their remit.

Interviews are face-to-face verbal exchanges, the purpose of which is to discover as much information as possible about the matter in hand. At work, interviews are used for a variety of purposes including staff recruitment, hearing staff grievances and complaints, disciplinary action, performance appraisal, and other matters concerned with management staff relations. They also occur when sales representatives see potential customers, public relations officers deal with the media, organisational and operational research, staff surveys, and other information gathering activities.

In general, in interviewing situations, one person will have authority over the other. This authority may be overt, as in the case of an employer interviewing an applicant for appointment; or it may be implicit but not stated, as with a researcher carrying out an organisational survey of some sort.

Special skills and qualities are required for extreme forms of interview. For example, counselling interviews should only be carried out by someone in whom the interviewee has full confidence; and serious problem counselling should only be carried out by persons with professional qualifications. More generally, it is still necessary for those handling angry and aggrieved customers to have special skills and qualities, as well as organisational authority to put a complaint right.

15.10   The key elements of an interview

In order that the interviewer may derive the utmost benefit from an interview much care must be exercised before and during the meeting. It might be said that there are four elements to a successful interview: planning it, conducting it, making assessments during it and at its conclusion, and making a decision based on factors brought out by the interview.

(a) **Proper planning** must be carried out prior to the meeting, as without a clear plan the interview will be less than completely successful. The purpose for holding the interview must be definite and certain. What, precisely, do we wish to find out? What sort of questions should we put to the interviewee and in what order? How are we going to put them? Which is the most suitable place to hold the interview?

Many interviewers prefer to have a structured interview – that is, one in which a specific list of topics with, perhaps important questions, is prepared, probably on a form that can be completed as the interviewee answers. Others are content with a list of headings that act as a guide during the meeting, but which, nevertheless, keep the interview on course. Either method is preferable to an interview where the interviewer has no plan but asks questions *ad hoc*. Such an interview is likely to miss many important pieces of information that will allow a well-considered decision.

The interview should be conducted in accordance with the plan that has been previously formulated. However, the plan must be viewed as a flexible guide rather than a rigid set of rules, and it must be modified as circumstances require during the course of an interview.

An interview is a human situation. This being so, the personality of the interviewee must be taken into account and accommodated so far as the other requirements of the interview will allow. Only in this way will the most benefit be gained from the interview. It must also be remembered that in most cases the interviewer is in a position of command, and this produces different reactions in different interviewees.

(b) **Assessment** is not, generally, something that happens at a particular point in an interview. Rather is it the result of continuous appraisal from the moment the interview begins. Information will be gathered from the interviewee during the course of the meeting, adding to the knowledge being gained bit by bit. Gradually an assessment emerges based on this knowledge and on the impression made by the interviewee through personality, attitude and apparent motivation. When this moment of final assessment is reached the discussion should be terminated; no useful purpose can be served by prolonging it and in some cases further conversation may interfere with the clear decision already made. In the case of the salesman/customer interview, for example, the customer may quite well be talked out of a favourable assessment of the product if the salesman continues to expound its virtues after the buyer has made up their mind to buy.

(c) **Decision** on the course of action to take normally comes very soon after the final assessment. Sometimes the decision comes simultaneously with the assessment. The temptation to arrive at a conclusion during the course of assessment, and before the termination of the interview, should be firmly resisted, because in such a case a verdict is probably being taken before all the evidence has been presented. The decision should be objective: if it is made without the full information being presented it will probably be in some measure quite subjective, perhaps influenced by the interviewee's dress, accent or other personal trait.

Where possible, interviewees should be informed of the decision at once. Otherwise they should be given the result as soon after the meeting as possible. In the latter case it is courteous to tell the person concerned when they may expect to hear the outcome of the interview. However, if the announcement of the decision is to be delayed it is most unwise to give any hint as to the possible outcome in advance. In the case of an applicant for a job, for instance, hopes may be raised that subsequently have to be dashed to the ground.

15.11   Interviewing techniques

So important is the question of interviewing skills that it is advisable to look at some of the techniques that help to make a successful interview.

(a) The environment

Except for certain circumstances, such as a sales/customer interview, all interviews should be held in private. All possible steps should be taken to avoid interruptions, such as informing the telephone switchboard operator to avoid putting telephone calls through, and asking colleagues to respect your privacy for the duration of the interview. Interruptions, even minor ones, can reduce the effectiveness of an interview by impeding the flow of thought and inhibiting conversation. Where a series of interviews has to take place, such as a selection of an applicant for a job from among a number of interviewees, sufficient time should be allocated for this purpose and be made sacrosanct.

The physical arrangements are also of extreme importance, and must be such that they put the interviewee at ease. The room should be pleasant and evenly lit. The chairs should be businesslike but comfortable, and prefer-ably the same for each party. Both people should be able to see each other easily. Interviewees should never be at a disadvantage against the inter-viewer. They should not be positioned so that they face a window directly, thus putting them fully in the light whilst the interviewer is less well lighted. Such a condition simply makes the interviewee feel selfconscious and puts an obstacle in the way of the free flow of conversation. Where possible there should be no physical barrier between the two people, such as a desk, as this tends to produce a barrier against the free flow of thought as well as a barrier in the physical sense. Rather, if a desk is necessary to the interviewer, the interviewee should be seated at the side of it.

(b) Interviewer's behaviour

Because they are in control of the interview, the interviewer has a position of authority, and this they must not abuse. They must, therefore, be especially careful to put the interviewee at ease and to give confidence. The inter-viewer's attitude should be one of understanding and of wanting to be of assistance. Above all, the interviewer must not be overbearing, thus creating apprehension or nervousness in the mind of the interviewee. Neither must the interviewer put personal and irrelevant questions. Unless the intervie-wee has a calm and relaxed mind communication will be hindered and the interview will be less than successful.

(c) Information flow

The purpose of an interview is the gathering and interchange of informa-tion, and this can come about only if a smooth, two-way communication is established from the very beginning. Mutual trust and confidence are essen-tial, as is a relaxed and friendly atmosphere. One way to generate these con-ditions is for the interviewer to introduce a non-controversial topic of mutual interest at the start of the interview and so establish a rapport between the parties. This will make subsequent conversation much easier and will lessen any nervousness the interviewee may feel. The questions to be asked during the interview should have been decided upon during the planning stage; the form in which they are put will be governed by the cir-cumstances that develop during the interview.

It must be remembered that it is desirable to check the answers and information that the interviewee gives during the interview, though this requires tact. There are a number of ways of doing this. For example, a ques-tion may be put in a different manner at a later point in the interview and the response checked with the previous answer. A response may be referred to again, casually, later and re-examined; or an alteration of approach may be adopted round a topic. It is important, however, not to doubt the inter-viewee's integrity; confidence must be maintained throughout.

(d) The theme of the interview

An interview is an exercise in the meeting of minds, as mentioned earlier. If this is successfully achieved, as it should be in a fruitful interview, then there may be a tendency to discuss interesting topics irrelevant to the objectives of the interview. This must be resisted firmly, except, perhaps, at the beginning of the meeting when it is necessary to induce a friendly and relaxed atmosphere. Thus, the purpose of the interview must be kept firmly in mind throughout the discussion, and no extraneous subjects allowed to intrude. If the interview has been carefully planned this should not be very difficult. An unstructured interview, however, may allow the conversation to wander off the point with the result that insufficient information is gathered about the interviewee and a conclusion come to based on inadequate data. More often than not such a situation results in decisions being taken that prove unsatisfactory.

(e) Behaviour interviewers should avoid

The effectiveness and success of an interview depend almost totally on the behaviour of the interviewers. At the beginning of this section we looked at some of the things they should do, and we must now examine some of the things they should avoid doing:

1 They should not let personal reactions to the interviewee influence the assessment. In particular, first impressions should not be allowed to colour the interviewer's attitude, otherwise a great deal of the objectivity of the interview will be lost. An open mind as to dress, accent, physical appearance and mannerisms must be maintained unless any of these is fundamental to the objective of the interview.

2 The interviewer should, at all costs, avoid asking leading questions which could indicate to the interviewee what answers are expected: not, for example, 'You can do a trial balance, can't you?', but rather 'How far can you take the books of account?'

3 Too much talking by the interviewer is detrimental to the interview. This is not an uncommon fault, but must be resisted. The interviewee must be allowed sufficient time, and without having to compete for time with the interviewer.

4 Conversely, interviewers must not be guilty of being taciturn. If they are uncommunicative the interviewee may be hindered from speaking freely, or may feel compelled to talk too much to avoid embarrassing pauses. In either case the interview will be less than effective. Interviewers are always in charge of the interview and it is their responsibility to keep it flowing along the planned course; this means that they must make a reasonable contribution throughout.

5 Just as it is necessary to avoid putting leading questions, so is it important not to give information that can give an indication to the interviewee what sort of attitude and response are expected. At a job interview, for instance, if the interviewer extols the special virtues of the previous occupant of the post, the interviewee may be inclined to claim the same virtues.

6 The interviewer should very carefully avoid constantly interrupting the interviewee's answers and comments, or cutting them short. In addition to resulting in a less than fully effective interview, this practice may also

cause interviewees to feel that the interviewer has little interest in them or their views. A personal rapport must be generated and maintained all through the meeting, and this includes showing interviewees that they have the interviewer's interest all the time.

7 No questions should be put that can be answered simply by 'Yes' or 'No': interviewees should be required to express themselves fully at all times.

8 Interviewees have as much interest in the interview as the interviewer, otherwise they would not be there. The interview should not be closed, therefore, without giving the interviewee the opportunity to seek all the information required. Failure to do this frequently results in misunderstanding and subsequent grievance.

15.12 Addressing an audience

It is often necessary for a manager to give a speech to a group of people, sometimes a large group and sometimes a small one. There are certain guidelines that can be followed to make this task easier than it may first appear, particularly if it is necessary to address a large gathering.

(a) Some general points

- The first step towards a successful speech is knowledge of the subject. A thorough grasp of the topic or topics to be dealt with is essential and gives confidence to the speaker. If necessary the subject should be researched to fill any gaps in the speaker's knowledge. This is particularly desirable if the subject or point of view is at all controversial.

- There are almost certain to be questions put by the audience or group being addressed and the speaker must be prepared to answer them. Any lack of knowledge displayed may lose the confidence of the audience. However, it is quite acceptable to admit being unable to answer a question that is very much outside the main theme of the talk. In the case of an intimate or informal group a promise to supply the answer later is usually welcome.

- Language can be a problem to speakers. They should ascertain beforehand what kind of groups they are to address, assuming they are not colleagues. The kind of language used to address a board of directors is not the kind to use when addressing a meeting of production workers.

- In any case, anyone giving a speech should always know their audience, both size and nature. The key to all effective speech-making is understanding – that the audience will understand what it is that the speaker is trying to put across.

(b) Notes

Very few speakers can deliver a first-class speech without notes in one form or another. There should, therefore, be no reticence about taking notes on to the platform, and to be seen to be consulting them. The problem lies in the manner of the notes. They are needed as memory aids and to keep the talk flowing logically from step-to-step and to avoid omission of important points.

The overall key to success is knowing the material and the audience. In this way, the necessary material can be put across in ways that the audience understand. Experienced and expert speakers always do this; and they always have some form of prompt or bullet point card to which to refer during the course of the speech.

Methods to be avoided are as follows:

1 Writing the speech verbatim: a read speech is almost always boring to the listeners. Speakers are concerned with keeping their place on the page rather than being lively and vital. They also have to keep their eyes on the notes, and therefore lose eye contact with the audience. Moreover, written language is more stilted than spoken language and the speech is therefore likely to lack freshness and spontaneity. Worst of all, if speakers lose their place, there may be an embarrassing pause or silence.

2 Writing out the speech and memorising it: in which the exercise becomes a memory test rather than effective communication.

3 Impromptu speaking: off-the-cuff remarks, ill considered or improperly thought out, often cause quite as many problems as they resolve. If for any reason it becomes necessary to make an 'off-the-cuff' remark – e.g. in response to a question – this should always be made absolutely clear; and wherever possible, this should be followed with the speaker determining to provide full and accurate information afterwards.

Where lengthy, detailed, statistical or other numerical information is required, this should be issued as a hand-out. Reference can then be made to it as necessary. Indeed, many speakers issue hand-outs covering the broader scope of the material that they wish to cover; they then use the speech to draw attention to salient points, and to enlarge upon them if necessary.

(c) Preparing a speech

Having looked at the question of content of the speech, and how the notes should be prepared, the steps required in the actual preparation of the speech must now be examined:

1 Fix the purpose and aim of the speech. Is it to be informative, persuasive or evocative? Is it intended to offer new knowledge, to examine existing knowledge or to alter current thinking? Is it to instruct, to train or to further interest? Answers to these questions will set the tone and pattern of the speech.

2 Ascertain, or fix, the length of time of the speech.

3 Gather ideas, as suggested at the beginning of this chapter.

4 Write the main headings and fill in with the outline of the talk, as explained under (b) above.

5 Familiarise yourself with the main pattern of what you will say, guided by your notes as in 4.

6 Set time limits to each section of the speech. This will ensure that each part is given its appropriate quota of time. More important, it will help to

avoid over-running the total allotted time or, worse still, to avoid running out of material before the allotted span.

7 Consider whether the talk could be more informative or more entertaining if some form of visual aids were used rather than relying entirely on speech.

8 Leave time for questions.

A chart such as that shown in Figure 15.3 is a valuable aid to structuring a speech; where visual and other aids are to be used these are noted against the section heading in a column ruled for them. Inspection of this chart before the meeting will act as a reminder of what aids must be available, and the various times should be marked on the actual notes to be used for the speech. As a planning aid, this chart can be invaluable.

It cannot be overstated that the greater the care taken in preparing for a speech, the better the speech is likely to be.

15.13 Report writing

According to the dictionary a report is 'an account given or opinion formally expressed, after investigation or consideration'. It will be seen from this

Title: Communications

Date . . . .   Time . . . .   Venue . . . .

Timing	Topic	Aid
10.00 – 10.15	Introduction – Dictionary definition	—
10.15 – 10.25	Two-way nature of communication	Chart on O/H projector
10.25 – 10.40	Factors affecting communication	Hand-out
10.40 – 11.00	Perception and experience	2" x 2" slides
11.30 – 11.40	Summary of main points Questions	

Figure 15.3 A specimen scheme for a talk

definition that a report is reckoned to be formal, and is required to give an account of the matter covered or to state an opinion on it: sometimes both are required. In most cases, moreover, conclusions have to be drawn by the compiler of the report and, often, recommendations given.

(b) Basic principles

Whatever form a report takes, it will be subject to a set of basic rules or principles. These are to ensure that the report is logically constructed, and they encourage the writer to present it in an accepted format. The basic principles are as follows.

1　A title – indicative of the content of the report.
2　The report should be addressed to the people or person for whom it is intended.
3　The terms of reference, coverage or remit, under which the report has been prepared should be stated. Where it is a regular routine report, headings are often pre-printed; and it is only necessary to amend them if they change.
4　Some sort of introduction, preamble or background is useful before the main body of the report.
5　The body of the report should contain:
    (1)　the nature of any investigations carried out;
    (2)　any limiting factors;
    (3)　a statement of the sources of information used;
    (4)　a statement of facts and opinions discovered during the investigations;
    (5)　clear arguments and hypotheses arising from the investigations.
6　Conclusions should be indicated if these are called for. They should be the subject of a separate heading or section. All conclusions should be supportable from the main research carried out.
7　It is also usual for recommendations to be made. These should also be put separately under proper headings.

　　Both the conclusions and recommendations should be: prioritised; timescaled; giving indication of resources required; and brief support (though again, the recommendations will flow from the work previously carried out).
8　The report should be dated and signed, and the author's name appended.
9　It is often necessary to include various charts, statistics, graphs and other supporting material, and where these are extensive, they can be included as appendices. Where necessary also, other resources or bodies of information should be included as appendices.
10 Where reports are extensive, it is usual to give an executive summary, and summary of conclusions and recommendations, right at the start.
11 It is also useful to give a table of contents.

　　The purpose of taking this approach is to make the report easy and accessible to the reader; and especially easy and accessible to the reader who may only require parts of it but not the whole.

(b) Planning and preparing a report

The planning and preparation of reports reflects the principles indicated above. The normal procedure for planning and preparing reports is as follows.

1 **Terms of reference** A report, especially a formal one, is always commissioned for a specific purpose, and the extent of the brief must always be clearly known by the investigator. This is given in the terms of reference, and these terms must never be exceeded. Where, during the investigation, pertinent matters are uncovered that go beyond the terms of reference, these must on no account be included in the report, but must form the subject of a supplementary communication.

2 **For whom intended** It is necessary for the writer of a report to know for whom the report is intended and why it is required. This information will help the writer to decide which parts of the matter collected should be included in the report and which should be omitted. Such discrimination is an essential talent for any investigator or writer, and is highly desirable in the sphere of report writing. For example, if a report is required on a new machine tool, the board of directors of the company will be interested in different data from the works maintenance engineer.

Similarly, the language in which the report is couched will be different according to its destination. Highly technical language will be in order for the works engineer, but not for the board of directors.

3 **Headings** As with other written communication, the report should flow logically from one point to another, and should develop in an orderly and easily understood fashion. With this aim in view it is of great assistance if the headings and subheadings of the various sections of the report are laid down first so that a proper framework is constructed. The writing of the full account can then be undertaken in the sure knowledge that a logical arrangement has been established. Further, this method helps to avoid the accidental omission of important points that have to be made.

4 **Drafts** For any report other than a fairly brief one, it is almost always essential to prepare a draft first, so that it can be carefully edited before it is produced in its final form. In fact, a lengthy report may require more than one edited draft before it is considered satisfactory. Where the report is to contain any statements or opinions by experts, it is necessary to have these verified by the experts themselves, particularly in the context in which they are to appear. Drafts of these parts of the report will most certainly be required, therefore, to submit to the authorities in question for verification.

5 **Meeting the required date** Not only is a report required for a specific purpose, it will almost certainly be required by a specified date. This must be known at the outset and must be met at all costs. A report that is not ready when needed is worthless.

6 **Style** The style in which a report is written is important. It should be authoritative, and positive statements should be employed wherever possible. Negative statements should not be used unless there is no way of avoiding them. Particularly, if part of the purpose of the report is to stimulate action,

positive statements will encourage a positive approach in the reader whereas negative statements are inclined to lead to apathy.

7   **Preparation** The way the report is presented in its final form will depend upon its length, upon the number of copies required and, not least, upon the impression it is sought to have on its readers. It may be typewritten, duplicated or printed, therefore. A lengthy, formal report will normally be printed, and bound in book form, whilst a short, informal one may be duplicated and stapled together. If it is required to impress a potential client, a short, formal report on some project may be carefully typed, and bound in an attractive cover by one of the modern binding devices to be found in most offices nowadays. Presentation, then, is a matter of length and targeting.

The Nonsuch Company Plc.
Oldville,
Anyshire, AY32 BOX
Phone: (01975) 292850
Fax: (01975) 810738
30th October, ..

The Board of Directors.

Subject: Modernisation of Motorcar Fleet

As instructed I have investigated the condition of the motorcars now used by our salesmen, and have to report as follows:

Present position:	The fleet of motorcars used by our salesforce comprises 10 vehicles. Of these, two are over five years old, six are three years old and the remaining two were acquired six months ago: all are Ford Escorts of 1300 c.c. capacity.
Condition of vehicles:	The two oldest vehicles have done over 100 000 miles and are overdue for replacement. Of the six three-year old cars, four have done over 60 000 miles and the remaining two nearly 50 000 miles. The two six-month-old vehicles have both done under 15 000 miles.
Other findings:	The six three-year-old cars are performing reliably at the present time, but are beginning to require constant maintenance to keep their performance up to par. Further, four of them will require an expensive major overhaul in the very near future, and in the opinion of our maintenance engineer the other two are likely to be in this category within the next three or four months.
	All eight salesmen driving the oldest cars have expressed dissatisfaction that they have not been allocated up-to-date vehicles in line with those driven by their competitors.
Recommendations:	In order to modernise our salesmen's motorcar fleet, the eight cars of three years old and older should be replaced by current models of the same make and capacity. Competitive quotes should be obtained from three fleet dealers, and orders placed on the basis of best selling price coupled with best trade-in prices for our existing vehicles. Immediate delivery is desirable but not essential provided the delay is not more than two months.

Car Fleet Manager

Fig.ure15.4   A specimen report

Figure 15.4 is a specimen of a short, formal report. Examples of long, official reports are held at most public libraries and may be seen on request.

15.14   Sources of information

There are very many occasions when it is necessary to consult outside sources to gather information.

An ever-increasing volume of information is published nowadays on every subject from accountancy to zoology, and each has its own standard works which should be the first to be consulted for basic knowledge. So rapid is the advance of knowledge these days, however, that it is necessary to supplement basic reading of standard works with consultation of other writings on the same subject. It is also essential to consult the latest editions of all publications.

(a) The public library

The most convenient source of textbooks and technical works is the public library. If the library does not have the book required, it will always obtain these. It is also possible to approach the British Library in London which, for a fee, will provide any work published.

Libraries also have a vast amount of knowledge at their fingertips of where to look for information, and many libraries have extensive reference sections. Increasingly, public and specialist libraries have access to electronic databases, and can provide references for and access to the Internet.

(b) Specialist journals and newspapers

In addition to books, libraries keep good ranges of specialist newspapers and journals; and university libraries have very extensive resources for the acquisition of these. Moreover, all professional and technical societies publish journals devoted to their particular speciality and in addition, there are scores of such magazines put out by independent publishers catering for both professional and the amateur practitioner. Most industries have their own trade press. Many organisations subscribe to these, and indeed contribute articles and features to them.

(c) Specialist bodies

The most up-to-date information on any specialist subject is inevitably held by the professional, trade association or institution specialising in that particular area. Thus, the very latest knowledge about accountancy is likely to be obtainable from the Institute of Chartered Accountants or the Chartered Association of Certified Accountants. Similarly, current thinking on human resource management and industrial relations is likely to come from the Institute of Personnel and Development. The Institute of Management publishes a range of journals on all aspects of management. From such bodies, both fact and opinion can be obtained as well as possible future trends. Most professional and trade associations are quite willing to provide information and advice to non-members.

(d) Government sources

Facts and opinions may also be solicited from government departments, local authorities, educational institutions, and other public bodies which have an interest in the subject under investigation.

(e) Abstract services

Because of the great range of information available, a number of information management consultancies and database search experts have come into being. These services will produce summaries of articles appearing in various specialist journals so that it is possible for the researcher to keep abreast of essential information without the need to read through long articles. Some of these services are free; others require the user to subscribe on a period basis.

15.15   Effective reading

Managers are often inundated with material to read and it is important, therefore, that they do this effectively.

- It is essential that everything is first sorted. How this is done will vary between individual managers: what is essential is to have some system that orders material into priorities; deadlines; urgency; importance; value; and interest. Managers increasingly ask their staff to get involved in the reading workload.

    Managers also inevitably receive newspapers and journals from both the professional management sector, and also from the industrial or commercial sector in which they happen to be working. It is part of being a professional manager to keep abreast of the latest developments in both the management and the operational field.
- Within these constraints, effective reading consists of a combination of speed and understanding. There is only so much information that anyone can deal with effectively and when this barrier is reached, the phrase 'information overload' is used.
- There is a direct relationship between effectiveness in reading and the purpose for which we are doing it. We are much more likely to read quickly and comprehend fully and promptly something that interests us. This reinforces the point made earlier that the best reports and presentations are those that are written with the reader in mind.
- With practice, it is possible to increase the capacity for absorbing and understanding information, and this is a key management skill which should be practised by people as they become more experienced. Organisations require ever-greater returns on their investment in managerial and supervisory activities, and it is a great organisational help if all managers and supervisors can understand and grasp information quickly.
- To be an effective reader, it is essential to be able to concentrate fully on the matter in hand when necessary. Managers and supervisors need, therefore, to be able to set aside certain periods of time in order to read. Such a period of

time need not – will not – necessarily be long, but it is essential if particular matters are to be grasped fully.

- Skim reading or skimming is a skill that should be acquired by managers and supervisors. This is the art of 'running your eyes over' a piece of writing so that the general sense of what is written is picked up. That way, the particular manager or supervisor will keep themselves generally informed, and will at least be aware of the particular matter, even if they do not know about it in-depth. It is also a key feature of managerial technique to know which items should be contracted on, and which are capable of being skimmed, or ignored altogether.

- It is also a key feature of managerial quality to take an active interest in everything that passes over the desk or through the department. Managers and supervisors must be interested in developments in the profession of management, and also of their sphere of operations and industrial, commercial or public service sector, as a prerequisite to being an effective manager. Because of the volume of information currently available, it is therefore essential to become an effective reader as a condition of undertaking a managerial role.

15.16 Listening and hearing

Listening is a key managerial attribute. All managers are required to listen effectively at many stages throughout their working day; and faulty listening, receiving only part of the message, or general misunderstanding can, and does, lead to serious problems.

Listening is conscious or active hearing, and this means concentrating on what is being said, rather than merely being aware of it.

It is not always easy to maintain concentration when listening, and so when it is essential that undivided attention is given, time should be set aside and a quiet place also.

It is also essential to be interested in what is being said. It is part of the managerial duty to take an active interest in the hopes, fears and aspirations of all members of the department's staff; and any lapse in this is a mark of disrespect, as well as a barrier to effective listening.

Other barriers to effective listening are:

(a) **Length and duration:** this is especially a problem when trying to listen to a formal talk or lecture. It is difficult to maintain full concentration on a speaker for more than twenty minutes at a time. Skilled speakers indeed quite consciously intersperse their talks with small diversions every now and then in order that this barrier is overcome.

(b) **Emotional disturbance:** it is very difficult to get people to concentrate on anything if they have had unpleasant personal news or a quarrel in the recent past. Their concentration is entirely on the previous upheaval; and so anything that anyone tries to tell them subsequently will be diluted.

(c) **Dislike of the speaker:** if we like someone, we are inclined to accept what they say and to listen to them; conversely, if we dislike someone, we are likely to adopt a negative attitude to them and this will colour what we hear.

(d) Tone of voice: the way something is said in many cases is as important as what is said; and words take on a great variety of different meanings depending on the tone of voice used, facial expression, other reinforcements (e.g. pointing the finger, banging the desk).

(e) Distractions: outside noises, smells, and the like always tend to divert people's attention away from what is being said.

(f) Speech lag: while the average talking speed is 120 words per minute, the average possible hearing speed is nearer 400 words per minute. This means that the listener's mind has to slow down to keep pace with the speaker. This again reinforces the point that everything that has to be said should be stated with the listener in mind; and that the interest of the listener should be engaged beforehand.

The path to effective listening is not easy. It needs attention and concerted effort. Many organisations now send their managers on effective listening courses; and effective listening is now invariably a part of basic communication courses.

15.17 Non-verbal communication

Non-verbal communication either gives an impression of ourselves to someone else without our saying anything, or else it reinforces what we are saying. The main components are:

(a) Appearance: for example, age, gender, hair, face, body shape and size, height, bearing, national and racial characteristics, and clothing. Each of these aspects on its own, and the combined effect, has great implications for: interviewing; public images; creating impressions; advertising; public relations; salesmanship; confidence; and presentation.

(b) Manner: this indicates behaviour, the range of emotions, levels of confidence, levels of confidence, levels of certainty or sureness (or uncertainty and unsureness), levels of contentment/anxiety.

(c) Expression: after the initial meeting and first impression, facial expression becomes the focus of our attention and we concentrate most on this.

(d) Eye contact: regular eye contact demonstrates interest, trust, concern, affection and sympathy. The depth of expression in the eyes generates a deeper perception of feelings – anger, sorrow, love, hatred, joy.

(e) Clothing: this is also an important carrier of meaning in all face-to-face situations, and people provide an instant summing up based on this.

(f) Pose: this is either static or active. It is generally used to reinforce the total manner. It helps convey the overall impression such as relaxation, activity or passivity, anger, leisure, nervousness and so on.

(g) Activity: this is also important when meanings are being given emphasis.

(h) Positional communication: the closeness with which people are standing or sitting to each other; the presence of chairs, tables and other props; props such as desks and chairs are often used to emphasise superior–subordinate relationships.

(i) Other props and settings: these are used to convey impressions of luxury, casualness, formality, opulence and other meanings in different situations.
(j) Touch: this signifies and reinforces a wide range of perceptions. Consider the difference between different people's handshakes and the impressions that these convey. Touching also reinforces other communications – someone banging their fist on the table; someone meticulously rearranging their clothes.

15.18 Other aspects of communication

As stated at the beginning of the Chapter, all managers should be effective communicators. It is an essential part of the job. When things go wrong, therefore, managers need to reflect on why a particular communication was ineffective. The most common problems are:
(a) Failing to deliver that which was promised; failing to follow up with action that which was stated.
(b) The language used – where it is simple and direct, understanding accrues much more easily than if matters are dressed up in imprecise and (unfortunately all too often) 'mealy-mouthed' terms of phrase.
(c) Where non-verbal communication exists alongside verbal, the non-verbal should reinforce what is stated. For example, if someone is using direct and positive language, but their body conveys anxiety or uncertainty, then the latter message is that which comes across.
(d) If people use only formal channels of communication or committee systems to put the message across, then the message will get distorted and lost; the formal should be reinforced through the informal and the direct.
(e) If people use phrases such as 'he is only a secretary', 'she is only a cleaner', then this is a mark of lack of respect, and this attitude will come to be known and understood.

Communication is a continuous process. People at work need constantly to be told and re-told things; and it is a matter of human behaviour, that they lose confidence whenever they are not told things, however mundane those responsible may consider the matters to be. Effective communication is also a mark of organisational and managerial integrity, openness and honesty.

QUESTIONS

1 'To be of any value a meeting must be fully effective.' What are the characteristics of an effective meeting?
How can an administrator prepare and conduct meetings to ensure they possess these characteristics? (ICSA)
2 How important is the role of chairman in ensuring the effectiveness of a committee? (ICSA)
3 What are the roles of the meeting and the committee in the communication and decision-making process within the organisation? (ACCA)

4 What are the main characteristics of a properly organised and well-conducted interview? How can an interviewer apply these characteristics in order to monitor and improve his/her performance? (ICSA)

5 What are the basic problems which affect both the interviewer and the interviewee in a job regarding/promotion interview? How would you as the interviewer ensure that the interview was fair and objective? (IAM)

6 'What matters at an interview is not what is said, but how it is heard.' How far do you think this is true? (ICSA)

7 Enumerate the essential features of a good report. Illustrate your answer by writing a brief report to your managing director on a subject of your own choosing. (IComA)

8 Draw up a draft outline guide to writing reports to management and clients. This draft is required for discussion and eventual use in your organisation as training material in the induction of newly employed graduates and part-qualified staff. (ACCA)

9 What do you understand by either 'effective reading' or 'effective listening'? Discuss how this skill may be acquired and developed. (ICSA)

▪ ⫿ 16 The manager

Management, which has been the subject of the preceding chapters, is carried out by people; these people are the managers. It becomes necessary therefore to discuss what a manager is.

The term itself has become somewhat debased recently in that many people who are given the title of manager are, in fact, not managers but supervisors or administrators at junior management level. The distinction can be a fine one. The main distinction is one of discretion. A supervisor will make decisions in accordance with rules that are laid down, little or no discretion being required or, indeed, allowed. Problems that cannot be solved within the established rules have to be referred to the supervisor's superior. A manager, on the other hand, will have the authority to use discretion in making decisions and the limits to this discretion indicate the manager's place on the management ladder. A person's title within an organisation, therefore, is not necessarily indicative of that person's real position from the point of view of management. Thus an accounts manager may be nothing more than an accounts supervisor, having no authority at all to vary the terms of credit with customers nor to negotiate terms with suppliers. Someone in another organisation, with the title of chief clerk, may on the other hand have the authority and discretionary power of a middle or senior manager.

16.1 Management qualities

The question as to what constitute 'management qualities' and 'management potential' has been the subject of much discussion by many authorities over a very long period without any total consensus having been achieved. There is, of course, no specific answer possible because different people have different attributes and are able to learn to use them effectively often to the extent of overcoming any lack in other ways. For example, a person who lacks the desirable quality of stamina may develop a latent capacity for organisation so that his or her day's work is planned to conserve personal energy. The list of desirable characteristics is a long one if the suggestions of all the important authorities are taken into account, but among them are the following:

(a) **Self-confidence:** the belief in one's own ability to succeed in solving problems and dealing effectively with difficult situations.

(b) **Drive:** the urge and enthusiasm to stimulate action, both personal and in other people.

(c) **Initiative:** the ability to lead action without waiting to be prompted and to bring fresh thought to old problems.

(d) **Decisiveness:** the ability to think positively and without vacillation and to act in the same way.

(e) **Willingness to accept responsibility:** this includes the acceptance of accountability for one's decisions and the consequent acts of oneself and one's staff.

(f) **Ability to delegate:** this also includes (e).

(g) **Integrity:** this includes trusthworthiness and loyalty to one's organisation and one's staff.

(h) **Judgement:** the ability to analyse a situation and formulate appropriate action. This includes choosing between different possible courses of action where choices present themselves.

(i) **Adaptability:** the ability to change one's outlook as circumstances change and to alter one's actions in the light of what is necessary in changed circumstances. This is a most valuable characteristic in the modern world which is subject to such rapid change.

(j) **Organising ability.**

(k) **Stamina:** the ability to work long and hard without undue strain or stress.

(l) **Emotional maturity:** includes self-discipline and self-control and the ability to analyse a situation without prejudice.

(m) **Human understanding:** the ability to work with other people with understanding and sympathy; the willingness to listen to staff problems.

(n) **Personality:** this is difficult to define, but the personality required in an effective manager might be said to include the ability to communicate easily at all levels, to exude confidence, to be approachable and open, and to be able to carry staff and other members of the management team with him. An open-minded approach to problems may be said to be part of personality, with no hint of vacillation on difficult questions.

(o) **Being supportive of staff:** ensuring that all are treated equally fairly; encouraging them and supporting them in their career ambitions.

(p) **Adequate educational standard:** this does not mean, necessarily, the holding of a university degree, but rather a development of the mind that enables one to think positively and without prejudging a situation, and also to communicate effectively.

This list of attributes is by no means exhaustive; neither are all these qualities likely to be found together in one person. Again, they are not necessarily conspicuous in everyone who is considered to have management potential. In fact, most of the desirable attributes are likely to be latent at the beginning of a manager's career, and developed through training and experience. Management skills are on the whole largely practical and virtually any man or woman can be effectively trained for management provided the necessary latent talents are possessed.

16.2 Leadership

This is the quality that enables a manager to exert a positive influence over the behaviour of subordinates. It is difficult of definition but is, nevertheless, important to the success of any group activity whether this is a small group in a department or the whole of an undertaking.

- The qualities that make a good leader will be determined to a large extent by the circumstances under which the leadership has to be exercised; or rather the attributes that are actually brought into play will be so determined. In other words different situations will require the display of different qualities from the same individual. Very generally the qualities that a leader, needs to possess are those given under 16.1 above for a manager because to all intents and purposes being a manager also entails being a leader, and equally a leader needs to be a manager. In point of fact, in management studies it is unnecessary and pointless to try to draw any distinction between the two.
- There is argument as to whether leaders (or managers) are born or made and the same answer can be given as that given earlier in this chapter – leadership can be developed provided that the latent capabilities are there. There are two elements that are acknowledged as being necessary to an understanding of leadership. The first is that it is essentially a group situation where members of the group have a common purpose, and the second that the authority of the leader must be accepted by all members of the group if that leadership is to be effective.
- The steps involved in the exercise of management or leadership skills can be illustrated in Figure 16.1.

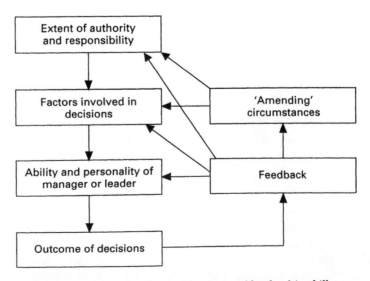

Figure 16.1 Exercise in management and leadership skills

16.3 Styles of leadership or management

Leadership is concerned with the human aspect of management. It therefore follows that the style of leadership has a direct bearing on the overall management style. It is therefore necessary to know and understand the variety of different leadership and management styles available.

- It is first necessary to understand the effects of particular situations on management style. This must not affect the fundamental integrity of the approach. However, the management content and approach necessary to manage a group of untrained school-leavers is very different from that required to direct a co-ordinated team of skilled people all expert in their work and accustomed to working together. In the first case, close and sympathetic attention will be required, whereas in the second case, leadership is likely to consist only of general guidance and acceptance of ultimate responsibility.
- Within all situations, and given the vagaries of departmental management, there must be a guiding set of core principles on which the management style, both of the organisation as a whole, and also of its departments, is based. This is in turn, reinforced through: procedures and manuals; relations between staff and managers; relationships between departments, divisions and functions; and direction from the top.

Within these confines, it is possible to define the following.

(a) Authoritarian management

This is the traditional view of a leader or manager where power is in the hands of one authority whose word is law. Orders are issued and are expected to be obeyed without question.

This rarely works. It creates a resentful work-force, which in turn, leads to low productivity and output.

(b) Other forms of autocracy

It is true that autocratic forms of management do exist, and can be more effective. However, their continued effectiveness is dependent upon: the extent to which those in charge continue to be prepared to take an enlightened view of the world; and their capability not to become corrupted by the very position of their own autocracy. For example, Richard Branson runs the Virgin Group as an autocracy, and the reason why he remains so successful is because he continues to surround himself with expert advice, guidance and direction on the business initiatives that he proposes and undertakes. On the other hand, Robert Maxwell created a publishing empire through surrounding himself with similar expertise; and it then, in turn, became ruined due to loss of principles and integrity.

(c) Paternal management

Common chiefly in small concerns, paternal management endeavours to create a family atmosphere where the leader likes to be regarded by the workers as a parent figure. In a suitable organisation, this style works very well and in most cases, motivation of staff is excellent. Staff generally become very loyal to their management, and people who do not like this form of working generally move on.

(d) Democratic management

A great weakness of the democratic style of management is the propensity of those supposedly in charge to abdicate their responsibilities. In operational terms, democracy – management by the people for the people, and management by vote – may not be the recipe necessary for long-term success and effectiveness. As with all votes, greatest resentments arise where the vote is very narrow, for example, where 53 per cent of those voting want one thing and 47 per cent want another. Moreover a majority of people may simply vote for the wrong course of action in the circumstances.

(e) Participative management

Participative management exists where everyone involved is kept informed of decisions and progress at every stage. People therefore understand why those responsible for the long-term future and success of the organisation have taken the decisions that they have taken. It also becomes very much easier to understand unpleasant decisions (e.g. those concerned with redundancies), even on the part of those directly affected. The participative style is also the most effective vehicle for change currently discovered; and this is of especial value in the current state of the business and management world.

(f) Management by committee

The great weakness of the committee approach to management is that decisions tend to get diluted or delayed. It also happens that the decision that is taken is the one that nobody did not want – and this also tends to lead to organisational inertia. Also when things go wrong, there is a tendency to blame the other members of the committee for not having done what was necessary, rather than accepting responsibility one's self (this is also a weakness of all democratic forms of management).

Figure 16.2 illustrates the continuum of leadership styles.

16.4   The Leadership Grid®

Whilst it is true that leadership must concentrate on the problems of human relationships to achieve set goals, it is also concerned with the question of non-human resources.

* To a considerable extent the style of management adopted will result from how much emphasis is given to one or the other. Recognising this dichotomy, Dr. R. R. Blake of the University of Texas conducted research into the problem, the results of which he first published in 1964, and he defined two main concepts of management: (a) concern for people and (b) concern for results or production. These two aspects of management he expressed on a graph which he originally called the Managerial Grid® or as it is labelled in its latest form, the Leadership Grid (Blake and McCanse, 1991), where points 1

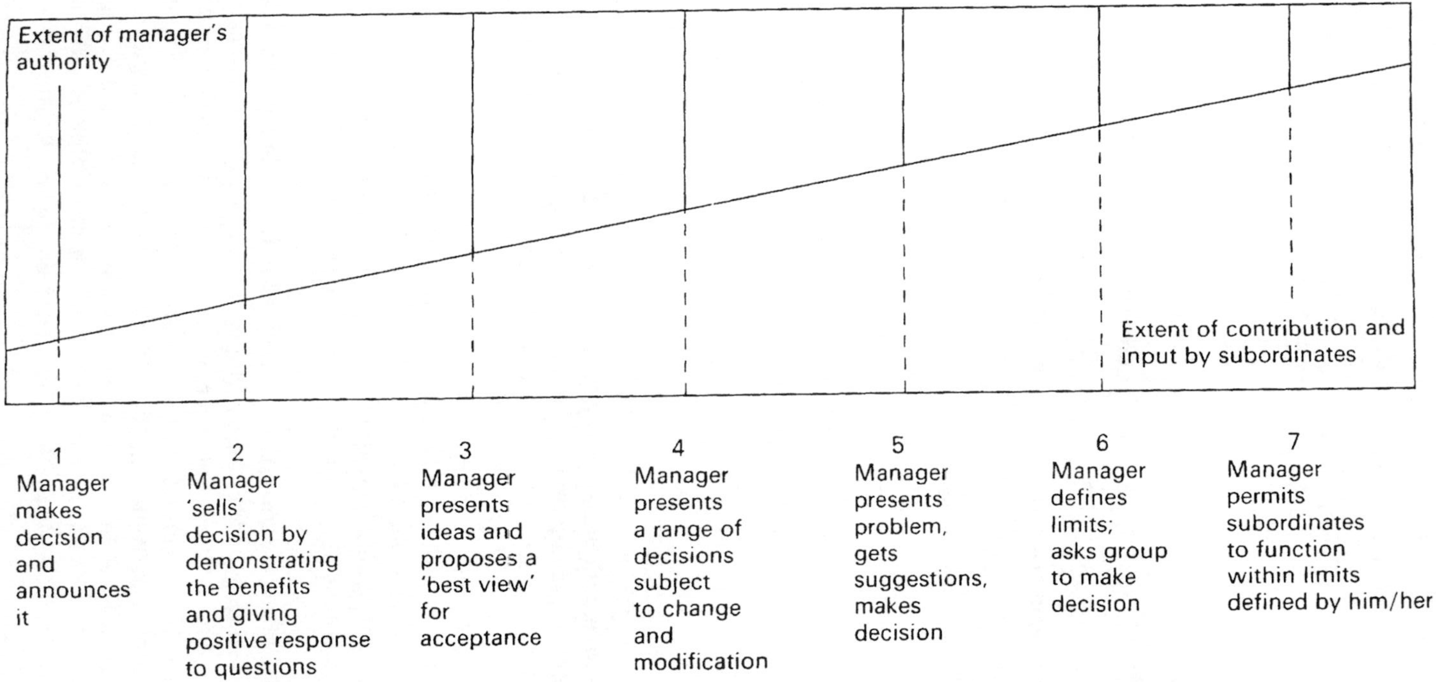

Extent of manager's authority

Extent of contribution and input by subordinates

1	2	3	4	5	6	7
Manager makes decision and announces it	Manager 'sells' decision by demonstrating the benefits and giving positive response to questions	Manager presents ideas and proposes a 'best view' for acceptance	Manager presents a range of decisions subject to change and modification	Manager presents problem, gets suggestions, makes decision	Manager defines limits; asks group to make decision	Manager permits subordinates to function within limits defined by him/her

Purpose: illustration of the autocratic–participative range that is available in organisational and managerial decision-making. It also provides a sound basis for forethought. Certain types of decision will be better understood, and accepted, it they are delivered in particular ways.

Figure 16.2   A decision-making model: the autocratic–participative range
Source: R. Tannenbaum and W. Schmidt (1958) 'How to choose leadership pattern', *Harvard Business Review*.

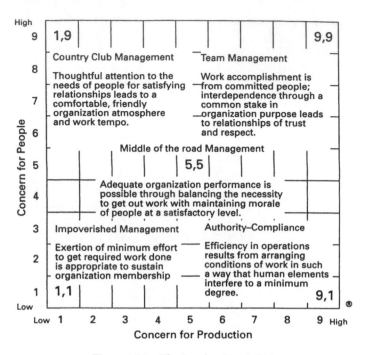

Figure 16.3 The Leadership Grid®

to 9 are plotted vertically for concern for people and similarly points 1 to 9 are plotted horizontally for concern for results. Concern is weakest in each case at 1 and strongest at 9. Concern for production is conventionally stated first so that a manager whose rating shows 1,9 has very high regard for people and one whose rating is 9,1 shows an extremely strong concern for production and little for people.

- Dr Blake actually defined five leadership styles from 1,1 which indicates minimum interest in both aspects to 9,9 which indicates high production achievements from dedicated staff. Rating 5,5 on the Grid shows an adequate and balanced management performance with both human and material resources of equal concern. A specimen of the Leadership Grid is given in Figure 16.3.
- The concept of what is now known as the Leadership Grid is the first step of a programme of management training developed by Dr Blake and his colleague Dr J. S. Mouton, and it shows how management styles can be depicted to indicate the basic philosophy of the management concerned. A full exposition of the concepts surrounding the management training programme involving the Leadership Grid can be found in Robert R. Blake and Anne Adams McCanse, *Leadership Dilemmas – Grid Solutions* (Gulf Publishing, 1991), which also explains the five basic management styles identified by the authors in more detail.

16.5 System 4

The System 4 approach to management was developed by Rensis Likert in the 1960s alongside the work of Blake and Mouton. Likert's contribution arose from his work with high performing managers; managers and supervisors who achieved high levels of productivity, low levels of cost, and high levels of employee motivation, participation and involvement at their places of work. The work demonstrated a correlation between this success, and the style and structure of the work-groups that they created, and the ways in which they managed them. The groups achieved high levels of economic output and therefore high wage and salary levels. They were also heavily involved in both group maintenance activities and the design and definition of work patterns. This was underpinned by supportive style of supervision and management; and the generation of a sense of personal worth, importance and value in belonging to the group itself. The System 4 model arose from this work. Likert identified four styles or systems of management.

- System 1: exploitative authoritative – where power and direction come from the top downwards and where there is no participation, consultation or involvement on the part of the work-force. Work-force compliance is therefore based on fear. Unfavourable attitudes are generated. There is little confidence and trust.
- System 2: benevolent authoritative – similar to System 1 but which allows some upward opportunity for consultation and participation in some areas. Again, attitudes tend to be generally unfavourable, and confidence, trust and communication remain at low levels.

    In both Systems 1 and 2 productivity may be high over the short run, when targets can be achieved by a combination of coercion, and bonus and overtime payments. However, both productivity and earnings are demonstrably low over the long run; there is also high absenteeism and labour turnover.
- System 3: consultative – where aims and objectives are set after discussion and consultation with subordinates; where communication is two-way and where teamwork is encouraged at least in some areas. Attitudes towards both superiors and the organisation tend to be favourable when the oroganisation is working steadily.
- System 4: participative – in which three basic concepts have a very important effect on performance – the use by the manager of the pronciple of supportive relationships throughout the work group; the use of group-based methods of decision-making and supervision; and the setting of high performance targets and ambitious goals for the department and the organisation overall.

    System 4 was Likert's preferred system, the one that his research demonstrated worked best in the long run. The openness of System 4 also meant that problems were identified earlier and dealt with before they became crises. it also became very much easier to consult with, and gain agreement on, reorganisations, changes and developments when these became necessary.

    A specimen of a System 4 is given in Figure 16.2.

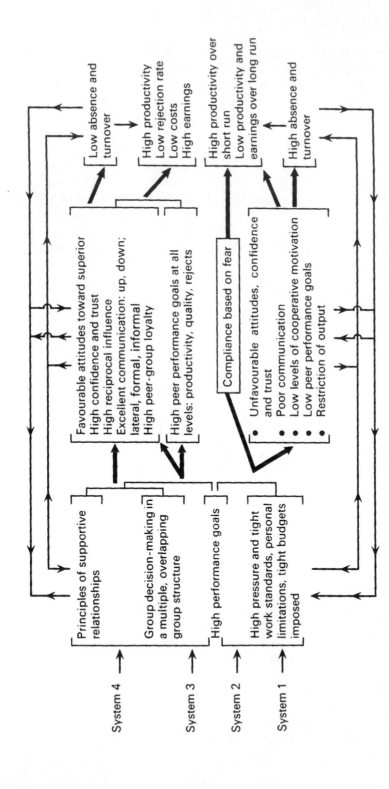

Purpose: to demonstrate the interrelationship and interaction of the critical factors indicated in the text

Figure 16.4 System 4

Source: R. Likert (1961) *The Human Organization* (New York: McGraw-Hill).

16.6   Management education, training and development

The management trainee is a common phenomenon both in private industries and in public services. It is a sign that the training of future managers is being taken seriously by all but the worst organisations. Currently, the principal concern of all organisations is that their managers have:

(a) Understanding of a broad range of knowledge, dealing with the theoretical aspects of management, and giving an indication of the application of this theory in practical circumstances.
(b) Departmental, divisional and functional expertise and understanding, gained through practical work experience.
(c) Potential to develop this knowledge and understanding into substantial expertise for the future.

This is increasingly carried out through formal course of study. The MBA, together with diplomas and certificates in management, and other professional body qualifications, once had extremely high value; now each is becoming commonplace, a prerequisite for access to any substantial managerial post at all. Other courses in business and management studies are available at diploma and undergraduate level. Sandwich courses, where students spend part of their time at college sandwiched with periods of actual work experience, are also regarded as extremely valuable.

Those accepted on management developed programmes are expected to spend time, both during periods of study and during periods of planned work experience, gaining as full and wide-ranging functional knowledge as possible. This is not to say that managers must be expert accountants, mathematicians or operational research practitioners. However, they must be aware of these techniques and their uses and be able to use the services of experts when required. Many management training schemes also require their trainees to gain experience of the different functions in their organisation – accounting, marketing, production and so on – so that they gain a balanced view of all of the aspects of the enterprise, and understand both operations and their supervision and management in action.

In addition, management trainees are also expected to become proficient in 'core skills' during the period of their training. These core skills normally include: leadership; decision-making; communication in all forms; information analysis; negotiating; policy planning, objective and target setting.

In this way, it is seen that management is becoming increasingly regarded as a trade and profession in its own right. Most organisations now both value the expertise and potential of their managers, and also draw a direct relationship between the expertise of their managers and the effectiveness of the performance of the organisation as a whole.

16.7 Management development programmes

The purpose of engaging in management development programmes is to ensure that the pool of talent available is developed to its full potential, to ensure continuity of high and improving levels of managerial expertise.

In practice, this is very difficult to achieve. For, in order to gain and maintain the interest in having people develop, future opportunities have to be held open for them. Because of the turbulent nature of the business and public service world, this is not always possible in practice. Organisations operating in a permanent steady-state are increasingly hard to come by; and by the same token, succession plans based on orderly progress are also very difficult to achieve in practice.

The emphasis in management development has therefore shifted from precise paths of succession, into the development of all-round capabilities and expertise, so that a pool of talent is available for any opportunity that comes up – whether or not this can be forecast.

A further complication may arise when management trainees are found to be in competition for promotions and appointments, with those who have risen through the functional and operational ranks. Great care has to be taken to ensure that everyone is given the same opportunity.

- Management development must therefore be a properly planned operation involving all levels of management from the very top down to junior managers and supervisors. It needs to be a key feature of the corporate plans and policy of the organisation. As indicated above, this works best when opportunities for development are universally accorded; and where the broadest approach is taken to management development, as distinct from narrow functional promotional paths which may cease to exist at some time in the future.
- For this to be effective, periodic reviews are required. Effective appraisal schemes are also required. Managers must have incorporated into their duties, a remit to develop their subordinates, so that both organisational and individual requirements are met.
- Much of this sounds idealistic or utopian; and indeed, there are dangers that should be recognised so that steps may be taken to minimise their effects. The main difficulties are:
  1 lack of support, resources and direction from top management.
  2 uncertainty as to precisely what the development programme policy and activities should contain, and what its ultimate objectives are;
  3 the programme is too restricted as to the number of staff it includes;
  4 raising unreal hopes and expectations on the part of the staff being trained; above all, no new position should be promised to anyone if it cannot be delivered;
  5 adequate appraisal reviews are not instituted; this aspect of the programme is a key component;
  6 insufficient attention is paid to wastage, drop-out rates, and other aspects of the development programme that are not working;

7 the mix of internal development, and the bringing in of outside talent is out of balance. Too great an emphasis on internal development can breed introversion; too great a dependence on external recruitment can breed resentment and frustration;

8 managers and supervisors refuse to identify talent and potential within their existing staff, and refuse to recommend them or support them on management development programmes;

9 managers order their staff on to development programmes against the will of the individual, or without sufficient consultation.

Some organisations also resent the resources that are spent on developing potential and talent, only for the individual then to leave. This has to be seen in context. Some labour turnover is inevitable during management training and development programmes, and from graduate recruitment schemes, exactly the same as from all aspects of organisational activity. Moreover, insisting that people remain in an organisation against their will, is both detrimental to the individual, and ultimately damaging to the morale of those with whom he or she comes into contact.

16.8 Appraisal

Some form of control is essential to ensure that all training programmes throughout an undertaking are achieving their objectives and to measure to what extent the staff involved are performing adequately. Management training and development programmes are no exception, and all staff who are involved in such programmes must have their performances assessed to ensure that expectations are being achieved and that their potential is being suitably developed. Such appraisal will also indicate where a manager or potential manager has reached the limits of performance, and whether some revision of the individual's career development might be advisable.

- Such appraisals cover two areas – achieved performance and future potential – and are carried out by continuous assessment by the subject's immediate superior supported by records of work. Almost always appraisal interviews are also conducted at regular intervals. This is virtually essential to assess the changes in attitudes, social skills, managerial skills and increased technical knowledge which should be brought about by a successful programme and work experience. Performance record and improvements in managerial qualities will indicate the potential for promotion and the route of the subject's future career within the organisation. At the same time the need for changes in the individual's programme to improve the subject's capabilities can be discerned.

- The areas most likely to be covered in the appraisal are:
  (a) The ability to recognise, isolate and solve problems.
  (b) The ability to plan and organise work programmes, both personal and for subordinates.
  (c) The ability to communicate effectively both vertically and horizontally.

(d) The ability to create and maintain good relations with superiors and with staff, and to establish and sustain a co-operative attitude with other sections of the organisation.

(e) The development of personal qualities such as decisiveness, ability to lead, willingness to listen, ability to accept responsibility for errors, a positive attitude to change and so on.

(f) The extent of the individual's technical knowledge and ability and the improvements that have taken place since the previous appraisal.

(g) Setting goals and objectives for the individual for the coming period.

- The areas subject to appraisal ideally will be dealt with in depth. In many cases, organisations use appraisal forms which include scales of performance and potential. The greatest weakness with this approach is that it becomes purely a paperwork exercise, and as a consequence, the appraisal process falls into disrepute. The ability to measure performance is a key managerial skill, and one which should be developed as component of all management development programmes.

16.9   Stress

In recent years, stress has come to be recognised as a major occupational hazard in many organisations and areas. Managers at all organisational levels, and those in other professions also, suffer from stress; and this is understood to be caused through having too great a work-load, together with pressure from the individual's superiors. Stress may also be caused by factors over which the manager has little or no control – outside pressures, loss of markets, loss of a key member of staff, and so on. Stress is also caused as the result of redundancies and reorganisations, and through crises and emergencies.

- Symptoms of stress include fear of not being able to cope with the work, real or perceived work overload, unsatisfactory personal relations with staff or superiors, lack of sufficient information for the purposes of decision-making, and persistent under-performance. The most serious symptoms of stress are indecision and operational mistakes – whereby the individual spends all their time worrying what is to be done, rather than taking their normal steps to do it.

- Where it is apparent that there is too heavy a work-load, efforts should be made to delegate more or to redesign jobs so that they take less time. Feelings of lack of knowledge can be reduced by taking positive steps to increase knowledge. Indecision requires the capability and confidence to seek advice and support from elsewhere, without abdicating responsibility for the decision.

- Stress, ultimately, is extremely destructive if it is not managed. Those individuals affected increasingly resent having their health ruined by the demands of an organisation; and there is increasing resort to litigation, and the seeking of damages. This is especially true in the cases of bullying, victimisation and harassment, which cause great stress to those who are the victims of these activities; it should be clear to all managers that, quite apart from anything else, bullying, victimisation and harassment are against the law. Where incidences are proven, damages are very heavy indeed.

- It is clear, therefore, that there is a world of difference between ensuring that people work hard and productively for the hours of their employment, and working under intolerable pressures and strains. Managers need to recognise the causes and symptoms, and take positive steps to nip these in the bud. Once it becomes apparent that people are working under extended periods of stress and strain, this is damaging both to the morale of those involved, and also to the output of the organisation.

QUESTIONS

1 The size of an organisation is often considered to influence managerial style, organisational climate and employee attitudes. Do you accept this view? State your reasons? (ICSA)

2 What do you understand to be the special skills required in management to-day? (IComA)

3 (a) What are the potential disadvantages of a participative style of management?
(b) How could such disadvantages be overcome or minimised? (IAM)

4 You are required
(a) o describe the structure of MbO (Management by Objectives);
(b) to assess its advantages over other methods of direction;
(c) to suggest reasons for its comparatively rare use. (CIMA)

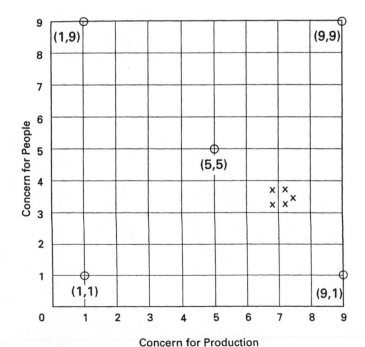

Concern for Production

5 'The word "leadership" is sometimes used as if it were an attribute of personality, sometimes as if it were a characteristic of certain positions within an organisation, and sometimes as an aspect of behaviour.' Discuss. (ICSA)

6 In a changing world, senior managers face many pressures and uncertainties. Why do managers keep on managing? What motivates people to perform effectively in senior management positions? (ICSA)

7 (a) Identify, with brief examples, four organisational causes of individual stress.
  (b) Make recommendations for the management of stress in the work situation.
    (IAM)

8 Making the transition from sales representative to sales manager can be traumatic. Explain the tensions involved and suggest ways in which such personal promotion can be achieved effectively. (CIM)

9 Six supervisors from accountancy departments are on a management development course. A, one of them, has reported his proposals about a case which they have been studying. The other five have rated A by placing crosses on Blake and Mouton's Managerial Grid [now known as The Blake and McCanse Leadership Grid]. The results are as shown.
  You are required to
  (a) explain what the consultant in charge should tell the group about the significance of the result;
  (b) make seven suggestions as to how A could improve his management style.
    (CIMA)

▪ ⅴ **17** Functional management

So far this work has concentrated on general management, its theory, practice and some of its techniques. Many managers, particularly senior executives, are certainly concerned with these areas exclusively. Their working days are devoted to planning their organisation's future, setting objectives and generally concentrating on survival and progress. When they are members of the board of directors or other governing body they are responsible for formulating policy and making the final decisions on corporate planning and corporate strategy. Yet all the planning and strategy is of no account without the work of the functional departments of the organisation. These are the sections of the undertaking which actually make it work on a practical basis.

It is at the functional level that management expertise has to be married to technical expertise, and where functional technical knowledge is as important as managerial skills: this was pointed out in Chapter 1 where it was suggested that at the level of principal officer, or senior manager, the proportion of skills may be somewhere in the region of 50 per cent managerial and 50 per cent technical.

17.1 **The need for managerial expertise**

Although the operation of functional departments requires function knowledge and expertise it does not follow that a person highly qualified in the technical sense will necessarily turn out to be a good functional manager. An efficient factory superintendent, highly effective in the mechanics of running a factory, may not prove a success as a production manager where much more managerial skill is needed. A competent sales representative may prove quite unsuccessful if promoted to the position of area sales manager. In fact, it is the transition from the purely technical level to one where a certain amount of true managerial skill is needed that is frequently the most difficult. Years of study and of practice in a purely technical capacity can narrow the view of many people in this situation, and it often demands a real change of attitude and outlook for such a person to become a competent functional manager. Here the term 'technical' is used in its widest sense and includes such areas as accounting, marketing, purchasing and so on. Once any sort of supervisory or managerial element is present in a job then the occupant of that post must start to practice management skills in addition to technical skills. A foreman bricklayer on a building contract is responsible for managing the team of bricklayers, of planning their work-load, their activities and their material resources and equipment. The element of management is small, but is there. Such foremen may be less of a craftsman than the best bricklayer but their managerial capacity, though relatively small, makes them better foremen than the best bricklayer who has no managerial talent or skill.

17.2   The need for technical expertise

Nevertheless, a functional department will not be efficiently managed unless the manager has technical knowledge of a high order. This is for two reasons. Subordinate staff have more respect for a manager who is fully competent in the technical aspects of their department, and a properly qualified manager is able to solve technical problems with authority and confidence. Unless subordinate staff respect their manager's technical understanding, they are unlikely to respect any managerial capacity, however great this may be.

- It is a fact that practically all functions are now served by professional bodies which lay down minimum standards of knowledge and experience for membership and which require qualification by examination for their members. They also require a minimum standard of ethical conduct in order to maintain public confidence in the work of their members.

  In Britain, some professional bodies have gained a statutory recognition, or chartered status; while others are so highly regarded that senior posts in many organisations are reserved for members of those bodies. These include accountancy, purchasing, marketing and human resource management; and it is increasingly common to find people with engineering and technological qualifications at the top of those organisations that operate in these fields.
- It is also true that as the statutory requirements of the European Union begin to take effect, formal qualifications will be required of people aspiring to certain functional management positions; and indeed basic qualifications and prescribed periods of training are certain to become more prevalent for anyone in any management or supervisory role at all.

17.3   The scope of the functional manager

The manager in charge of a functional department, for example purchasing, should have total control of the function and be responsible for all aspects of its operation in respect of its technical performance. However, the department must be operated within the framework of the organisation as a whole. The functional manager is therefore subject to all of the constraints set out for the general running of the undertaking. These include adhering to budgets, co-ordinating the department's operations with the needs of other functions, and working with the advice of experts and committees when required.

It is also essential that functional managers understand the scale and scope of the activities carried out by all of the staff in their departments. A key contribution of periods of on-the-job training for managers lies in understanding the ways in which the particular department works, the pressures under which the staff operate, and the resources necessary to do the job effectively.

17.4 Management fads and fashions

Functional and operational management is clearly a highly complex occupation, requiring a great complexity of skills, qualities and attributes. In recent years, there have been moves to try and simplify all this by offering directive and prescriptive approaches to management issues and problems. Some examples are as follows.

(a) Business Process Re-engineering (BPR)

Attention to administration, supervision and procedures for the purposes of simplicity, clarification and speed of operation. In practice, BPR tends to be applied prescriptively to all functions without reference to organisational effectiveness, the prevailing environment, or broader aspects of individual operations and functions.

(b) Total Quality Management (TQM)

Attention to every aspect of organisational practice in pursuit of continuous improvement. In practice, TQM tends to be prescriptive in approach and dominated by paperwork and administration systems rather than attention to products and customers. It therefore tends to over-complicate the lives of functional managers rather than simplify them.

(c) Benchmarking

Benchmarks set standards of activity against which other activities can be compared and rated. In practice, of course, every activity needs its own individual standards to be set. Benchmarking activities tend to cloud and complicate the functional manager's activities, rather than simplifying them.

(d) Management by Objectives (MbO)

MbO takes the view that every activity can be broken down into a set or series of objectives which can then be attained. Again, this tends to complicate rather than simplify – writing everything down in this way produces great proliferation of paperwork; and writing anything down for the medium to long term, means inevitably that the objectives will be changed or modified.

In practice therefore, it is much better to recognise the complexity of the functional manager's situation, rather than to try and produce universal prescription in these (and many other) ways. Indeed, the functional manager's job is complex enough without imposing the additional layers of work that these forms of approach inevitably generate.

In fact, the role of the functional expert has become increasingly complex as new techniques and concepts have been introduced. Even top management, where the requirement of technical expertise is at its lowest, must at least understand operational and functional problems. Chapters 18–23 are therefore devoted to introducing the principal functions to be found in most organisations.

QUESTIONS

1 What is meant by 'functional management', and how does it differ from general management?

2 Why is it important that a functional manager should be seen to be technically competent?

3 Would you say that an expert craftsman would make an efficient supervisor? Give reasons for your answer.

4 In many jobs where technology changes rapidly managers may have subordinates who have greater technical competence than this one. How can you reconcile this apparent conflict between knowledge and authority? (ICSA)

5 What are the main organisational and environmental factors which limit the managerial discretion of the manager of a functional department in an organisation? (ICSA)

6 What are the main managerial issues to be faced by a functional manager wishing to achieve effective control over one of the following:
(a) a production or operations department;
(b) a marketing department;
(c) a research and development department;
(d) a sales department (either in manufacturing or service or retail). (ICSA)

▪ ⅴ 18 Marketing

Marketing is defined by the Chartered Institute of Marketing as 'the management process responsible for identifying, anticipating and satisfying customer requirements profitably'.

The idea of a producer, first investigating and them producing goods for customer requirements rather than endeavouring to sell goods already produced is at variance with the British tradition of deciding which goods to produce and then finding a market for them. In many industries and sectors, this has involved a radical alteration to corporate management approaches.

This approach is covered by the term 'marketing concept', and it has in turn, given rise to various ways of assessing customers and consumers' needs and wants, and has resulted in great changes in market research, and advertising and promotional activities.

The traditional view in Britain was always that marketing was equated with selling. Marketing embraces every activity required to find customers for, introduce, inform about, create a desire for, and actually supply the goods or services required. Selling is therefore only one aspect of marketing, involving the effort of finding the actual customers and then persuading them to buy. Many marketers indeed take the view that in order for effective and profitable business to be sustained in the long term, nobody actually sells anything – customers and consumers choose to buy (and also, therefore, choose not to buy).

18.1 Marketing strategy and direction

Effective marketing strategies are devised in accordance with overall organisational policy and direction. Within this context, some useful definitions exists as follows.

(a) **Pioneering or first in field:** opening up new markets or outlets for existing products, or new products for existing outlets.

(b) **Follow the leader:** the great benefit of not being first in the field, is to learn from the mistakes and experience of the pioneer so that informed judgements can be taken about the nature of the involvement considered.

(c) **Me too or all-comers:** where the market is wide open, where it is easy to get into the market, where the products or services in question are universal or general.

(d) Supply-led: the traditional British approach of producing products and services because the organisation has complete faith in their ability to sell them.

(e) Technology-led: where the organisation finds itself in a particular line of business because it has at its disposal a particular type of technology which can be turned to productive and profitable advantage in a variety of sectors.

(f) Staff-led: because of the skills, qualities and preferences of the staff of the organisation; this is very prevalent in the small business sphere.

(g) Market-led: where the organisation looks first at a range of markets, then assesses their requirements and finally decides which of these it can most valuably and profitably operate in and fill (most akin to 'the marketing concept').

18.2 Customer and consumer satisfaction

When people buy a product or service, what they are actually buying are the benefits, value and satisfaction afforded by ownership or consumption.

Customer and consumer satisfaction is based on the extent to which their expectations are satisfied through the benefit and value accruing as the result of ownership or consumption. Part of this also concerns ever-increasing expectations: people now expect ever-greater levels of customer service; no quibble, money-back guarantees; prompt attention to complaints; prompt service from restaurants and bars; and prompt service in dealings with public bodies (e.g. education, health, social service, the Inland Revenue). For larger and more considered purchases – e.g. cars, electrical goods – people now expect enduring and prompt after-sales service, maintenance and repairs when necessary.

Once customer expectations have been raised, it is very difficult to reduce them. Certainly something has to be conceded in return – e.g. a substantial reduction in price, or some other form of free extras.

Expert marketers also now understand that it is much easier to keep a customer, than to gain one. Thus for example, food supermarkets offer no quibble refunds and product replacements; they take the view that it is much better for business to keep a customer satisfied than to risk losing them, and they also understand that a dissatisfied customer is much more likely to tell others about their dissatisfaction, and thereby influence others to go somewhere else also.

18.3 Marketing and the non-profit-making sector

The need for effective marketing of public sector services has come about as the result of:

(a) Statutory requirements to improve those services and their delivery.
(b) Ever-greater public accountability on the part of those delivering the services.

(c) Known poor performance in specific areas – e.g. hospital waiting lists, inability to claim social security benefits.

These services have to be marketed to the people concerned, both to inform them of the existence of the services and benefits, and to persuade those entitled to make their claims. Many statutory services now have a formally constituted ombudsman, whose function it is to put right any mistakes, to offer redress, and to ensure satisfaction.

- Organisations in the voluntary sector – charities – have also to be expert marketers. The big charities, such as Oxfam, Help the Aged, NSPCC, are themselves large and complex organisations. They have therefore to engage in expert marketing, especially advertising and public relations activities, to raise funds for their special projects. It is no longer enough to appeal for funds – successful, effective, long-term fund-raising is now based on highly professional marketing.

18.4 The marketing mix

The various elements of marketing need to be carefully employed in order to achieve the greatest success, and it is necessary to combine them in the most effective way given the circumstances at any particular time. The combination of these elements is known as the marketing mix, and is graphically portrayed in Figure 18.1.

- There is no universal list of the particular aspects of the marketing function that go into the marketing mix, but they fall under four main headings with subdivisions providing an analysis of the mix. The main headings are:

  (a) **Promotion** This includes advertising, selling, public relations and the creation of a brand image where this is advantageous. Promotional activities are often referred to as 'marketing communications'.

  (b) **Product** This includes product design, the quality of manufacture and, where the product requires it, after-sales service.

  (c) **Price** This must relate to product quality and the particular market aimed at. The policy on granting credit also falls under this heading.

  (d) **Place** This involves the channels of distribution to be used, e.g. sales through agents, wholesalers, direct, and so on.

- The particular marketing mix used at any one time will depend upon many circumstances such as the economic climate, the strength of competition and sometimes the need for an improved inflow of revenue. Different organisations, even in the same industry, will use different mixes successfully because their particular circumstances demand a particular mix. For instance, in an intensively competitive industry, where there is very little difference between the various makers' products within a general price range, heavy promotion on a particular aspect of its product may be engaged in by a manufacturer to emphasise a particularly attractive feature which may or may not be present in

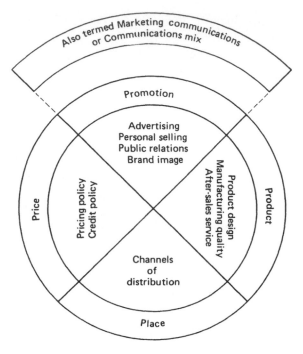

Figure 18.1 The marketing mix

the products of competitors. A typical example comes from the photographic industry where the Pentax camera was, and still is, heavily promoted on the basis of its handling qualities. 'Simply hold a Pentax' created a brand image of a very desirable camera, though it is probably no better or no worse than other cameras of its class in other directions. However, it is a feature most potential buyers now examine carefully in all cameras they handle with a view to buying.

• Similarly, pricing may be an important marketing feature where quality is not of paramount importance. It is generally conceded that intending customers equate low prices with low quality and are likely to question the quality of a product selling for substantially less than its equivalent competitors. If a top-quality product is offered at a very low price suspicion is aroused as to whether a new and improved model is about to be introduced. Often a manufacturer or supplier may price a product or range of products at substantially reduced prices simply because of a fall in cash intake and this is the only way to generate revenue quickly.

These two examples are sufficient to show how a marketing manager may constitute the marketing mix to suit prevailing objectives or conditions.

18.5   Market research

Before launching a new product or improving an existing one it is desirable to discover its potential sales volume in order that the resources to be devoted to it may not be wasted in a vain attempt to find a substantial enough market. The activity used to try to establish whether the potential customers are likely to buy, and to discover the best form the product should take, is market research.

- By various means the market researcher endeavours to establish what is likely to attract buyers in a particular product line in sufficient numbers, in regard to design, size, price and other relevant features that go into a customer's buying decision. For instance, if it is decided by a radio manufacturer to launch a new portable radio on to the popular market, it will be necessary to know as accurately as possible what physical size the equipment should be, its frequency range, its output volume and quality, and so on. If this receiver is to replace an existing model, it will also be useful to know what the public's opinion is of the present set, what improvements should be made and what features should be retained. By researching these matters the chances of a successful launch are better than if no such research is carried out.
- Similarly, if an organisation is in the retail trade the opening of a new store will be contemplated only after research into the population of the selected area, the proportion of this likely to become active customers, the average income of the area, the normal buying habits of the potential customers, their particular tastes and so on. Only if it can be shown by this research that enough people will be likely to patronise the potential store, and that its revenue will thus be sufficient to justify the required capital expenditure, will the project proceed.
- Even in the non-profit-making sector similar research should be carried out. Thus, for example, a local authority should set up an advice bureau only after having assured itself by proper research that there will be enough clients to justify the costs of establishing and running it.
- Market research can be divided into desk research and field research.

(a) Desk research

This involves researching past records, both internal and external, on matters relating to the proposed project. Past sales and other records, past reports from sales representatives and other data are used to form an estimate of possible sales based on past sales volume, customer complaints, and suggestions gathered by sales representatives during their calls. Information can be gathered from external sources such as government publications and statistics, technical and trade journals and the sales literature of competitors to give indications of market trends, technical innovations and what competitors have to offer.

(b) Field research

This involves active fieldwork in interviewing potential customers, preparing questionnaires and having them completed by the public at large or by selected sections of the public, offering samples, or having selected categories of potential customers carry out tests by using the product or prototypes of the product and reporting on specially prepared questionnaire forms.

- How the active or field research is done will depend almost entirely on what type of product is to be launched. The distribution of free samples is common in research on foodstuffs (new breakfast cereals, instant tea and the like) and cleaning materials such as washing powders, whereas high-cost capital equipment requires research through personal contact with potential buyers, the preparation of detailed specifications and analysis of the reactions of the potential buyers.
- The quality of market and marketing research has greatly improved in recent years. Properly conducted, it is highly statistical, requiring expert knowledge and experience if it is to be at all reliable. It is difficult enough to predict changes in customer and consumer behaviour on this basis; and, therefore, the higher the quality of the market research the more likely there is to be a full understanding of the vagaries of the situation.
- Market research should always be conducted alongside wider issues, including research and evaluation of opportunities, analysis of various promotional and selling methods, evaluation of advertising media and their effectiveness, consideration of different methods of distribution, as well as continued research into existing and potential customers' desires and needs. Market and marketing research should also include evaluating existing marketing methods, product research and sales policy, assessing their effectiveness and suggesting improvements. This is sometimes called a 'marketing audit'.

18.6 Market segmentation

- To market successfully an organisation must first know what the total potential market is for its products or services and then try to identify the various divisions or segments of the market. Having broken down the market into segments it can then decide its best policies in regard to exploiting either the total market or desirable segments of it. For example, the total market for lamp-posts for street lighting includes columns made of steel and of concrete, to supply them and to erect them, wherever they can be sold. In Great Britain the total market spans the whole of England, Scotland and Wales, and customers include local government authorities, building contractors and concerns needing lighting for yards, transport depots, wharves and similar areas. A street lighting column manufacturer can, therefore, decide to undertake to carry out all the activities concerned with the total, or whole, market or can decide to try to serve only one or more sections, or segments, of it. In one instance a maker of concrete lamp-posts serving the supply-only segment to the local authority section decided to embrace the erection segment as well. Eventually this same concern covered the total market. The ability to serve the total market, however, is very difficult unless the possible market is fairly limited (as it is for street lighting) or the undertaking has enormous resources.
- Market segmentation is, properly, the term used for dividing the market into categories according to type of customer, by age, by sex, by income, by region, or by any other logical division that suits the product or service. In the

example above, for instance, local government authorities are a particular category of customer. Additionally, such general classifications can be further broken down or combined so that a manufacturer may make clothes for girls between the ages of 5 and 10, a shoe manufacturer may produce shoes for both sexes up to the age of 11. However, 'market segmentation' is the term often used to cover product segmentation.

18.7   Product segmentation

- This is a newer classification than market segmentation, which explains why the latter term is often used instead. Product segmentation follows market segmentation in that, having classified the customer categories to aim for, the undertaking then classifies these segments according to the products which it can exploit within each customer category. An example of this is the publishing of women's magazines. A publisher may decide to serve the segment of the market containing young women between the ages of 18 and 30. Some will be single, some married, some with low incomes and some with high incomes. In consequence, a single publisher publishes magazines that interest the single and low-paid, the career girl, the young wife on a low income, the young middle-class home-maker and so on throughout the range of categories.
- The conventional approach to product segmentation is branding. This means giving the product a perceived distinctive identity in the minds of the customers, a summary of its qualities, value and perceived satisfaction. This form of product segmentation is heavily dependent upon promotion: this is the means by which people come to recognise instantly the product and the benefits that it has to offer. The returns on successful branding in commercial terms are enormous – Coca Cola and McDonalds for example, can be found everywhere in the world, and everybody knows (or thinks they know) what they are. Other companies carry out this form of branding in their own sectors – e.g. Caterpillar is a well regarded brand in the plant hire sector; British Airways in the air travel sector; Spode in the pottery sector; Dartington in the glass sector; and so on.
- Some organisations use their existing brand strength to enter other markets. For example, the Virgin Group had a strong reputation as a music company and it built on this reputation when it went into the airline business. This reputation was also used to gain a foothold in the railway business; it is worth noting, however, that should any of these individual businesses fail, this may lead to wider damage to the brand as a whole.
- Some companies segment their products as: products that attract; products that sell; products that make money. The car industry is very heavily based on this. Car advertising and salerooms normally have the most powerful, top-of-the-range cars as their features, and this is what draws people to the company in the first place. Having been attracted by the glamorous car, the customer then buys the standard offering. And the company makes money from selling the finance plans that normally underwrite such purchases.

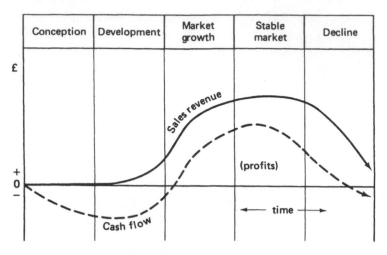

Conception	Development	Market growth	Stable market	Decline

Figure 18.2 Product life-cycle

18.9 The product life-cycle

The product life-cycle is a useful way of considering the span of existence for all products. Products are deemed to pass through the various stages of conception, development and growth, periods of maturity and stability, and then suffer decline and eventual disappearance from the market. Products may also be rejuvenated or re-presented through different packaging and promotional activities at different stages, especially at the time of maturity and around the point of decline. A very simplified graphical representation of this phenomenon is given in Figure 18.2. This also illustrates the initial outflow of cash and subsequent inflow of profits during this time. These stages can be described as follows:

(a) Conception
It is at this stage that careful research has to be conducted into market potential, and expense is incurred against which there is no revenue.

(b) Development
This second stage also demands the investment of considerable resources with a view to return in the future. Product development will lean heavily on the findings of market research, technical innovation and design expertise.

(c) Market growth
Assuming a successful product, sales increase and the product becomes increasingly accepted by the market. If it is completely innovative, once its novelty has been accepted and it proves dependable, market growth may be very rapid and highly profitable because of the absence of competitors. The introduction of zip-fasteners and ball-point pens are cases in point.

(d) Stable market
Often termed the 'stage of maturity', at this time the product has become established and competitors have entered the market with similar products, often offering some improvements. Profitability tends to fall even against

level or rising sales because of the additional costs of selling, advertising and promotion required to challenge competing products.

(e) Decline
This is the point at which the market has become saturated either because demand has been virtually satisfied, or because new products have arrived to take its place.

- The product life-cycle is a useful general concept. It should be noted, however, that it is also influenced by the entry of substitute products and companies making them; and changes in customer taste (which, as we have seen, may or may not be rational).
- Companies concerned with their long-term existence, therefore, take steps to ensure that they have a steady stream of new products and developments on offer. They classify their products as:
  1 yesterday's breadwinners: products that were successful in the past, and which may have still an enduring reputation (e.g. the Mini car); but which no longer make a key contribution to the finances of the organisation;
  2 today's breadwinners: the main sources of current income:
  3 tomorrow's breadwinners: products that are being tested, marketed and piloted to gain acceptance and commercial standing.

     It should be noted however, that all companies investing in their future need to be aware that the great majority of new products fail. This again underlines the need for high quality and expert market research.
- Services, as well as goods, also suffer this life cycle. The professional laundry for example, is a very much reduced activity, and invisible mending is a service very hard to find indeed, having reached its peak when clothes were in short supply and expensive.

18.10   Pricing

There are various considerations necessary when setting a price for a product. These are as follows.

(a) The economic price
This is the lowest price that can be demanded to cover all costs involved in the production and distribution of the product or service in question. This is the true economic price that makes production worthwhile. Some companies follow strategies of 'cost leadership' in which they set out to become the lowest cost operator in the particular market so that, if necessary, they can compete on price alone because their cost base is the lowest.

- Some companies are able to charge higher than the economic price for their products or services, because of scarcity value or extreme desirability for example. This is known as 'economic rent', and is normally sustainable only until customers find substitutes and alternatives.
- 'Moral pricing' occurs where companies command a key product or service, and could charge much higher prices than they do. They either choose not to

do so, or are ordered or regulated into not doing so, because of moral, ethical and social concerns.

(b) Price and sales volume

This is higher than the true economic price but one that the market does not consider unreasonable. Research is conducted to establish the highest price that the consumer will pay that will, in turn, yield a satisfactory or desired sales volume.

(c) Price and value

This is the price that customers expect to pay. The term 'expect to pay' is significant, especially when the product is competing with similar goods. If it is pitched higher than the figure demanded by competitors, it may cause sales to suffer; if pitched lower, especially if the difference is significant, customers may question the quality of the product. Also if the price is pitched too low, customers often feel that they are buying something that is 'cheap' (which is negative), rather than something which is 'good value' (which is positive). People do not like to be associated with connotations of cheapness.

(d) Psychological pricing

Psychological pricing is used in a variety of different ways. Luxury goods such as jewellery, perfumes, high-class watches and similar goods are most often bought as gifts. Here, the buyer expects to pay high prices because they want something of high value to give to the receiver.

The second approach is the one which sounds lower than it really is. Thus, an article marked at £9.99 sounds cheaper than if it was marked at £10.00, and the psychological bargain is reinforced by the fact that it will inevitably be paid for with a £10.00 note, with the customer receiving change. This approach was originally developed by Marks & Spencer in the late 1960s in order to make sure that the staff recorded sales through the tills, and it had a major commercial and marketing spin-off.

The third approach is that increasingly adopted in hire purchase situations. For example, some cars are marketed on the basis that it is possible to own them for £15.00 per month; and this is very much more attractive than the asking price which may be up to £13,000.

The fourth main aspect concerns the marketing of industrial services. For example, management, commercial consultants and specialists charge very high levels of fees and this gives the impression that they are top-quality operators. Also, high fee levels put a psychological pressure on the customer or client to accept and implement the consultants' recommendations. The customer or client therefore knows that they are going to have their problems solved (for good or ill) as the result of spending this money; whereas if they spend a lesser amount, they would consider the opinion of the specialist more closely and may have to decide what to do about the issue for themselves.

(e) New product pricing

A new product that is in competition will existing similar products always has to be carefully priced. If the price charged is too similar to the competition, it may lose its identity; if it is priced too low, it will be seen as a cheap alternative, while if it is priced too high, this may give connotations of quality that are simply not warranted in the particular segment. Pricing of new products has, therefore, normally to be conducted as a part of the broader marketing necessary to launch a new product successfully. At the initial launch however, there may be a price incentive offered so that people will at least look favourably upon it in the first instance. Or it may be that the product is offered at a comparable price, but with enhanced guarantees and after-sales provision ahead of the competitors.

- The pricing of a completely new product is of especial difficulty, particularly if it is an innovation. In such a case, initial pricing is often very high and is reduced only when competitors enter the field. Colour televisions, camcorders, and the ball-point pen, were all initially very expensive and only after many years of competition, improvement and mass availability, have prices come down.
- It may also be necessary to recover research and development costs as the consequence of launching a completely new product.

18.11   Advertising

Advertising is concerned with presenting an organisation's goods or services to best advantage. It can be said to perform the following functions:

- *To inform*
  The first task of advertising is to make the public aware of an organisation's products or services.
- *To persuade*
  Advertising's second task is to generate the desire for the product being offered and to turn the desire into a need that must be satisfied. In this area, the appeal is very much to the emotions rather than to reason and to the practical worth of the product. It is normally full of strong visual images, and is sometimes known as selling dreams.
- *To convince*
  The third task of advertising is to convince the potential buyer that the product advertised is the only one that will satisfactorily fill that desire.
- *To retain*
  The fourth task of advertising is to convince the customer that future purchases should be of the same brand as the only way of achieving continued satisfaction.

18.12   Common advertising media

The main advertising media are: the press, comprising daily and weekly national newspapers, local newspapers, magazines and journals, including the trade press; commercial and satellite television, commercial radio, and cinema and theatre advertising; direct mail advertising and promotion; sponsorship; and increasing use of electronic media and the Internet.

Posters on hoardings and other sites are also a much used medium and are especially effective at the 'inform' stage; and this is now being extended to include the panels on trains, buses, lorries and taxis. The media chosen depends upon a number of factors, including the market aimed at and the type of product or service being promoted. The overall purpose is to 'differentiate' the product or service on offer from those of competitors, substitutes, or near equivalents. Many organisations operating in mass markets, or with a large number of individual customers and consumers, constantly adopt strategies of differentiation as the cornerstone of their marketing policy.

1 The market aimed at
Food products will be advertised in women's magazines and papers read by women; contractors' plant will be advertised in building trade journals; and investment opportunities in the financial papers. An advertiser could expect little response from an advertisement for excavator hire appearing in a fashion magazine.

2 Is the market local or national?
A local newspaper or local commercial radio will serve the local market quite adequately in most cases. Commercial television, national newspapers and national magazines will serve the national market.

3 Section of the public aimed at
Where specialist products are advertised this is best done in specialist publications, e.g. angling anoraks in angling magazines. Products of general interest will be advertised through media with general appeal.

4 Availability of names and addresses
Where up-to-date and reliable lists of the names and addresses of potential customers are available direct-mail and e-mail advertising may be used. Often these lists provide details of specific segments of the market, enabling advertisers to aim precisely at the people they hope to influence.

5 Would a moving advertisement be advantageous?
Where a product or service lends itself to a moving presentation then television or video may be considered.

6 Past effectiveness of the medium
A successful medium will obviously be used again and again. The problem is how the response from any particular medium can be measured. Coupons, department numbers or names and other devices are pressed into service in this connection but there is as yet no really reliable and accurate way of assessing the effectiveness of any particular medium.

7 The budget allocation for advertising
A careful assessment must be made of the expected gain in sales and profit against the proposed advertising expenditure. Again, however, measure-

ment of sales gain against advertising cost is incapable of accurate measurement.

8 What type of sales are aimed for?

It must be determined whether increased sales are expected to come from the existing market or whether a new market is the target. A case in point is the advertising of wines in photographic magazines rather than, or in addition to, advertising them in food and related journals.

9 Advertising and price

As we saw above, pricing – especially psychological pricing – is used as an advertising tool in itself. Beyond this, it must be determined how customers and consumers tend to pay for their purchases. For example, if the intended market mostly makes cash purchases, then the price needs to be set at such a level so as to ensure that customers are able to make the purchases at their own convenience with the cash that they have in their pocket or wallet. If credit cards, hire purchase, or other non-cash payment terms are to be used, then the onus is on the advertiser to make sure that these facilities are available for the convenience of the customer.

10 Ethical dimensions

Some people see both the role and content of advertising as having detrimental effects on the interests of consumers. In particular, advertising must not make or imply claims for the products and services that cannot be supported by their actual performance. Emphasis on images such as sex, youth, glamour and vitality – and especially the role of women in advertising – have caused strong legal, moral and ethical objections in various quarters. As well as presenting products and services in the best possible light, therefore, effective advertising is increasingly dependent upon consideration of a much broader range of factors.

18.13   Public relations

Public relations, or PR, is defined by the Institute of Public Relations as 'the deliberate, planned and sustained effort to establish and maintain mutual positive understanding between an organisation and its public'. This definition has been taken many stages further in many cases, as an ever-greater range of information is available about organisation's products, services and activities. Good public relations are now considered essential between an organisation and its employees, customers and consumers, the public at large, political and social bodies, and lobbies and vested interest groups.

- Goodwill and good reputation are not easily acquired. They take a lot of time and trouble to build up. Conversely, they are very easily and quickly destroyed, and once gone, take a much longer time to rebuild. Confidence, once lost, is not easily regained. Even relatively minor incidents such as an impolite representative or an unhelpful telephone operator can mar the organisation's public image.

- Public relations may be placed in the hand of a senior member of the organisation, or a member of the marketing team, or it can be handled by outside consultants; however it is done, this must be effective. A large part of the work of a public relations team is to deal with complaints and criticisms from customers and from the public at large, and from vested interest groups and lobbies. Great skill is required to provide satisfactory answers and explanations so that criticisms are accepted as being answered, and not explained away.

- However, public relations is charged with more than simply protecting the organisation's reputation. It also holds a key responsibility in informing the public about the organisation's actions and policies, especially where they may affect the physical and social environment. In these cases especially, the need to deal effectively with pressure groups, lobbies and vested interests is paramount.

- The key function of public relations is to show to the world at large that the particular organisation is socially aware and responsible, and that whatever it does, is being carried out to the highest standards in the particular circumstances. Many companies take this a stage further, donating money and resources to charity, and sponsoring sporting and cultural events in the same way as wealthy individual patrons in the past.

18.14   Distribution channels

The marketing function's ultimate objective is to ensure that the product ends up in the hands of the customer. If this does not happen all else has been in vain. It is essential, therefore, to use some form of distribution channel to achieve this. There are four main ways in which distribution is accomplished.

(a) Direct sales

In these cases products are sold direct from the producer to the consumer. This is the common method adopted for capital goods of high value or made to individual specification such as aircraft, machine tools and similar goods. It is also used by many manufacturers of retail consumer goods such as household requisites which are sold door-to-door by sales representatives. One of the world's largest cosmetics firms sells its products this way.

Another method of direct selling is by the establishment of retail outlets by manufacturers and suppliers. Many department stores and supermarkets make and sell their own goods, as well as distributing those of other firms.

Services such as insurance have always been sold direct through agents and intense competition has led to the opening of what are really retail shops in many busy shopping areas. These services also increasingly avail themselves of direct targeted mailings, and telesales.

(b) Through a third party

In this case suppliers use intermediaries to channel their wares, usually an appointed agent. This is common in the retail area and some examples are domestic equipment such as washing-machines and refrigerators where the manufacturer appoints special retail shops to act as agents. In this way the manufacturer retain some control over the quality of the service the ultimate buyers obtain. A service example is that of insurance, which is often sold through agents such as banks and through brokers. Supermarkets who buy direct from food manufacturers form part of this pattern of distribution.

(c) The distribution chain

This involves more than one party between the source of the goods and the consumer and is the traditional way in which many staple goods such as food and household requisites are sold. The chain usually consists of producer, wholesaler, retailer and consumer, but on occasion there may be more than one party between the producer and the retailer.

(d) Mail order

Mail order takes two forms: direct sales by the manufacturer to the user; and sales by mail order houses, mainly through advertisements and catalogues, and on the Internet.

The great advantage of all mail order is that it can be carried out from the convenience of the customer. Products and services can be purchased over the telephone or via the Internet from the mail order companies. The extent of services offered in this way has greatly increased in recent years and now includes: insurance; motor services; financial services; retail banking; as well as the well-established range of products offered through catalogues. Contact is made with the customer either through display advertisements in the press and magazines, by direct mail advertising, or through inserts in newspapers and magazines.

(e) Electronic distribution

As yet in its early stages, electronic distribution is expected to become a significant niche player in the distribution aspect of marketing. Either through the Internet, or through computer and television displays, customers may choose products and services from a wide variety of sources. The independent television Ceefax service already offers a huge range of travel products and package holidays; and there are currently pioneering activities in the field concerning the order of electrical goods and foodstuffs. As an example, Curry Dixons, the retail electrical goods chain, has set up its own computer ordering facility; as yet in its infancy, the company anticipates that by the year 2010, the electronic facility will be responsible for about 5 per cent of the company's business. While this may not seem to be all that large, the company anticipates that 5 per cent of its business at that time is likely to represent a value and turnover of approximately £40 million.

The method of distribution chosen depends largely upon the type of market aimed at and the type of goods or services offered. Many producers find it profitable to use more than one method. Above all, however, it is becoming increasingly necessary at least to consider alternative outlets to those traditionally used on the grounds that customers and consumers are being offered an ever-greater range of points of access for the products and services that they require.

QUESTIONS

1 Explain the marketing concept. Discuss the factors which have caused companies to become marketing oriented. (CIM)
2 Explain the concept of the marketing mix and write a brief account of each of the four elements into which it may be divided. (IComA)
3 Define market research. Write an account of the activities which are covered by the term. (IComA)
4 Distinguish, with examples, between market research and marketing research. (CIM)
5 How might increased consumer concern about environmental issues affect markets and market segmentation in the future? (CIM)
6 Assess the contribution of market segmentation to marketing mix planning. (CIM)
7 Describe the stages in the product life-cycle. (CIM)
8 Discuss the value and limitations of the product life-cycle concept. (CIM)
9 A marketing director is planning to launch a product into a competitive but growing market. It is claimed to be of superior quality to the existing products. What factors should he bear in mind when setting the price? (IComA)
10 You are required
   (a) to explain how a marketing specialist may have regard to the benefits which potential buyers perceive in a product when determining its selling price;
   (b) to assess the importance of product quality to a buyer of consumer goods;
   (c) to explain why a direct relationship between the costs of production and a selling price may be inappropriate as a pricing strategy. (CIMA)
11 Discuss the role and purpose of the public relations function. (IAM)
12 What do you understand by the term 'an organisation's image' so far as it relates to the local community? How may a positive image be developed? (ICSA)
13 Is advertising in the public interest? (ACCA)
14 'Ensuring a high quality of service to the client or customer is the key to the success of any enterprise.' Discuss. (ICSA)

▮ Ⅳ 19 Production

In Chapter 18 it was stated that effective marketing is vital to the survival of an organisation, in whatever sphere it operates. If goods are to be sold or services provided, however, then it is essential that they be available. So far as goods are concerned in the manufacturing industries, whether in the private or public sector, this involves production, the conversion of raw materials into usable commodities. In this sense the term 'raw materials' is used to indicate the basic input to a production process, though this input may be anything from a primary material such as iron ore to a finished component such as a length of cloth. In the first instance the iron ore is the raw material for the manufacturer of iron and in the second the cloth, already a finished article in its own right, is the raw material for a manufacturer of garments. In fact it is commonly the case that the finished output of one manufacturer is the input, or raw material, for another.

19.1 Types of production

Production methods are conventionally divided into three types: job or unit production, mass or flow-line production, and batch production.

(a) Job production
- In this type jobs are carried out individually and usually to the specific order of a customer. Job production can range from small units such as the production of an individually designed piece of pottery to the building of a large cargo ship, from made-to-measure clothing to bridge-building.
- Job production is usually very labour intensive since it does not easily lend itself to mechanisation. Further, the labour employed has to be highly skilled for the most part, and supervision must be constant and very technically competent. There is little opportunity for the use of highly specialised machinery, and the machinery that is used must be versatile and able to cope with varying work.
- It is unusual for an organisation to be able to make for stock as each order will be different from previous orders and from future ones. In many cases, such as a bridge-building or in road construction, there can be no question of making for stock. Continuity of work for both labour and equipment depends, therefore, on effective marketing and under this heading must be included competitive tendering.

- Where jobs of high value and extended timespan are the rule, problems are often experienced with financing the projects, especially in view of the high labour content which means that large sums for wages have to be regularly found.

(b) Mass production

- This method, which is also known as flow-line production, is a process of continuous production where large numbers of more or less identical units are manufactured continuously. It is the exact opposite of job production. Little or no individuality can be introduced into the product, and the processes are extremely capital intensive. The labour content is relatively small compared to the capital investment, and most of it is unskilled or semi-skilled. Highly specialised machinery is used and in the most modern mass-production plants practically all of the work and machines are controlled by computer. The small proportion of skilled labour required is employed to set up the machines for production, and is highly paid. This small, very skilled, work-force is a vital element in continuing production and disruption of their operations normally causes severe setbacks in manufacturing volume, and can cause production to cease altogether.
- Mass-produced products, which range from such items as breakfast cereals and paper products to motor-cars, are manufactured in advance of sales, and sales forecasting and marketing of a high order are essential for the success of the manufacturing enterprise.
- A distinction is usually made between two aspects of this method of production. The term 'mass production' (or 'flow-line production') is used for the continuous production of manufactured goods such as those just mentioned. Where the nature of the product is the result of formulations such as petro-chemical products, adhesives and jams, process production or continuous-flow process production are the terms normally used.
- In order to remain profitable it is necessary for enterprises employing mass-production methods to utilise machinery to virtually full capacity. When orders fall short of full capacity it is often more advantageous to keep the plant running and to produce for stock rather than to reduce the volume of output. An example of this is the stock-piling of motor-cars when sales are low. This situation cannot, of course, continue indefinitely. In the case of domestic consumables, such as washing-powders, attempts are made to stimulate sales by a variety of means including 'special offers', competitions and free gifts.
- Mass production is often criticised because of the poor quality of life it imposes on the workers. The content of the individual job of a worker may be severely limited, sometimes even being reduced to one repetitive operation. The use of a conveyer belt gives the worker no control over the pace of the work and diminishes opportunities to communicate with fellow workers. This has an adverse psychological effect on the workers leading to boredom and lack of job satisfaction. The result is a high rate of absenteeism, general work stoppages and possibly defective working owing to a low level of interest in the job. Group working as set out in 19.2(c), (d) and (e) below is practised

by some manufacturers to obviate or alleviate these problems, and the increasing use of robots is advantageous in this respect, though it has the social disadvantage of causing redundancies.

(c) Batch production

- This is a method that falls between job and mass production, and may be said to be repeated production but not continuous production. It is employed where orders consist of a significant number of similar items but these orders are not sufficient to justify continuous manufacture.
- Industries offering choices of design or sophistication in their products make use of batch production, a notable one being the furniture industry. A batch of one design will be made and then a batch of another, and then perhaps the first will be run again. Labour is more skilled in this method of production than in mass production because of the variety of the work entailed, and machines are more versatile. It uses more labour, proportionately, than mass production and less machinery.
- Whether goods are made in advance of orders or subsequent to them depends not so much on the type of production method as on the situation in the market. Manufacturers using batch production will set up a production run when orders for a particular item are received, but have the problem of making the run economically viable; in other words producing sufficient quantity to make the run profitable. They do this by adding a stock quantity to the ordered quantity. One of the most difficult problems in batch production is deciding on the economic batch size.
- Batch production can offer some of the cost saving advantages of mass production, but also allows the manufacturer to satisfy individual job orders if necessary because of more versatile machinery and skilled workers.

19.2　Developments in the types of production

While the principles indicated in 19.1 still basically hold good, great developments have taken place in many spheres of activity. These include changes in production methods and also changes brought about as the result of the great proliferation of the service sector.

(a) Information production

The great advantage of the information industry is that companies working within it can be located anywhere. Information can be transmitted to all parts of the world within a matter of minutes, and this applies to both electronic and paper transmissions (for example, through modem and fax). Those wishing to work in the information industry can therefore locate in their own preferred place, and acquire the technology which can then be very easily installed and connected up to the global communication systems.

It is also not necessary to have all those working in the company in the same location – by the same token as above, they too can work anywhere.

This also applies to those companies that create database, and manufacture computer software.

Many well-established organisations in mainstream activities are also increasingly finding that information and database work can be carried out either by their own staff or sub-contractors working off-site, from home, or from business centres, and the like.

(b) Commercial service production

Commercial service production encompasses: retail and distribution; financial services; agency services such as travel; and professional services, e.g. architecture, management services.

1 In retail and distribution, the principles of 'production' organisation are akin to those for mass or batch production. Even the smallest shop has to have a great variety of products available for consumption. The principles of supermarket organisation are very akin to those for mass production; the stores are designed to afford the best possible use of space, including income per square metre; income per till or cash-point; while at the same time optimising customer convenience and choice.

2 Travel agencies and financial services offer a wide range – or batches – of products or services, and these are then tailored to meet individual needs where necessary, or the individual makes a choice from the range on offer.

3 Professional services are akin to jobbing production in that every customer or client will require the expert to bring their specialism to bear on an individual problem or issue.

(c) Public service production

Managers in public services are faced with two overwhelming problems. What should constitute a given aspect of public service, and how this should be delivered and paid for. Traditionally, giant organisations were created to make national provisions and these, in turn, then managed the schools, hospitals, essential services and emergency services in their own particular areas. Organisations in these sectors have therefore to reconcile the public requirement to offer the highest possible standards, with the political drive to make these as individual as possible, and the universal requirement to keep costs down. In many cases, therefore, public services fall between the traditional pillars of jobbing, mass and batch production; and may therefore be seen to operate in something of a void, uncertain of the necessary direction or approach.

This is directly at variance for example, with private health care or social services, for which the individual hospital or organisation concerned makes specific charges for a limited range of activity. A key priority facing those responsible for managing core public services is to arrive at a set of principles, and to deliver these in accordance with local demands.

(d) Voluntary service production

As stated above (Chapter 18), voluntary services have become much more professional in their outlook; the largest charities are now highly expert and effective marketeers.

This has alienated many of their traditional supporters. People who were happy to undertake small collections in their locality on the part of these institutions now find themselves swamped by mass professional marketing techniques. Big charities now need to raise ever-greater quantities of resources, above all money, and have therefore to compete for this in the commercial world.

Many charities have also had to accept the responsibility for privatised public services; for example, Help the Aged now runs much of the old people's provision in Britain that was previously run by social services in many areas. This again, has required a professionalisation and commercialisation of operations management, and again, has not met with universal approval (and this is quite apart from the dilemmas surrounding the privatisations themselves).

(e) Project production

Project production comes in two basic forms. The first is a version of small group working, whereby production line activities are organised so that the maximum job rotation and work involvement is possible.

The second is a reflection of the approach required to major capital investment. Originally, the preserve of building and civil engineering, it is now the approach favoured when installing major new information and electronic communication systems.

For both, the approach is fundamentally the same in that those working on the projects are required to have a wide variety of skills, qualities and expertise, and a willingness of attitude to apply these in whatever the circumstances. Especially in the completion of mega projects and others formed and financed through joint ventures between different companies, and often different countries, unforeseen circumstances are certain to occur, and the ways in which these are overcome are a matter for the application of ingenuity and creativity as much as the availability of financial and other resources.

Project production often requires the resources and scale of capitalisation necessary for mass and flow activities; its application is very much on a jobbing basis in that no two projects are ever exactly the same.

(f) Core and peripheral approaches

As organisations become more efficient and effective in their production processes, they find that they have spare capacity. This has led to many becoming involved in peripheral activities, or niche or secondary markets. The main problem to be addressed here is reconciling the fact that while these are secondary markets for the product or service, the customers and clients being served nevertheless require the same primacy of treatment that they would get from other places. The great danger of going down the peripheral market and activity route is that either the customers and clients get an inferior level of product or service, or that the peripheral route sucks other resources in and dilutes the primary effort.

19.3   Determining production conditions

- The first decision a producer has to make is to choose the location of production. This used to be done either on the basis of proximity to raw materials and power where the product lost weight during production; or near the market, where the product gained weight during production. These simple criteria now apply to a much lesser extent because of the better transport facilities and communications, and because of inducements and grants to move to areas of high unemployment and economic stagnation. These are also increased legal restrictions being placed on where industrial and commercial development may take place.
- The method of determining the lay-out of the point of production is still the prerogative of the particular organisation. There are some basic ways that should be considered.

(a) Lay-out by process of production
This is the conventional approach and it is still very widely practised. Groups of machines of activities are clustered together, often on a single premises, and the product or service on offer is delivered through people working out of these premises.

For manufacturing processes, the production line is kept as straight as possible because this reduces handling charges. Stages in the process are also kept as closely grouped as possible, as this too keeps costs to a minimum.

(b) Lay-out by production technology
This is of greatest importance in mass and flow-production activities. Large sites are required to house the sheer size, scale and complexity of the technology required. In these cases, the greatest attention is to the choice and location of site; everything else is secondary to that. It especially affects industries such as oil, chemicals, mass motor-car manufacturing, and the production of electrical and white goods.

(c) Group working and cell production
In this arrangement, which is very like production lay-out, machines and workers are arranged in self-contained groups to make complete units or components, and they enjoy considerable autonomy not provided by other methods. Each group is, in effect, a small self-contained unit or cell with virtually full control over its own planning and output.

(d) Group technology
This is where particular machines require a group of workers to operate them, rather than an individual. The end result is very much the same as in group and cell working and production, but the starting point is the tech-

nology itself rather than the finished product. Especially in the service sectors, technology allows work – and therefore workers – to be located anywhere of choice. In many cases technology is fully portable and fully flexible

19.4   Production and operations management

- Many organisations favour a balance between production expertise and marketing effectiveness. For example, Japanese car and electrical goods manufacturers pride themselves on constantly anticipating demand for ever-improved product quality and development, and they therefore concentrate as much on product excellence as marketing output. Travel agents also concentrate on improving the quality of the products that they know they can sell, and then concentrate on marketing needs to best advantage.
- Production and marketing management are therefore closely intertwined. On the one hand, production management is influenced by what the market is persuaded that it wants; on the other hand, some marketing effort is concerned with certainty of product and service quality and durability, as well as by the generation of more positive general images.

19.5   Production and service planning

This follows decisions concerning policy and direction. It covers the requirement to plan the manufacture of products and delivery of services. All production activities, whether manufacturing or service, are placed under the control of an operations manager, by whatever title that is assumed in the organisation (e.g. production planning manager, travel agency manager).

The activities covered by production and service planning are:

(a) to determine when the production should be put in hand and the timescale involved;
(b) the preparation of work and materials' schedules to ensure labour and materials are available at the right times and in the right quantities;
(c) the preparation of machine technology and information utilisation schedules; this is commonly termed 'loading,' and this is to ensure that whatever the product or service in question, both technology and operators are available at the right time and when demanded;
(d) to maintain close liaison with suppliers, designers, sales and marketing so that, again where the product or service is being considered, the right quality and volume of offerings is available when required.

Effective production planning ensures smooth production runs. Disruptions due to material and component shortages (manufacturing), products being out-of-stock (retail), or non-availability of hotel rooms or airline seats (travel agency), are therefore kept to a minimum. By considering the broader picture, moreover, other matters such as staff shortages can also be anticipated and rectified.

19.6   Production and service control

This is an extension of production planning and is increasingly organised under one function.

- The principal form of production control in all situation is monitoring – progress against targets and objectives; returns against projected returns; and demand against projected demand. When delays and deviations are discovered then corrective action can be taken, or the reasons for the delays and deviations assessed.
- In industrial and manufacturing situations, it is also usual to check frequency and density of machine utilisation; the regularity with which delivery schedules are met; and labour and machine downtime as a percentage of total working time.
- The travel industry will tend to check regularity and frequency of late departures; frequency with which trains, coaches, ships and planes are fully loaded, and different percentage points below full loading; frequency of delays and diversions and the reason for these.
- Health services control their output through monitoring appointment waiting times; waiting lists; patient throughput; the extent to which treatment is able to be carried out in one go, and the extent to which return visits are necessary or desirable.

Whatever the *product* therefore, forms of monitoring and evaluation of actual results against projected results is essential.

Alongside this, it is certain that some form of inspection, testing, or other quality assurance procedure will be in place.

19.7   Production technology

All activities now have an ever-greater range and quality of technology and equipment at their disposal. Production, public service and information technology are constantly being upgraded and updated, and what is suitable and adequate for particular purposes at present may not last all that long for the future.

- It is increasingly being seen, as a key part of production operations and financial management, that investment in technology may have to be made as and when new technology becomes available, rather than depreciating or gaining anticipated returns on existing machinery and databases. Technology and equipment has effectively become a fixed cost, rather than an investment on which there are 'certain' returns.
- This also has implications for training and retraining of work-forces. It is now in the interests of everyone concerned that there is a universal commitment to continuous updating and development, both in the interests of protecting the employment of those present, and also to ensure that the particular organisation remains competitive and credible in its particular field.

- In industrial production, components are produced to an ever-greater quality; production technology is much more precise and accurate than in the past, and this is set to improve much further; wastage rates can be greatly reduced; and where faults do occur, the source of these can be quickly identified and remedied. Industrial production also requires a far smaller work-force than in the past, though this requires to be far more highly trained and flexible.
- Those working in public services also have a much greater range of technology at their disposal. For example, surgeons now have to become computer operators in the pursuit of development in such things as keyhole surgery; and as the result of advances in microtechnology, it is now far easier to pinpoint accurately the treatment that is necessary for a patient, and to deliver this quickly and effectively. Schools, colleges and universities have a much greater access to databases, laboratories and information services, and those who work in these areas must be proficient in their use.
- Those working in commercial services have information technology and databases as a primary tool, and as the result of this, customers expect to find out whether they can have the holiday, the travel ticket, or the financial plan of their choice, either as the result of visiting the agency, or as the result of a telephone call.

In all of these cases, production technology has raised the expectations of everyone concerned – companies and organisations working in these fields are able to deliver their outputs to a much greater quality standard, and much more quickly; and at the same time, customer, consumer and client expectations have been raised in the same way.

19.8   Inspection and quality assurance

(a) The function of inspection and quality assurance

It is in no-one's interests to produce output without regard to its quality, volume, access, or the timescales in which it is required. Checking is therefore required so that absolute standards in each of these areas are maintained. It is known by a variety of names – inspection, quality assurance, quality control, product and service guarantee functions, are all familiar terms.

Before quality assurance can effectively take place, standards must be set and these stem from those required and determined upon by organisational policy and direction. The standards required are therefore a matter for the senior management of each organisation; increasingly, they will tend towards the highest possible standards, because if they do not, then they will lose out to competitors who do.

(b) When to inspect?

Defects need to be discovered as early as possible. As these can occur at all stages of industrial production, commercial service delivery and public services, some form of checking should therefore be carried out at each stage. It is therefore necessary to have some form of monitoring and evaluation at at least the following stages:

1 on receipt of inputs, bought-in components, quality of database;
2 upon receipt of production technology, to make sure that those responsible for it can use it;
3 before a production or service output run, to ensure that the technology can deliver what is required, when it is required;
4 during the production and service output, to ensure that what was envisaged is being delivered;
5 if pilot schemes or prototypes are being envisaged, during and at the end of these runs, to ensure that what was envisaged is again being produced;
6 final testing which is carried out on the finished product or service so that it is ready for delivery to the point of sale.

It is also most important that any defects which will be hidden by subsequent work are discovered before the fault is concealed. In an industrial situation, such a case would be where a flaw in a metal part will be covered by paint and subsequently invisible. For a travel brochure, it may only subsequently become apparent that there is a flaw with the particular package on offer – the hotel is incomplete, or there is a food poisoning scare; and this therefore will require constant checking.

(c) Quality assurance

- The best and surest check is, of course, 100 per cent testing and inspection. In most cases, this is not possible.
- It is most usual therefore to sample products and services. This may be done through random sampling techniques; spot samples; and through the incidence of customer feedback, and especially complaints.

(d) Where to inspect

Inspection and quality assurance should be carried out as follows.

- With work groups, as part of the wider process of performance monitoring.
- With suppliers, ensuring the continued delivery of the required quality and quantity of components, information and technology.
- With distributers and outlets, to ensure that they are not receiving volumes of customer complaints of which the manufacturer or service deliverer is not aware.
- Centrally as a corporate function, to make sure that overall organisation standards are being maintained.
- At the point of manufacture or service delivery, as a part of 'managing by walking about' so that those responsible can actually see for themselves.
- In response to customer, client and end-user surveys, to understand where they see the strengths and weaknesses of the product or service lying.

In normal circumstances, organisations adopt a mixture of each of the above. This gives the best possible chance for identifying faults early and remedying them, before they lead to loss of consumer and customer satisfaction and confidence.

(e) Responsibility for inspection and quality assurance

Opinions differ as to where this should lie. Some prefer distinctive quality assurance departments, while others contend that this should be carried out by production and service operational teams at the point of their activities. Japanese companies certainly tend to favour the latter – customer complaints are referred directly to the production team or crew that produced the item. On the other hand, the National Health Service carries a separate audit office, and this looks at the quality of medical care on offer as well as budget expenditure. Whichever is chosen, it is important that there is an active responsibility taken to identify and remedy faults as quickly as possible.

19.9   Internal and external production

- In industrial production and manufacturing, this is known as 'the make or buy' decision. For all sectors, the decision has to be taken as to which components, information and service parts are to be manufactured, created or owned by the organisation, and which are to be bought in.
- In manufacturing and industrial production, some organisations consider it an advantage to be able to produce many of their own components so that they can guarantee absolutely the quality and availability of these. At the same time, however, other manufacturers take the view that by going to a high-quality component supplier, they get the quality anyway, and can concentrate on what they do best.
- Commercial services, information services, and professional services all have to come to the view as to whether it is better to create their own databases and have a wide range of expertise available on the premises, or whether to be able to gain access to these as and when necessary. Many organisations take the latter view, and this has led to contracting arrangements between agencies and database providers, and to certain specialists – e.g. surgeons, architects – working extensively as sub-contractors, rather than as employees.
- The building, civil engineering and construction industries have traditionally taken the view that it is better to sub-contract certain specialist operations – e.g. drainage, earthworks – for those with expertise in those areas.
- In industrial production, there is now a variation on the traditional approach which may be defined as 'make, assemble or buy'. Again, this is an innovation brought about by the incursion of Japanese industrial practices into the West. Japanese car and electrical goods companies either manufacture their own components, or else they buy these in from expert sources in Japan; and these are then shipped to their factory locations in the West for assembly close to the local markets. Any local provider that they subsequently choose to use has to meet the quality and delivery assurance standards of their own in-house providers.

It is necessary to stress that there is no one right answer. So long as the matter is a conscious and positive corporate decision, its effectiveness can be monitored, and remedies and improvements made where necessary.

QUESTIONS

1 What are the four main divisions in the work undertaken in any company under the general heading of production Administration? (IComA)
2 What are the principal responsibilities of the production planning and control department in a manufacturing concern? (IComA)
3 The use of the assembly line for a manufacturing operation is justified in terms of specialisation and higher efficiency achieved. Examine the factors which a company should evaluate before introducing an assembly-line system of production, or when considering the abandonment of an existing assembly-line system. (ACCA)
4 Flow- or assembly-line production has been the subject of considerable criticism. Explain the difficulties to which this system of production gives rise and consider suggestions which have been made to overcome them. (IComA)
5 A manufacturer is faced with a decision whether to produce components for his product within his own organisation or to buy them from outside specialist suppliers. Discuss the points which he should consider in arriving at a decision. (IComA)
6 (a) What may the advantages and disadvantages of cohesive work groups be?
   (b) How can managers reduce or avoid the disadvantages? (CIMA)
7 Explain how the level of demand for a company's products influences the way in which its production system is organised. (CIM)
8 In manufacturing industries, inspection takes place to ensure a satisfactory standard of quality in the finished product. Such inspection is not concerned only with the finished article. Describe four other areas where inspection may take place in a manufacturing process. (CIM)

■ ꙮ **20** Purchasing

Purchasing used to be a peripheral and *ad hoc* activity that enjoyed very little status or importance in the organisation. In recent years, however, with the opening up of global markets and much greater access to a variety of sources of supply, the purchasing activity has grown in stature and now makes a major contribution to the success, effectiveness and profitability of every enterprise.

Purchasing is concerned with the buying in of raw materials, components and service features. These are all variable costs. An expert top-quality purchaser therefore makes an enormous contribution to the well-being of their organisation through their capabilities in keeping these costs down, while at the same point ensuring the reliability and quality of the supplies.

- It used to be accepted that the purchasing function differed from many others in that those carrying out this work were to a large extent tied to their own industry. It was always considered, for example, that purchasing wood required expert technical knowledge of a high order to ensure that the correct wood was being bought, each batch varying from sample to sample; and that therefore it was impossible to be an expert purchaser of wood without an extensive grounding in that trade.

  Today, those perceptions have changed. The expert purchaser is required to have negotiating and financial skills; and the capability to ensure regularity of supplies, together with access to alternative sources, in whatever sector they may find themselves. It is therefore rather incumbent upon the purchaser a) to acquire these skills; and b) to ensure that they become expert in their particular sector before they envisage moving into it, and once they get installed.

  There are therefore many activities within the purchasing function common to all industrial and commercial sectors, and also to public services.

20.1 Common purchasing activities

Activities common to most sectors are:
(a) All buyers will need to have a wide knowledge of the markets from which they have to make their purchases, whether these are raw materials, manufactured components or, as in wholesale and retail trading, finished goods. The knowledge will extend to how the suppliers perform in regard to reliability and delivery performance.

(b) In manufacturing and kindred industries buyers will have to liaise closely with the production department to ascertain their precise requirements. In retail selling the buyer has a key role in the success of the enterprise in that he or she must be closely attuned to consumer taste and demand.

(c) Though stock control may or may not be the direct responsibility of purchasing officers, they are primarily responsible for ensuring that sufficient supplies of materials or components are available to maintain continuity of manufacture or sales. The buyer may do this by contracts with suppliers for regular deliveries or by building up stocks to be called off as required. The former keeps a minimum of capital tied up in stores and storage space but entails the risk of suppliers not keeping to delivery undertakings, while the latter does tie up capital but ensures that materials or components are readily available.

It is probably true to say that in the retail trade no one knows how many sales are lost to an organisation because of articles not being in stock. Most consumers nowadays demand instant satisfaction and are disinclined to wait even a short while for delivery, preferring to go to another retailer who can supply immediately.

(d) In most organisations the purchasing department will be responsible for negotiating purchase prices and terms of credit.

(e) Purchasing will also generally be responsible for ensuring that the goods ordered and invoiced are actually received and that the prices charged are those quoted. This is an area where fraud is not difficult and procedures should be instituted to minimise this risk, such as having the necessary checks carried out by different staff from those directly involved in placing the orders.

(f) Purchasing will constantly monitor expected deliveries to ensure that suppliers adhere to their undertakings regarding quality and delivery dates.

(g) Purchasing will constantly investigate the market
   1 to seek better products, prices, terms or deliveries;
   2 to seek out alternative suppliers to ensure continuity of deliveries should the principal source unexpectedly fail for any reason;
   3 to ensure a multiplicity of suppliers, where appropriate, to maintain competitiveness;
   4 to be aware of new suppliers coming into the markets;
   5 to be aware of the prevailing state of suppliers' businesses, so that any problems can be anticipated and dealt with early.

20.2   Different approaches to purchasing

As stated previously, great advances have been made in the scope and expertise of the purchasing function. Expert purchasers now need to be aware of the following approaches to purchasing and supply.

1 By now, pay later – and other extended credit terms.
2 Pay now, buy later – so that costs can be established for the given period of time, even though payment has been made in advance.

3 Discounts, preferred supplier/preferred customer relationships – so that advantageous terms, and priority treatment, can be ensured.

4 Just-in-Time (JiT) – so that rather than stockpiling and using expensive storage space, supplies are made in small batches regularly and frequently.

5 Retainer systems – so that in return for a regularity of payment, supplies can be guaranteed whenever they are required. This is especially prevalent when purchasing expertise and information.

6 The use of futures and international financial instruments – for overseas buying. A 'future' is a financial device that secures a guaranteed currency exchange rate for a given period in the future.

7 Extended credit and debit schemes – to enable payments to be spread over a period of time; and again, to enable some measure of control and certainty over financial commitments in this area.

- Purchasing is therefore clearly very much to do with finance: the buying department is a major spender in any organisation. Its link with accounting functions is therefore clear. In many cases, credit terms in regard to payment times and cash discounts will be as important as the actual purchases. Judicious timing of purchases can have a beneficial effect on working capital and cash-flow. Other similar approaches will also be used according to the particular circumstances. Very often, for example, the buyer may be able to strike a particularly favourable bargain to the advantage of the organisation, and expert purchasing officers will constantly have this at the front of their minds.

20.3 Purchasing policy

As with all functions, policy and direction will be laid down for purchasing. This remain the responsibility of top management, and is carried out in support of the wider objectives and direction of the organisation.

- A key factor of purchasing policy is the level of stocks to be carried. Will stock-holding be restricted to goods and service components for immediate and current usage or should buffer stocks be held? If the latter, what quantities should be held? The normal pattern of deliveries by suppliers may determine this. If supplies are generally constant then reliance can be placed on a continuing receipt of goods ordered, but if they are erratic it may be more prudent to establish a stock to ensure regular input to production. Costs of holding stores, quantity discounts, the possible financial implications of production stoppages, and vulnerability to deterioration and to theft will all play a part in making this decision.

- Second, is speculative buying to be indulged in? Certain raw materials in particular experience wide price fluctuations and it may be both prudent and profitable to purchase large quantities when they become available at low prices. There are two advantages in doing this. (1) production gains the benefit of low-priced inputs which can reflect in lower selling prices, giving the final products a competitive price edge, or alternatively the lower cost can be seen as an opportunity to gain higher profits particularly where a sufficiently large part of the market is already assured. (2) when raw-material prices rise the organisation may be able to dispose of its surplus stocks at a profit, thus experiencing a gain just by holding the stocks.

- Third, is entering into short- or long-term contracts for the purchase of materials to be part of the purchasing policy, or is it to be the policy to go to the market as and when materials are actually required? When prices generally are rising, or when supplies are difficult or uncertain, such a practice has its attractions. On the other hand, being committed to one supplier at fixed prices may inhibit more adventurous buying and may also turn out to be detrimental if prices fall unexpectedly or supplies from the contractor fail for one reason or another.

- Fourth – and this applies especially to the service sectors – if the choice is made not to retain expertise and information access, will it still be available when it is required? Scarce and specific expertise may well be in high demand as well as short supply, and if one organisation fails to snap it up, or put it on some form of retainer, it may get taken on by someone else.

These are the key questions that have to be asked when formulating buying and purchasing policy. The mix, approach and priority of each will vary between sectors, though the principles remain largely the same.

20.4　Objectives of effective purchasing

The objectives of effective purchasing can be set out in the seven rights which may be expressed as follows.

The right goods, expertise, information and components, at the right price, in the right quantity, of the right quality, at the right time, delivered to the right place, on the right terms.

This is a simple framework, and critical to the success of all purchasing and supply activities.

20.5　Centralised purchasing

- Where the operations of the undertaking are on a large scale and relatively uniform centralised purchasing has much to commend it. It should result in a consistent buying policy, which means fewer problems for both buyer and supplier because fewer queries arise that need special attention. Large single orders resulting in bulk buying result in more power in the hands of the purchaser to influence suppliers in regard to prices and terms in favour of the buyer. Suppliers are also inclined to give better and more favoured attention to those organisations placing large orders because a large customer is a valuable customer the loss of whose business may be a serious matter. The purchasing department itself can develop specialist buyers who can concentrate on different parts of the market and so build up greater expertise than if they were required to spread their activities over many different purchasing needs. Finally, buying procedures can be made uniform with consequent convenience in administration and greater control of expenditure and over stocking.

- There are, of course, some disadvantages to centralised purchasing. This especially concerns loss of flexibility. Where a large enterprise is spread geographically over a wide area, or where there are many diverse activities carried on centralised purchasing can become a rigid operation and special individual requirements have to be refused on account of this. This may result in certain activities of the enterprise having to substitute slightly less effective materials or components for those which would be ideal. Thus in reinforced concrete component manufacture, for example, a steel of slightly greater or less diameter may be supplied by the purchasing department than that ideally specified because to buy an unusual size would cause greater expense or be inconvenient administratively. This in turn may necessitate an alteration to the specification of the concrete mix to accommodate the size of steel actually supplied, and in consequence become both expensive and damaging to the work in hand.

- Where centralised purchasing is practised it is common to find that user departments have practically no control over the procurement of their requirements. Where particular suppliers are specified this is often ignored by the buyer for reasons of convenience, being contracted to particular suppliers or because of cost. Therefore the user departments can take no responsibility in connection with the purchase of their requirements other than informing the buying department of their needs.

- Often centralised purchasing procedures become unwieldy and bureaucratic. This is unavoidable in a large organisation but it does lead to delays in authorising and placing orders. This can be to the detriment of the user department concerned.

- Departmental buying avoids the disadvantages of centralised buying in that it gives individual users control over their material and component inputs and brings grater operational experience to bear on their selection and acquisition. Orders are placed more quickly and followed up more effectively. There is less bureaucracy and thus less paperwork. Against these advantages must be set the disadvantages of a probable increase in material and component costs, the inability to bargain from the strength of large orders and the possibility of a greater opportunity for fraud.

20.6 Stock control

- The question of whether stocks of materials and components should be the responsibility of the purchasing function has no universal answer. Some undertakings have such stocks under the control of production on the basis that the physical availability of these items is part of the manufacturing function. Others assert that as the purchasing department is responsible for procurement then it is this department's responsibility to control and account for stocks. There is yet another school of thought that believes storage and stock control should be a department separate from either, particularly as the financial value of stocks held may be considerable.

- These three points of view are really relevant only where operations are conducted on one site or on a very small number of nearby sites, and appertain principally in the manufacturing field. Other industries and activities, such as building and construction, where operations are carried out on sites far removed from central administration, have the question answered for them. Every building and civil engineering site, for example, must of necessity have materials and components at hand under the direct control of the site manager.
- The main objectives of stockholding and stock control are to ensure an adequate flow of materials and components required for the organisation's operations, to keep minimum stocks commensurate with operational requirements, to ensure the good physical condition and safety of the stocks held and to reduce to the utmost the possibilities of fraud and theft. The procedures required to carry out these objectives will vary according to the types of stores held, their physical disposition and the rates of usage.
- The main objectives of stockholding and stock control in service sectors are to ensure an adequate flow of information, and an adequate volume of each aspect of the given service, to ensure that the total can be delivered when and where it is required. Much of this stockholding and stock control is therefore concerned with maintaining access to existing databases, and ensuring access to new databases when these become available. As with industrial components, it is also essential to take the steps necessary to reduce to the utmost the possibilities of fraud and theft. Procedures are therefore required to ensure that these objectives are met, in the same way as with the control and storage of physical components and raw materials.

QUESTIONS

1 What are the main objectives of efficient purchasing? To what extent is it desirable or necessary that the purchasing activity should be carried out by a separate department? (CIM)
2 With which other managers and on what facets of business would the Purchasing Manager normally be involved and why? (IComA)
3 The scope of activities of the Purchasing Department may vary from company to company, but there are a number of common activities which are essential. Describe these vital activities. (CIM)
4 What might be the objectives of a Purchasing Department? (CIM)
5 What are the main factors on which the purchasing manager of a manufacturing company would base their decision, in awarding business to one of several competing suppliers of production materials? (CIM)
6 The purchasing function may be organised in various ways. It may also be a separate department or part of another department (e.g. accounts or production). Discuss with reference to the purchasing functions of centralisation or decentralisation. (IAM)

7 P Ltd is a company producing a number of different products and services from five sites which are located quite near to each other. At each site several departments are involved in creating the products and services of that site. All the equipment used, the materials and components for production as well as general purpose supplies, are bought for the whole company by a central purchasing department. The company's performance is below target. This is partly due to sales being lost because of long delivery dates and delayed deliveries, and partly due to quality problems. The operating departments blame these problems on the failure of up-to-date and suitable supplies of good quality to reach them according to the agreed plans. You are required to

(a) describe what the objectives of a purchasing function might be;

(b) recommend how the purchasing of the materials and components could be reorganised to improve the situation described above. (CIMA)

■ ⛿ **21** Research and development

Because of continually increasing technological knowledge, ever-greater competitiveness, and enhancements in product and service delivery, all organisations have to produce new and improved products and services if they are to remain effective, successful and profitable.

- Manufacturers who rely on their existing range of products, however successful, will eventually find that they have been overtaken by others who have exploited new methods, new materials and improved designs. In the service industries, organisations cannot stand still, and institutions such as banks and building societies now provide facilities such as electronic cashpoints for the withdrawal of money outside opening hours, and they have also had to enlarge and enhance their range of products and services, and their attention to customer satisfaction in order to remain competitive. Research and development is therefore required by all organisations to a greater or lesser extent.
- Organisational attitudes to research and development are a function of corporate direction, planning and strategy. These are concerned with the further development of existing markets, and the exploitation of new markets, improving existing products and services, and developing new products and services. Alongside this, there is the corporate approach to research and development, reflected in the nature and level of investment that is made available.

21.1   Research

Research can be divided into three basic areas – pure or fundamental research, applied research, and derived research, though in practice there is normally some overlap.

(a) Pure research
This is concerned, essentially, with furthering basic knowledge and is principally exploratory. It is not pursued with any idea of exploitation or specific practical application and seeks only to add to the fund of human knowledge. That is not to say that out of pure research nothing of practical or commercial value ever flows. In fact the origins of new materials, methods and applications that eventually become common place can be traced in

almost all cases back to such research. What is true is that researchers engaged in fundamental research have no aims in the direction of exploitation. This being the case, nearly all pure research is carried out by government agencies and universities where no financial return is expected from the necessary investment. Industry, however, does not make some contribution. Many of the very large industrial concerns do carry on some pure research in their laboratories while others make contributions by way of donations to universities.

(b) Applied research

It is in the area of applied research that industry is heavily involved. This research is concerned with investigating and solving an identified problem or project with a view to ultimate commercial exploitation. There is little scope for pure exploration in this type of research and interesting lines of investigation must not be pursued unless some positive outcome can be made apparent. It is, in fact, problem orientated, the problems arising through the need for improved products, entirely new ones, or simply the necessity to keep ahead of the competition. A good example of this is that of the electronic pocket calculator where all the successful manufacturers have found it necessary to carry out continuous research to make their product even smaller, lighter and with ever more functions. Those who fall behind in this effort just lose their markets.

(c) Derived research

Derived research occurs where, as the result of some activity being undertaken, further research becomes necessary. For example, when the viability of the Channel Tunnel was being researched, this, in turn, made it necessary to research the viability and operational potential of the equipment that would be needed to actually dig the tunnel. The invention of high-quality calculator technology led companies to look for other applications for this and they found that cheap and accurate wrist watches could be produced. This last example led to the collapse of the Swiss watch industry; and as a consequence, companies in that field had to undertake their own derived research as the result of the loss of their existing market, to see where else, and how else, their products could be sold.

21.2 Development

Research throws up the basic elements of a new material or product, or an improvement to an existing one: development is the process of translating these basic findings into practical application.

- Very often development is a long and expensive business and there is a temptation for a manufacturer to launch a new product before development is absolutely complete in order to be first in the field, particularly if it is known or suspected that a competitor is also engaged in a similar project. This action is understandable when it is realised just how much time and financial investment may have been expended on the project. However, the benefits of what is really a premature launch can be easily outweighed by loss of customer confidence if the product fails to live up to expectations.

- The amount of development and necessary testing required of a new product will depend entirely upon what kind of product it is, its cost and how it affects the health and safety of the user. Thus pharmaceutical companies, in developing new drugs, may engage in testing for many years in order to be satisfied with the safety and effectiveness of new products. A new motor-car may also take years to develop because of the considerable pressures on the manufacturer in regard to safety, economy and the minimising of pollution, in addition to taking account of what the customer demands and what the competition has to offer.

- Once a new product has been marketed other manufacturers will follow suit with as little delay as possible and a sort of 'leap-frogging' then takes place as minor improvements are developed and added as time goes on. This is well illustrated by the motor-car industry where the first really effective small car, the Austin-Morris Mini, set a new trend in car design. Most of the other major manufacturers followed suit with equivalent but better equipped models, and all added small refinements from time to time, each vying with the other to develop a car to beat the competition and be more attractive to the motoring public.

21.3 Design

Design is the ultimate stage in the development of a a new product before it enters the production phase, while in an existing one it is a continuous process to effect improvements

- The dividing-line as to where development stops and design begins is a very thin one, and in some organisations both terms are used interchangeably. Design is, in fact, recognised nowadays as a skill in its own right and can be studied separately. What it attempts to do is to translate the project as developed into a product acceptable to the market, and it does this by being concerned with the function of the product and with its appearance. In some cases function is the more important and in others appearance. An example of this can again be taken from the automotive industry. Owing to London's special road conditions, for the London taxicab function is the overriding importance and appearance second. However, a sports car must give the appearance of being very fast and aggressive even if performance does not match its looks.

- Much research has gone into design in recent years, especially in regard to functional products such as machines. For example, human physiological and anatomical characteristics are taken account of in regard to sizes, shapes and placing of controls. Industrial and office seating is ergonomically designed and the colour and material qualities of office furniture carefully selected on scientific principles. In some industries such as food and cosmetics the appearance of the actual products is important and colour in particular allies design with marketing (strawberry jam that was not rich red and had no pips would be unlikely to sell well, neither would margarine that was its natural white instead of butter color). In many cases packaging is even more important. An enormous amount of design skill is engaged in designing packages for cosmetics to create an attractive and enticing image, to the extent that in some instances the package costs more than its contents.

- Just as good design can enhance a product both in performance and in attractiveness so poor design can damage a product's chances of success, and many a sound and effective product has failed in the market-place simply because its design was clumsy, unattractive or old-fashioned. It is often said that a book should not be judged by its cover; but it often is!

- While it is true to some extent that a designer can work on many diverse products, an instance being the designing of a modern camera by the designers of a famous sports car, nevertheless it is essential that a designer be well acquainted with the properties of the materials involved and the ultimate use to which the product will be put.

21.4   Innovation

The introduction of new products is a necessary element in the continued existence of an organization in the manufacturing and allied industries. In fact it is sometimes stated that innovation is the only way to survival, but this must be taken as an exaggeration. Nevertheless, very often unless new and adventurous thinking is applied to the products of an enterprise it will begin to run down and eventually fail.

- To some extent the type of industry determines whether and how much innovation is necessary. For example, the building industry is extremely resistant to innovation and the many projects put forward from time to time to increase the speed of construction or to reduce costs in house-building have failed lamentably. Only those innovations that have followed traditional patterns have superseded the old ways. An example of this is the use of plaster board for ceilings instead of traditional plastering and this is probably because plaster is still the basic material of plaster board, and this innovation was probably encouraged by the scarcity and high cost of skilled plasterers. Blocks of flats and offices and industrial buildings have seen more innovations, but many of these have been only reluctantly accepted by building contractors on the grounds of speed and cost.

- On the other hand, if the photographic industry is examined it will be found that that innovation is the order of the day both in regard to design and to materials. The development of integral exposure measurement, automatic exposure, electronic operation, the use of advanced plastics for camera bodies instead of metal, and many other innovations have changed cameras almost out of recognition over the last two decades, and there seems to be no end to new developments and fresh design ideas. Any camera manufacturer who fails to keep pace with the innovations now going on will soon find failure ahead. In other spheres such as manufactured or processed foodstuffs innovation is necessary to maintain the required share of the market essential to ensure continued profitability. A prime example here is breakfast cereals where new, or apparently new, products are continually being offered to whet the appetite and to keep abreast of the competition. In fact the word 'new' is an overworked description used in connection with the promotion of very many household items in the struggle for increased sales.

- Innovation is also shown in the packaging of goods. New ways are found to present products so that they are more attractive or easier to use. A garden insecticide, for example, may be marketed in an ordinary bottle from which the liquid has to be transferred to a spray gun of some kind for use. The innovation of the aerosol can now enable this same insecticide to be presented in a container which allows of its immediate use without the bother of transfer to a spray. Innovations in packaging can be very important in promotion sales.

- The repackaging of existing products and services is also important. If successful, this provides a useful extension to the product life-cycle (see Chapter 18) and may have the effect of completely rejuvenating a product. Re-presentation may also work in the same way: for example, the Skoda car previously used to be thought as cheap; now, following the takeover of the Skoda company by Volkswagen, the cars have been successfully re-presented as 'good value'.

- Re-branding is also used in various circumstances to ensure product and service effectiveness. For example, when Sony wished to bring out a cheaper range of electrical goods, the company decided that, rather than market them under the Sony name, they would seek another, and so the brand 'Aiwa' was born. British Airways created their own 'good value' company which they called 'Go' – rather than risking perceptions of loss of quality on the part of those who continued to travel under the British Airways name. Other companies have different brand names for the same product in different countries – for example, the British 'Twix' chocolate bar is known as 'Raider' in France.

- Product and service enhancements also take place under the heading of innovation. For example, when lending money to house purchasers, some building societies and banks now arrange the legal process as part of the service. Some cars need servicing much less frequently than in the past because of enhanced quality and engineering performance. Many supermarkets now offer fresh bread, cakes and pastries in addition to pre-baked and pre-packaged items.

- Many products now have 'service extensions'. This includes cars and electrical goods with extended warranties; and an extending of guarantees at retail, food and hardware superstores. Many companies in the building industry now tender successfully for work on the basis that they will clear and landscape the sites as well as building the actual facility.

21.5   Financing research and development

So far as allocating financial resources to research and development is concerned, there can be no hard and fast rules. Organisations will take their own individual view on this. The prevailing approach is to look upon it as something between a fixed cost and an investment; and this has to be seen in the context that what goes on in one organisation may easily be overtaken by events in another. Any organisation that engages in research and development must therefore be prepared for some of the activity to come to nothing – a classic example of this is Sony's Betamax video system which the company spent extensive resources in developing, only to have it supplanted by the universal VHS system. The company took the view that there were valuable lessons to be learned from this, and that they had advanced the fund of their own general technical knowledge and expertise; and something along these lines is a necessary attitude when considering the financial of research and development.

The provision of finance for these activities is therefore one of great importance, and also one of considerable risk, and this is the context in which the following points have to be seen.

(a) How much can the organisation reasonably afford in this area? How much does the organisation wish to afford in this area? This is a matter for policy decision.

(b) Provisional estimates may be made, and subject to modification through review processes.

(c) The stages in the life cycles of current products and services may be examined so that the mix of product in terms of youth, vitality, currency, age and obsolescence may be established.

(d) A part of this consideration will include assessing the extent and nature of research and development being carried out by competitors and other players in the sector.

(e) Sources of outside expertise in the field may also be sought, such as that available at universities, sponsoring businesses, and relevant government departments.

● This all has to be seen in the context that the outcome of research and development work is rarely predictable and that there is unlikely to be a direct correlation between expenditure and results. However, unless all avenues are explored, which is a key function of research and development, the extent or otherwise of their practicability will not be discovered.

21.6   Other problems of research and development

The other problems that management have to consider in connection with research and development are as follows.

(a) Research staff, highly intelligent and mostly very dedicated, normally work primarily because of their interest in the work. It is often, consequently, very difficult to get them to recognise the importance and value of rules, restrictions and financial constraints.

(b) Because of the intensity of their interest in a particular project, researchers often take a very different view of financial and economic viability to those not directly concerned.

21.7 Value analysis and value engineering

Value analyses are techniques used to endeavour to reduce manufacturing and service delivery costs and charges without impairing the quality or use of the product, or availability of the service. As such, they belong very much within the realms of research, development and design, although many of these areas are now questioned by functional managers as a part of their day-to-day resource management activities.

- Value analyses are carried out by experts in research and development, purchasing, production, design and marketing. Every aspect, component, activity and material used is subject to scrutiny, and improvements sought where possible. In this way, alternatives of design material, expected life and finish may be assessed to establish where more effective or less costly materials, techniques and processes can be applied. The greatly extended use of plastics in many areas as replacements for other materials is a case in point. Many doors and windows are now made out of plastic, giving them a greatly enhanced lifespan with much lower maintenance requirements. Many lawnmowers for domestic use have plastic casings and grass boxes: not only are these easier and cheaper to product but they are free from rust. Fixtures and fittings in motor-cars are now made out of plastic rather than metal, which also means lower costs without loss of effectiveness.
- The same approach can also be taken to service delivery. This involves attention to procedures, reporting relationships, as well as to the databases, technology and equipment being used. Again, however, the purpose remains the same – improvements in the delivery of the service required, reductions in the time that this takes, and simplification (and therefore effectiveness) of procedures.
- This approach is being adopted as a key managerial task over many sectors. The view is taken that everything is capable of improvement; and that this improvement is a function of a combination of technological advance and human invention. It enables costs to be driven down, and quality, durability and value to be driven up. It is now to be found widely in all managerial functions under the headings of 'continuous innovation', 'continuous development' and, even in some cases, as part of 'organisation development'.

21.8   Product and service standardisation

Whether or not organisations use value analyses, some examination and revision of the nature and design of products and services from time to time is necessary. Some of this will be carried out on the basis of the organisation's own knowledge of what can be achieved; some of it will be carried out as the result of customer demands.

- The purpose of standardisation systems is to reduce the unneccesary diffrences in parts and components going into completed manufactured units; and the use of existing sources of information for as great a variety of purposes as possible.
- This philosophy is now common and has been extended to the standardisation of parts between products and product ranges. Thus, car handles tend to be common on most of the vehicles produced by one car manufacturer, and variation is limited usually only by the differences in price range.
- Standardisation also applies in industry overall. Thus it would be inconceivable for domestic light bulbs of any make not to fit the normal lampholder, or for any compact disc not to be playable on a normal CD-player. In fact where standardisation is not achieved in this sort of situation very often the industry concerned finds some difficulty in exploiting its products to the full. A good example of this occurred in the video recorder industry. Recording systems were developed by three different companies, none compatible with the others. The result was that potential customers, except real enthusiasts, were inhibited from buying while waiting to see which system would become standard. It is interesting to note that universal standardisation does not always result in the adoption of the best system. In the video example, for instance, there is strong opinion among experts that the now accepted VHS system is inferior to the two it superseded.
- It is, of course, very largely a matter for the design team, a part of research and development, to ensure standardisation whether it be within components or within completed products.

21.9   Product simplification

'Simplification' may be taken to mean making a product simpler and less complicated.

- Simplification of a particular product is often the result of value analysis, though it may come about without such an exercise. Generally speaking, however, the term is normally associated with a reduction in the variety of the products manufactured and is sometimes referred to as 'rationalisation'. It may apply to the products themselves or to the ways in which they are offered. Thus a paint manufacturer may restrict the number of packing sizes of the paint produced or may reduce the number of colours. Both of these decisions will result in simplication. In the first case if the existing packing sizes are 0.5 litre, 1 litre, 2 litres, 2.5 litres and 5 litres the manufacturer may feel that the 0.5-litre and the 2-litre tins are superfluous. The elimination of these saves in costs and stockholding space, but in regard to the smallest size may inconvenience customers. In the second case the existing range, of, say, 100 colours may be rationalised to 50. Again this will result in lower manufacturing and stockholding costs, and the inconvenience to the customer may be minimal since mixing of colours is possible to provide intermediate tints.

- It is not only manufacturers, however, who find simplification effective in saving costs and increasing efficiency. Retailers, especially in times of recession, rationalise their stocks by reducing the variety held. Food producers reduce the number of different varieties of fruit and other produce that they cultivate. Travel agencies restrict the number of holidays that they have on offer. Banks and buildings societies restrict the variety of mortgage offers that they will make to potential customers.

- It should be apparent from the content of this Chapter that research and development overlaps with a great many other organisational activities. Nowadays, most managers are expected to take active responsibility for genral developments in the efficiency and the effectiveness with which their departments, divisions and functions operate.

Research, development, improvement and innovation are all critical to future organisational success, in whatever sphere that organisation operates. It is therefore essential that all organisations make resources available for these purposes. Where the financial burden is creating in-house research, development and innovation functions and activities is considered too great, alternatives have to be sought. No organisation can operate in isolation from improvements and advances.

QUESTIONS

1 Describe the key problems associated with assessing the benefits from research and development activities, and exercising financial control over the resources employed. (ACCA)
2 What is 'value engineering' or 'value analysis'? Indicate the importance of this technique for a manufacturing concern. (ACCA)
3 Explain where the responsibility for 'innovation' within the organisation might be. Suggest how the performance of innovators could be measured. (IAM)
4 How can the expense of innovation be justified when a company is struggling to survive? (CIM)
5 (a) What is meant by the terms 'standardisation' and 'simplification', in relation to products and their components?
   (b) What implications would a greater emphasis on standardisation have for the marketing department of a company manufacturing fast-moving consumer durables? (CIM)
6 Where do you see R and D (research and development) activities fitting into long-term and short-term planning and control in a company manufacturing

consumer products? How would you implement accountability in these activities? (CIMA)

7 Many companies regard a flow of a new and successful products as essential to their continued prosperity, and spend large sums on Research and Development and design. What are the main factors to be borne in mind in the design of a new product? (CIM)

8 It is frequently complained that Research Departments develop new products without early consultation with other departments of the business. Explain, with reasons, the departments which should normally be involved? (IComA)

■ ⊻ **22** Finance

Success, survival or failure of all organisations sooner or later rests on their financial viability. Financial management, and the influence of the finance function, is therefore all-pervading. Whoever exercises financial control of an organisation therefore bears considerable responsibility and influence. The subject of finance and accounting is specialised and highly technical, and detailed study is outside the scope of any book devoted to basic general management. However, anyone who studies management needs to understand the scope of finance and accounting, and also to understand what is meant by financial management (as distinct from finance and accounting).

22.1   The scope of the finance function

The primary occupation of the financial function is to ensure that adequate funds are available for such capital expenditure as new plant and equipment and for working capital to meet revenue expenses such as wages and salaries, materials and all the inevitable administration expenses.

The need for capital expenditure will be ascertained from the long-range plans of the organisation which will have set out the objectives and targets to be achieved and the strategies and tactics required for success. It is the responsibility of the finance function to prepare regular capital budgets to ensure that funds are available for such expenditure and to advise on suitable sources of funds if these cannot be generated from within the concern. Similarly, the finance function is very concerned with a continuing flow of working capital to meet the revenue and running expenses of the organisation, and so must prepare cash-flow forecasts and cash budgets to ensure the availability of liquid funds for working capital purposes. Both capital and cash budgets must be subject to budgetary control. Budgets and budgetary control were discussed in Chapter 12 and need not be elaborated on here.

22.2   Sources of funds

The acquisition of funds resolves itself into three main categories: long-term funds which are to be applied to capital projects such as new buildings, plant and machinery; medium-term funds for smaller capital items; and short-term funds needed for use as working capital for expenditure on materials, labour and day-to-day expenses. While in practice some overlap is inevitable (current labour and materials, for example, being used to construct a capital project) separate consideration of the three is easier to present and understand.

(a) Long-term finance

This is the finance that is used to underwrite the permanence and stability of the organisation. In the private sector, long-term finance is raised through the sale of shares, and the realisation of profits from commercial activities. In the public sector, long-term finance is normally provided through taxation; in recent years, this has been topped up through charges made by public bodies for particular services (e.g. eye tests, public libraries, dental charges).

Other forms of long-term finance are also available, though these require repayment at some future time. These are as follows.

1 **Debentures.** These are really redeemable long-term loans at fixed interest and secured on the assets of the company. Debenture-holders secure certain rights over the borrower which in some cases involve the right to sell off assets to secure repayment in the event of the failure to meet interest payments when due.

2 **Ordinary loans.** These may be at fixed or variable rates of interest and are repayable at a specific date. They are normally secured either on some asset or assets, or on a personal guarantee of someone of substance. Such loans do not as a rule attract such severe rights to the lender as do debentures.

3 **Mortgages.** These are the same as ordinary loans, but are secured on property which can be realised in case of default.

4 **Sale and lease back.** This form of finance involves the borrower selling fixed assets such as buildings and then leasing them back from the purchaser for use. In effect it is the realising of a capital asset for funds and the regular expenditure of current revenue to pay for leasing.

In considering 1–3 above it must not be forgotten that the interest payments and other charges on this loan capital will be a continuing charge on the borrowing organisation until such time as the loan is paid off, and whether profits are earned or not. The proportion of loan (or fixed charge) capital to equity capital is known as gearing or leverage. A company with a high proportion of loan capital is high geared and, of course, it is low geared if the reverse obtains.

When trade in the company's industry is buoyant and high profits are earned this usually means that after the prior charges for loan capital are satisfied there remains a high proportion of the profits available for dividends to the equity shareholders in the case of high geared companies. However, in times of recession the payment of charges on loan capital may absorb all the available profits leaving none for ordinary shareholders. Where no profits are earned the lenders have to be paid out of reserves. It follows, therefore, that in severe cases the burden of interest charges can be fatal to the organisation.

(b) Medium-term finance

This is usually interpreted as finance over three to ten years and generally involves funds for small capital projects or the development of new products or markets, where the return on the investment is expected to began within two or three years. It is also used to finance the working capital requirements of a planned programme of growth. It is not considered suitable for the funding of normal working capital requirements. Funds are available as follows:

1 **Hire-purchase** from various finance houses. Hire-purchase relates to specific plant or equipment which is named in the contract. A common hire-purchase contract is that for a fleet of lorries, for example.

2 **Medium-term loans** from merchant banks, finance houses or commercial banks. Commercial banks tend to be less generous in the period of their loans than the other sources.

(c) Short-term finance

This is generally finance required for current working capital, to pay wages, current creditors and the like, when self-generated funds are short. In some industries revenue is cyclical although current expenditure continues all the year. An extreme example is that of arable farming where income is received perhaps only twice a year but farm workers have to be paid each week throughout the year. Sources of short-term finance are:

1 **Bank overdraft:** This is usually the simplest and cheapest external source of short-term funds, especially if the requirement is only very temporary. Short-term bank loans can be negotiated, and are sometimes insisted on by the bank, instead of taking an overdraft. However, two aspects of this course must be mentioned: (a) the time limit for a loan is finite and will need to be re-negotiated at the end of the term; and (b) the sum represented by an overdraft varies with the intake and expenditure of funds, so that the average sum borrowed in this way is less than the total negotiated, so saving interest.

2 **Extended credit:** Special payment terms can sometimes be negotiated with suppliers to extend credit thus conserving liquid funds. Careful timing of purchase can also help to improve cash flow.

3 **Credit factoring and invoice discounting:** These related methods of obtaining short-term finance involve selling book debts to special finance houses who specialise in this practice.

4 **Bills of exchange:** In certain industries such as export and import trading bills of exchange can be negotiated and discounted to provide funds in advance of the actual due date of settlement.

The sources of funds describe are the main external ones available to an enterprise and it is within the skill and experience of the chief finance officer to guide the organisation to the use of the most suitable one in the circumstances obtaining when the necessity arises. However, a prudent finance department should examine all forms of self-generated finance before going elsewhere, as such funds are cheaper and subject to fewer constraints than those from external sources.

(d) Self-generated finance

Funds generated within the organisation itself can be categorised as follows:

1 **Retained profits.** A prudent policy of retaining a proportion of the profits within the organisation instead of distributing them entirely as dividend or other earnings to owners can build up funds for working capital or short-term capital projects. These retained profits can be invested for a return until they are needed.

2 **Profitable use of funds.** The amount of stocks held, assets under-employed and unprofitable lines or ventures should all be examined to see how these can be reduced to free funds for more profitable use.

3 **Credit policy.** Clear and definite terms of credit should be agreed with customers and these terms should be strictly but diplomatically enforced. Debtors who delay payment are using their supplier's capital for their own purposes, usually free of charge. In fact it is an unfortunate common practice that large undertakings such as supermarkets delay paying their less powerful suppliers well beyond the due date, so providing themselves with what are in effect substantial interest-free loans, to the detriment of the financial health of their creditors. On the other hand the most advantageous terms should be negotiated with creditors and full advantage taken of them. There should be a rigorous credit control policy pursued to minimise bad debts. It is worthwhile to note that experience shows that the incidence of bad debts is lower where accounts are rendered to customers promptly than where there is a time lag between the order being fulfilled and the account being rendered.

4 **Surplus funds.** Surplus funds should always be put to profitable temporary use if they are not immediately required for the organisation's own operations. The earnings so derived are a useful addition to funds, and here the expertise of the finance officer will be invaluable.

22.3 Working capital

Working capital is the financial lifeblood of an enterprise and insufficient working capital is a frequent cause of failure. Maintenance of an adequate flow of working capital is, therefore, a first duty of the finance function to ensure funds for continued operation.

- The definition usually applied to working capital is that it is the excess of current assets over current liabilities. In other words it is the total of assets, liquid or easily made liquid such as cash, trade debtors, finished stocks of raw materials and semi-finished goods, over liabilities that have to be met at short notice or in the normal course of business (certainly within one year) such as trade creditors, rent, rates and similar commitments. Insufficient working capital may indicate over-trading and can result in the demise of the organisation. When profits and surplus cash have been turned into fixed assets in pursuit of expansion the result can be a lack of ready funds to meet immediate liabilities, technically a state of insolvency. The same conditions can arise by being too lenient with debtors or by over-stocking, and by incurring debts with suppliers or the bank which cannot be matched by incoming current revenue.

- The need to forecast the amount of working capital to be devoted to new projects is particularly important, and this should be provided for when cash budgets are being worked out. Failure to make adequate provision restricts the amount of research and development that can be financed and thus is detrimental to the continued success of the enterprise. Very often the development of a new product requires the design and development of special tools, jigs and ancillary equipment and the necessary expenditure on these aspects of a new project must be accepted as a charge on working capital rather than as a charge against capital expenditure. There are two reasons for this. The first is that the control of revenue expenditure is more easily delegated to a department than capital expenditure and second, that development costs usually arise piecemeal as their needs becomes apparent, and repeated applications for capital sums is an inconvenience administratively.

- Any estimates and budgets for working capital must taken into account two important factors: the current and probable future rates of interest; and the probable trends in inflation. Both of these factors are beyond the control of the finance function, but must be included in the calculations of future working capital needs. Inflation erodes the buying value of working capital and this reduction in purchasing power must be countered as far as possible by an adequate product pricing policy, the establishment of cost-reducing practices throughout the organisation, a strict control on credit and the wise investment of surplus funds. Borrowing, also, must be strictly regulated, especially in times of high interest rates.

22.4   Cost and profit centres

(a) Cost centres

While the finance function has overall responsibility for the financial activities of an organisation, it can enhance its understanding of expenditure through assessing the costs incurred in each activity; and in some cases, reinforce its control of expenditure by placing the responsibility for cost control where the costs are actually incurred.

- This is the basis of the concept of cost centres. In practice, this means that activities are designated as cost centres and the managers and supervisors responsible for operating these activities are required to account for, and justify, the costs incurred in these operations.

- The greatest contribution that the cost centre approach makes to the financially effective well-being of an organisation, is to understand where the variable and marginal cost expenditure is occurring. Once a procedure is established, variable and marginal expenditure can be monitored on a continuous basis; and assessments made at any point chosen.

- It is also becoming commonplace for organisations to look at the following as a variation on the cost centre approach;
  1 costs per square metre;
  2 costs per member of staff;
  3 costs per location;
  4 costs per activity;
  5 primary function costs as a proportion of support function costs; and so on. Whichever approach is taken, the information is only of value if it is used as an aid to management decision-making rather than as the driving force behind the organisation.

(b) Profit centres

Profit centres view the financial aspect of operations from the viewpoint of income and profit, rather than expenditure and cost.

- Within the organisation, sections are designated as profit centres. In some cases, agreed targets are established for each profit centre and it is the responsibility of the manager appointed to endeavour to ensure that the targets are achieved. Some profit centres tend to be much larger than cost centres, often complete divisions, and are largely free to operate independently within the broad framework of policy and guidelines laid down for them by the organisation as a whole. Decision-making and managerial responsibility are squarely on the shoulder of divisional managers whose objective is to try to produce the agreed profit target.
- Again, this should be the subject of constant monitoring and evaluation. The target profit approach to profit centres always fails when the target is either easily met, or else impossible to meet. Both these sets of circumstances may occur as the result of factors outside the manager's control.
- Again, a variation on the profit centre approach is to be found in terms of:
  1 income per square metre;
  2 income per member of staff;
  3 income per location;
  4 income per division;
  5 income per activity;
  6 income per product/product cluster/service/service cluster; and so on.

(c) Cost apportionment

Some organisations still favour apportioning fixed costs to different activities. As a management tool, the approach is largely discredited; though it is essential in the production of accurate accounts. When considering profit and cost centres, and if this approach is favoured, it is much better to keep fixed costs well away. To do otherwise causes feelings and perceptions of resentment and unfairness.

- Moreover, the supposition that a cost or profit centre manager is entirely in control of the centre's activities can be questioned. Many of the aspects of the operations are not within the manager's own discretion. Some examples are the existence of corporate plans within which it is necessary to work, restrictions on the scope of products and services as inputs to costs or output for revenue, the span of the market within which a profit centre may be allowed to work, and the effect of other cost and profit centres upon any particular one; for example, the obligation to take the output of an associated centre rather than to be able to go into the open market for supplies.

(d) Investment centres

Before leaving this topic of centres for financial control, a mention must be made of investment centres. These are essentially the same as profit centres but with a particular difference. The performance of a profit centre is gauged by its achievement of a target of profit and this target will be different for each profit centre. Investment centres, however, have return on capital employed (ROCE, see 22.5 below) as a measure of performance and this will normally be the same, as a percentage, for all investment centres.

22.5   Return on capital employed (ROCE)

The return on capital employed is an accepted measurement of the performance of an organisation. The term 'capital' is open to a number of different interpretations, i.e. proprietors' capital, which means the actual investment of the owners or shareholders; total capital, which means the whole of the resources of the concern including bank overdraft, monies owing to trade creditors and other very short-term liabilities; and net capital employed, which comprises owners' capital (share capital), reserves, debentures, and other long-term borrowings. Unfortunately there is no absolute agreement on the items to be included in net capital employed, an example being bank overdraft, which some accountants include and some do not. However, for all practical purposes the items as given are adequate provided there is consistency in the inclusions when comparisons are being made.

- The return on capital employed is expressed as a percentage on the net capital employed and is frequently referred to as 'ROCE'. It measures the performance of an organisation by the return earned on capital resources employed and in so doing affords comparisons with other organisations carrying on the same types of operations and also affords comparisons with other types of investment.
- The latter measurement is important where a company is contemplating going to the market for capital: investors will take ROCE very much into consideration when deciding where to place their funds. Consequently if a share issue is contemplated the ROCE will be one of the factors that will determine the price at which they can be offered. In general the ruling rates of interest will have a marked effect on share prices because investors will not put up risk capital for a return much less than they can obtain from safe interest-bearing investments. If the ROCE is low share prices must also be low, so that

the actual earnings per share reflect a percentage somewhere in keeping with the prevailing rates in the market.

22.6 Financial ratios

Much of the monitoring of the financial performance of an enterprise is done by means of ratios. These ratios are important in that they quantify financial and operational strengths and weaknesses so that appropriate action can be taken promptly where necessary. The variety of these ratios is large and a detailed study of all of them belongs in a specifically accounting text. However, mention must be made of the most important.

(a) Return on capital employed ratio

ROCE has already been explained in 22.5 above. The formula employed to show the result as a percentage is

$$\frac{\text{Profits}}{\text{Capital employed}} \times 100 = \text{ROCE\%}$$

(b) Working capital ratio

The importance of working capital has been dealt with in 22.3 above. The ratio employed here is how many times current liabilities are covered by current assets, expressed as follows:

$$\frac{\text{Current assets}}{\text{Current liabilities}} = \text{Working capital ratio}$$

The very minimum ratio is accepted as 1:1, in other words the current liabilities can just be paid out of current assets. As some assets, such as stock or work in progress may take longer to convert into cash than the creditors will allow, a ratio of 2:1 or more is considered to be desirable, with 2:1 as normal.

(c) Acid test ratio

Also termed the 'liquidity ratio', this measures the vulnerability of organisation – especially small organisations – to pressure by creditors and others for immediate payment of liabilities. The ratio takes into account only current assets that can be turned into cash immediately (sometimes referred to as 'quick assets') and so ignore stock and work in progress, which may take time to realise. The formula is:

$$\left. \begin{array}{c} \dfrac{\text{Cash} + \text{Debtors} + \text{Readily realisable securities}}{\text{Current liabilities}} \\[2ex] \textbf{or} \\[2ex] \dfrac{\text{Current assets}}{\text{Current liabilities}} \end{array} \right\} = \text{Acid test ratio}$$

Ideally the minimum ratio should be 1:1. This means that all liabilities can be met in full immediately. Although in many spheres of activity less than this can be considered acceptable, nevertheless in the event of failure of some debtors, for example, the organisation would be extremely vulnerable in the case of pressure by creditors. Conversely, if the ratio is much more than 1:1 the wisdom of holding what amounts to surplus funds could be questioned, as these could possibly be profitably used elsewhere.

(d) Earnings per share

This is particularly important to an organisation contemplating seeking additional outside capital. It expresses the earnings made on each share in monetary terms, the formula being:

$$\frac{\text{Total earnings after tax (£)}}{\text{Number of shares}} = \text{Earnings per share(£)}$$

Intending investors can compare this figure with the market price of the shares and obtain the price/earnings (P/E) ratio. This provides a coefficient of return that can be compared with other investments.

(e) Price/earnings ratio

While an existing shareholder can obtain a personal P/E ratio, the normal use for this ratio is against current market prices for shares, to enable investors to make comparisons between different investments. The formula is:

$$\frac{\text{Market price of share}}{\text{Current year's earnings per share}} = \text{P/E ratio}$$

It will be seen that this ratio actually states how many years at present earnings will be required to retrieve the capital outlay required to retrieve the capital outlay required to purchase a share at a particular price. There is no accepted norm for the P/E ratio, but it is assumed that the higher the ratio the greater the potential of the enterprise and thus the more attractive the investment for those looking to the future. Where this expectation fails a share becomes expensive.

The ratios already presented indicate primarily the financial health of the organisation and its potential in the market for new capital. Other ratios are also used to measure performance, the most common of which are:

(f) Gross profit to sales (GP)

This provides a measure of gross profit expressed as a percentage of sales, as follows:

$$\frac{\text{Gross profit}}{\text{Net sales}} \times 100 = \text{GP\%}$$

This makes period-by-period comparisons easy and provides a simple monitor of trading performance before the application of administration costs.

(g) Net profit to sales (NP)

Again this is a useful measure of performance and a period-to-period monitor of net profit; that is, gross profit *less* costs of administration. The ratio is expressed as a percentage of net sales, as follows:

$$\frac{\text{Net profit}}{\text{Net sales}} \times 100 = \text{NP\%}$$

Comparison of GP% to NP% also indicates how much of the trading profit is being absorbed by the costs of administration.

(h) Administration expenses to sales (AE)

This provides an indicator by percentage of how much sales revenue is absorbed by administration, and shows whether administration is too costly. It also gives a period-by-period comparison of the proportion of revenue so absorbed, thus providing a picture of the trend in this direction. The formula is:

$$\frac{\text{Administration expenses}}{\text{Net sales}} \times 100 = \text{AE\%}$$

(i) Selling expenses to sales (SE)

Finally, this ratio gives information about the percentage of sales revenue absorbed by the costs of actual selling, an important element in profitability. The formula is as simple as the previous three:

$$\frac{\text{Selling expenses}}{\text{Net sales}} \times 100 = \text{SE\%}$$

When using ratios, it is important to bear in mind the context in which they are being considered. For example, while ideally the working capital ratio requires that current liabilities can be paid out of current assets, in practice, large organisations simply take out bank overdrafts and short-term loans to realise this should they have to. In the same way, the acid test is of much greater concern to small organisations than to large companies. Each individual case has to be considered on is merits, therefore; there are no hard and fast managerial rules in the application of ratios.

It is above all essential that managers do not let accounting ratios become the driving force for the prioritisation of their functional and operational activities. From a management point of view, financial ratios – and indeed all aspects of finance and accounting – are simply further aids to the quality of their judgement, evaluation and decision-making.

22.7 Management accounting

Management accounting is a branch of the finance function dealing with internal resource management and is a professional activity in its own right. It purpose is to assist management in the formulation of policies and objectives and in the operation of the enterprise by presenting accounting information in a fashion easily usable by management.

- Management accounting grew out of cost accounting, which provided detailed information in regard to costs of manufacture, administration and other activities. The attitudes that costing engendered, that of inquiry and analysis, became harnessed to the need by management for accounting information beyond that provided by the purely financial records, and presented in a manner more in tune with management needs than that adopted by the financial accountant. It could be said that the emphasis of conventional accounting is on financial records, prevention of fraud, concern for financial statements of revenues and the like; while management accounting concerns itself with costs, the interpretation of accounting records, the isolation of variables and controls.
- The range of activities of the management accountant is very wide and overlaps some of the areas of financial accounting. Briefly, the principal areas of management accounting are:

(a) Budgetary control

This is fully discussed in Chapter 12.

(b) Standard costing

This is a method of control of manufacturing costs in which the production of a unit has a standard cost worked out for it based on previous experience or estimates. Actual costs during production are ascertained and these are compared with the standard costs. Variances are examined to establish the causes for discrepancies. This exercise is termed 'variance analysis' and is not unlike budgetary control procedures.

(c) Absorption costing

This method of costing is designed to ensure that all costs are allocated to and absorbed by the final product. Direct charges such as labour and materials present no problems, but it is also necessary to apportion all indirect costs such as factory rent, machine maintenances, administration costs and so on so that all are absorbed. This must be done on an equitable basis, often in relation to machine time, floor area or other measure.

(d) Marginal costing

This method recognises that there is a fixed cost for a manufactured unit which must be met before variable costs and profits can be satisfied. It follows, therefore, that the cost to manufacture one extra item after the fixed costs have been met is the amount of variable cost entailed in its production. This additional variable cost is the marginal cost. Marginal costing is a complete system of cost accounting which is commonly used; it includes the concept known as 'contribution', which is simply the amount by which sales revenue exceeds variable costs and thus contributes to fixed costs and profits.

Whichever the approach adopted, it is important to note the differences in requirements between accountants and managers. From an accountant's point of view for example, absorption costing is likely to be the favoured approach when calculating profits and losses; while from a manager's point of view, the marginal costing of the contribution approach is the most certain to find favour. It is essential that this diversity is fully understood. Failure to do so normally means that the one imposes its will on the other (or vice versa) and this leads to confusion in the overall direction of the organisation.

22.8   The finance function in the public sector

Overtly, the problems of financial management in the public sector are not dissimilar to those arising elsewhere. However, the public sector does suffer from various legal and political constraints.

- The need to increase public service expenditure, and therefore to put up taxes and charges, is likely to be at variance with the demands from the public at large for reductions in taxes and charges.
- Many publicly owned industries, including those in the defence and air traffic control sectors, that trade and thus come within the category of profit making concerns are normally required to finance capital expenditure through raising costs and charges to the consumer.
- Newly privatised industries that continue to make a loss – especially the railways – continue to require government subsidies.
- In public sector services, income is relatively fixed and expenditure targets are established by central government, both for their own and for local government services.
- Revenues raised on such things as the sale of council houses, income from leisure centres and sports centres, municipal theatres, and so on, are also often restricted by statute or directive on what they may be used for, especially if what is envisaged is not directly related to the source from which the income was derived.

Consequently, the finance function is more concerned with the management of expenditure and the control of costs rather than raising revenue. Financial management in the public sector is therefore very often concerned with reconciling ever-greater demands for increased expenditure on the one hand, with ever-greater pressures to reduce expenditure on the other.

22.9   Finance in the not-for-profit sector

Responsibility for the financial management, viability and well-being of not-for-profit and voluntary sector organisations is normally vested, either with a board of trustees or a management board. Their duties are as follows:

- To guarantee the application of funds in accordance with the objectives of the particular body.

- To ensure that monies raised from donors and the public at large are used in accordance with the objectives and remit of the organisation.
- To ensure that projects, activities and initiatives can be fully supported financially.
- In the same way as other organisations, to produce annual accounts as required.

Both the accounting functions, and also the financial management of the particular organisations, are carried out in the same ways as elsewhere. However, because of the nature of the particular organisations in this sector, there are very specific duties and constraints under which these activities have to be carried out.

QUESTIONS

1 Define the term 'working capital'. What are the major considerations that an organisation should bear in mind when calculating the amount of working capital needed to finance an additional product? (IAM)

2 Outline the implications for working capital management of periods of high inflation. (IAM)

3 Discuss the merits and demerits of using the profit centre and the cost centre: (a) as ways of measuring managerial performance, and (b) as aids to planning and control at all levels. You should relate your answer to an organisational situation of which you have some knowledge. (CIMA)

4 In a certain industrial company 'return on capital employed' (ROCE) is used. The company is organised into three distinct operating divisions treated as separate investment centres and assessed on the basis of ROCE. There has been criticism expressed by the divisional management teams about this measure of performance and, in particular, about what they feel is the rigidity in long-term plans of specifying this particular objective precisely and with the implication that each division should attempt to meet the same target.
   Express your views about the use of ROCE as the key financial objective in these circumstances and in this manner. (CIMA)

5 Write a brief explanatory note in relation to any three of the following financial terms:
   Absorption costing   Contribution
   Marginal costing   Break-even analysis (CIM)

6 Explain the purposes and application of any six of the commonly used financial ratios relating to the operation of a business. (CIM)

7 'Ratio analysis is a much used tool for appraising financial performance.' Discuss why ratio analysis is so commonly used, supporting your answer with reference to actual ratios. (IAM)

8 In what ways may extra financial resources be made available to an existing company without resorting to a share issue?

▓ ☑ **23** Human resource management

The personnel function – or human resource management, as it is now more or less universally known – grew out of increased attention to the human side of enterprise. Moreover, individual and collective employment rights are now protected, to a greater or lesser extent, by statute; and the European Union is determined to legislate further in this area. Most large organisations in all sectors therefore have specialist personnel or human resource management functions to deal with these matters. Smaller organisations either ensure that one of their staff is capable of handling them, or else by using the services of experts when these are required.

The scope of the personnel function is vast and varied. However, all organisations, whatever their size and nature of activities, will be involved in most of these activities at some stage or other.

23.1   **Recruitment**

- Recruitment of staff, at all levels, is normally carried out through a combination of the personnel function with the department where the new recruit or recruits are required. The reason for this is that there are absolute standards required which are the remit of the personnel function; and operational standards required which the particular department will know about much better. The areas with which the personnel function must concern itself are:

  (a) equality of treatment and opportunity;
  (b) lack of discrimination on the grounds of race, gender, disability or trade union membership;
  (c) evenness of application in the interview process; and also in the application of any tests or examinations necessary;
  (d) the production of a person specification against which the required qualities and attributes can be drawn up so that the functional department gets someone with the capabilities that it requires.

- The sources of recruitment to which the personnel department will address itself include:

  (a) Present staff, particularly where the vacancy is at supervisory or middle-management level and there is a policy of internal promotion.
  (b) Local schools, where beginners are needed.

(c) Universities and colleges of higher and further education, where potential management material and special aptitudes are required.

(d) Local employment agencies, both government and private. Many private employment bureaux are specialist agencies dealing with one or two types of profession or skill only, such as those for accountants, heavy vehicle drivers and so on.

(e) The professional bodies, many of whom maintain registers of members and student members for this purpose.

(f) Advertisements in the press both at national and at local level. Such advertisements will include particulars of the vacancy generally as set out in the job specification shown in 23.2 below.

(g) Advertisements in specialist journals, particularly trade journals and the journals of the professional bodies.

(h) Specialist agencies, often called 'head-hunters', who have a much greater expertise and knowledge when it comes to finding specialist, high-quality or high-calibre staff.

(i) Naming, where a known individual is required to come and take up the appointment; this is a precursor to seeking permission to approach the particular individual.

- The best organisations underwrite this with a recruitment policy which states: the balance and mix of recruitment activities; the extent to which persons are to be recruited from within the organisation, and when the organisation will seek elsewhere; and opportunities for training and development for individuals once they are on the organisation's payroll.
- It is also essential that organisations monitor and review their recruitment activities in exactly the same way as everything else. Recruiting wrong, bad or inappropriate members of staff is extremely disruptive, and it is also very expensive.

23.2 Selection

The key to productive and effective staff lies in proper selection. This, in turn, relies on a full understanding of what a job requires, and this is embodied in: a job or work specification, a job or work description, and a person specification. These sets out the requirements of the vacancy on the one hand, and the personal and professional qualities and expertise required of the individual on the other. Two standard approaches to this are the 'five point plan' and the 'seven point plan'. The 'five point plan' is as follows.

(a) **Physical requirement** These include such attributes as age, minimum height, eyesight, manual dexterity and so on.

(b) **Intelligence** This includes mental attributes such as thinking critically, an analytical attitude, discrimination and an inquiring mind.

(c) **Aptitudes** Everyone has natural leanings towards certain activities. Some jobs call for mechanical or manual aptitudes, while others require more academic aptitudes, perhaps towards mathematics or art.

(d) Attainments These can be divided into educational and training achievements, evidenced by technical or professional qualifications, and practical achievements obtained through experience.

(e) Personality and temperament These are easy to specify but difficult to judge in an applicant. Some jobs call for a bright and enthusing personality (some sales jobs, for example) while others demand a more placid approach. Honesty, resourcefulness, tenacity, enthusiasm and the qualities for potential leadership all come under this heading.

- The 'Seven-Point Plan' is, in effect, an extension of the 'Five-Point Plan':

(a) Physical attributes These include bearing, speech and appearance; and also demeanour and manner. Some indications of attitudes and motivation may also be inferred – though these should be tested for if important.

(b) Attainments These include education, professional and technical qualifications; trade and expert attainments; and other training and development.

(c) General intelligence This has to be inferred from the applicant's way of answering questions. If specific measures of intelligence are required, these have to be tested for.

(d) Special aptitudes these may again be inferred. If precise answers are required – for example on manual dexterity, public speaking – then again they must be tested for.

(e) Interests This concerns the range, nature and extent of other interests that the applicant has. It may be used to infer attitudes and motivation.

(f) Disposition This is concerned directly with attitudes, values, commitment and enthusiasm.

(g) Circumstances This is concerned with placing the job applicant in the context of career progress and development.

- By taking this approach (or an equivalent), the skills, qualities and expertise of every applicant can be plotted and compared. Applicants may then be required to complete application forms, or to send a curriculum vitae, so that information relative to the job, work and person specifications can be elicited. The forms are then scrutinised and a short-list for interview is drawn up.
- Interviewing is a skilled task and may be carried out by one interviewer, or by a combination of personnel and the department involved, or by a panel. In all cases, equality and fairness of treatment must abound. Questions asked of one interviewee must always be asked of others.
- In addition to interview, some organisations make prospective employees undergo a variety of personality, skill, dexterity, and aptitude tests, and tests of potential. Again, whatever is used, they must be designed to bring out qualities suitable and relevant for the work, and must be evenly applied.

- For key staff, an increasing number of organisations are now resorting to 'assessment centres' – and they use these both for internal promotions and external appointments. An assessment centre is a combination of structured interviews and tests carried out over a period of a half to two days. While this is very expensive on the face of it, organisations are increasingly taking the view that it is better to find out as much as possible about a candidate before they are appointed to a post for which they are entirely unsuitable.
- Many organisations are also coming round to the view that the presence of positive attitudes and commitment is of importance at least as great as expertise and experience. Many organisations would much rather have people of an excellent quality who wish to work for them, rather than superstars who do not.

23.3 Induction

- It is important for a new employee to be acquainted with the organisation, its policies, practices and general objectives as well as where the new entrant's job fits into the organisation and its importance to the department concerned and the undertaking as a whole. This aspect of induction is calculated to generate a personal interest in the organisation, an enthusiasm for the job and a general sense of loyalty: in other words it seeks to promote morale and identity.
- A second aspect of induction concerns the more personal and specific aspects of a newcomer's employment, such as names and status of the senior members of the organisation, the recruit's immediate supervisors and managers; and what authority they enjoy. Such matters as working procedures, the terms of the contract of employment, remuneration and promotion policy, welfare and recreational facilities will probably have been discussed at the interview and will almost certainly appear in the staff handbook. However, these matters should be reiterated in the induction programme.
- Where employees are recruited several at a time – for example, at school-leaving time – it is possible to arrange induction on a group basis. This facilitates the presentation of films on the organisation, its history and future, and also enables senior members of staff to give lectures or talks on more domestic matters such as safety regulations, personnel policy, security and so on. Where one recruit at a time is engaged a senior or semi-senior member of staff should be assigned to the newcomer to provide guidance and information about the undertaking. The more general aspects of the concern which are best presented by films and lectures or talks can then be dealt with in a much fuller context.
- Induction – or re-induction – is also essential when an employee is given a new post within their existing organisation; and when the organisation is subject to takeover, merger or other change of status. People need to know as quickly as possible where they stand in the new function, or under the new organisation ownership or direction.

23.4 Training

(a) The need for training

It is usual to consider training under the following headings.

1 Personal training: following chosen preferences.
2 Professional training: required as the result of being in a particular occupation.
3 Organisational job training: required as the result of being in a particular organisation.

To maintain personal and professional satisfaction, organisation training policies and programmes have to pay attention to all three.

- All organisations therefore need stated training policies and resources committed to staff, individual, departmental, divisional and organisational development. This is absolutely essential – the introduction of new technology requires training; improvements in service also require training; new medical techniques requiring training; new production technology requires training also. The best organisations commit themselves to training and development anyway. For all organisations, training and development are not optional, though many leave it too late!
- Training programmes at organisational, departmental, staff and individual levels must be based on:
  1 assessment and identification of the areas of need;
  2 planned and structured programmes meeting individual, professional, occupational, technical, technological and organisational needs;
  3 monitoring the effectiveness of the training activities;
  4 review and evaluation of the success, or otherwise, of the activities.
- Some organisations make the acceptance of a position with them conditional upon agreement to enter a training programme. This is becoming very much more prevalent as organisations have to engage in both their own development, and that of their staff, in order to survive in their particular sector.

(b) Types of training

Types of training can broadly be categorised as follows.

1 Craft training: entering into an apprenticeship or other period of preoccupational training resulting in gaining a qualification enabling the individual to practise a recognised skilled trade or craft.
2 Operative training: for less skilled workers and for those trades where no formal apprenticeship scheme exists. Much operative training is carried out 'on-the-job'.
3 Day release or block release: where the individual is given time off work to develop particular aspects of their job requirements, or to further their education.
4 Professional training: covering both technical and commercial training, and normally means qualifying by professional or national examinations. Some of the areas involved are mechanical engineering, accountancy, statistics, computer sciences and management.

5 University degrees: it is becoming increasingly commonplace for under-graduates to seek industrial and commercial sponsorship for the duration of their studies. Many postgraduate courses are now taught on day release and block release bases.

6 Skill and aptitude training: normally consisting of releasing the individual for a period of study or experience to build up a particular quality or expertise.

7 Project work and secondments: whereby the individual is given the opportunity to work elsewhere, or on a particular initiative, to develop their expertise in some area.

8 Continuous professional development: increasingly required by those wishing to continue in professional and technical areas. Professions – e.g. nursing, medicine, the law – are required to do this because they have a statutory duty to keep abreast of developments in their profession. Many other bodies now also require it – including the Institute of Personnel and Development, the Institute of Civil Engineering – as a condition of continued membership of that institution.

23.5 Work and staff planning

This used to be called manpower planning. It is based upon the twin principles of 'fitting the work to the people' and 'fitting the people to the work'. This has to be carried out in the context of the amount of work to be carried out; the variety, diversity and complexity of activities; and plans and projections for the future concerning possible increases and decreases in the composition and nature of the labour force required.

- In previous times, it was possible to plan much more accurately the numbers of people required, divided into categories of jobs and skills required. This is no longer possible. Skills, aptitudes and expertise requirements change so quickly that a fundamental shift of approach and emphasis has been necessary.

- Staffing and work-force planning is now, therefore, driven by such considerations as: flexible working; part-time and seasonal working; multi-skilling; and positive attitudes concerning the willingness to be trained and retrained. Staffing planning in organisations is increasingly concerned with 'core and peripheral' working arrangements, sub-contracting, and the use of agencies.

- As stated above (**23.2**) organisations are now increasingly concerned with the attitudes of those who come to work for them, provided that they have the skills and capabilities. For it is true to say that while unemployment levels remain extremely high, there are nevertheless skills and expertise shortages in many areas. Organisations competing for staff with such expertise need to be certain that the people who come to work for them do so because they want to, and not just purely because of the volume of money on offer.

- It remains possible to plan with more certainty for retirement, labour turnover, wastage rates from recruitment programmes, and the numbers required to enter into staff training programmes. It is not possible to plan for succession, promotion, or steady-state career paths with any certainty. And for each of these areas, organisations are having to broaden their field of intake from school and college leavers to include people from all age ranges and sectors of society. This is because of the reduction in birth rates, changes in expectations on the part of school- and college-leavers, and the availability of persons coming back into the work-force, either as the result of having taken part in retraining and further education, or when returning to work after bringing up children.

23.6   Remuneration

Effective systems of payment and reward must meet a variety of purposes and considerations. They must reward productive effort, expertise and output in whatever terms that are measured. They must provide an adequate level of income on a regular basis for those receiving it. They must motivate, encourage and provide incentive. They must meet the expectations of those carrying out the work. They must be fair and honest to all concerned.

- Rewards based on targets must be achievable. Rewards based on quality of performance must be measurable in some way. The criteria for specific payment systems such as commission, bonuses or merit increments should clearly be understood by all concerned. As long as objectives and targets are met, payment must be made.
- For some occupations, this is very straightforward. The sales executive working to a commission based on sales volume or income from sales has a clear ready-reckoner against which to work.
- For others, this is not so clear. Performance-related pay schemes for office, administrative, clerical, executive and professional staff have often fallen short of expectations because the criteria against which performance was to be measured were never made clear or fully understood by those concerned. In these cases, the scheme actually demotivates those affected and falls into disrepute and discredit.
- Five elements of pay and reward schemes can be isolated as follows.
  1 Payment: annual, quarterly, monthly, four-weekly, weekly, daily; commission, bonus, increments, fees; profit, performance and merit-related payments.
  2 Allowances: attendance, disturbance, shift, weekend, unsocial hours, training and development, location and relocation, absence from home.
  3 Benefits: loans (e.g. for season tickets), pension (contributory or non-contributory), subsidies (on company products, canteens, travel), car, telephone/car phone, private health care, training and development, luncheon vouchers.
  4 Chains of gold or super-benefits: school holidays (teachers), cheap loans (banks), free/cheap travel (railway, shipping, airlines), pension arrangements (for older or longer serving staff).
  5 Economic rent: high rates of pay for particular expertise (especially scarce expertise or that which is required at short notice).

The mixes of each adopted by organisations in the devising and implementation of reward strategies for different staff categories cover a variety of aims and purposes in response to particular situations. It is very difficult for organisations to be totally fair to all their staff at all times, and those responsible for devising and implementing pay and reward schemes must take steps to ensure that fairness is achieved as far as possible.

23.7 Job evaluation

The overall purpose of job and work evaluation is to assess and evaluate the nature of the work to be done in a particular job; the key tasks to be carried out; and the balance, difficulty, value, frequency, importance and contribution of these; the subordinate tasks to be carried out; and the marginal or infrequent tasks also measured against the same criteria.

- Skills, qualities, capabilities and attributes are matched up and a market value placed on them, with particular weightings as necessary or desirable. Some organisations also include desired attitudes in their job evaluation schemes.
- Jobs are then placed in a ranking order for the organisation. They are matched up against grades, job titles, salary scales and any other relevant factors. In large or complex organisations, these may be clustered according to staff, budget or capital responsibilities; spans of control; key results or objectives; flexibility, progress and innovation; and so on.
- Public and multinational organisations spend a lot of time and resources on job evaluation and many have permanent job evaluation panels and committees.
- The main organisational criteria essential to the success of any scheme of job evaluation concern fairness and equity of treatment for all staff, grades and occupations. Criteria must be clearly publicised and pre-set so that everybody involved understands them. The job evaluation process should be acceptable to all; the opportunity for representation and appeal should always be afforded. Job evaluation processes should operate as quickly as possible. Above all, there should be a process for resolving anomalies and differences as quickly as possible.

23.8 Health and safety at work

Managers and supervisors are directly responsible for all matters concerning health and safety within their own departments. There also exists a corporate responsibility for ensuring that overall a healthy and safe working environment is provided.

- At the staff induction stage, training and attitude formation in health and safety must be integrated. Emergency procedures must be taught. The importance of the use and wearing of any safety and protective clothing, and procedures that may be necessary in the work must also be taught.

- Safe behaviour patterns must also be devised. These support the required attitudes and give effect to the procedures. Above all, they ensure that any potential hazard in any part of the manager's or supervisor's domain is dealt with by whoever happens to be nearest to it.
- Reporting of accidents is a legal requirement in the UK and also elsewhere in the European Union. The purpose of doing this, from the manager's point of view, must be to provide information about work areas where accidents are occurring. These can then be assessed and analysed and remedial steps taken.
- In any department, there must be emphasis on prevention rather than cure. This ensures that actual levels of accidents are kept to a minimum.
- In Britain, this is underpinned, above all, by the Health and Safety at Work Act 1974. This is called 'enabling' legislation – and this means that, rather than setting precise legal standards to which all organisations have to conform, organisations must set their own standards, and be prepared to justify these and defend them if necessary. The European Union also continues to legislate in the area of health and safety.

23.9 Staff welfare

The best organisations have always paid close attention to the continued welfare and well-being of their staff. This is increasingly becoming a legal, as well as a social and moral, responsibility.

- The work environment must be organised in such a way as to be as healthy and safe as possible. This obligation also includes attention to:
  1 temperature levels: proper training and clothing must be provided for those who have to work in extreme heat or cold;
  2 lighting: which must be adequate to work without strains on the eyesight of the workforce;
  3 ventilation: of all work premises;
  4 sanitary accommodation: for all, including separate conveniences for each gender and for the disabled; and related provision of washing and drinking water facilities;
  5 specific attention: to any organisational or operational factors, such as the potential for repetitive strain injuries, or eyesight damage, caused through extensive work at particular workstations;
  6 access to medical facilities: as and when required. Larger organisations often have their own doctor or nurse; speedy access is required for medical treatment for all staff when necessary.
- Many organisations take a still broader view of this obligation. Of special current concern are organisational policies on smoking, alcohol, drugs and HIV. Some organisations ban smoking on their premises altogether; others forbid their staff from drinking alcohol during their lunch hour. Whatever the

case, organisations should make clear the stance to be adopted on each, giving a clear lead to both managers and staff. Whatever the outcome, it should reflect organisational requirements, and be capable of support and justification. When necessary, levels of support for staff through programmes and periods of treatment will be directed at both treating the matter in hand, and also rehabilitating staff, getting them back into productive and effective work.

23.10　Staff promotion

Promotion used to be regarded as one of the most effective ways to encourage positive staff motivation; and it remains true that many people do look forward to eventual promotion with the accompanying increased earnings and higher status. However, this has increasingly to be seen in the following context.

1　Excellence of past performance does not guarantee excellence of present or future performance.
2　Technical excellence does not equate with managerial excellence. Especially where people are promoted 'from the ranks' to a supervisory or managerial position, this should always be underpinned by extensive training.
3　Promotion beyond the level of competence, known as the 'Peter Principle', has now come to be widely recognised.
4　Many people put in for promotions because of the higher earnings and status, and then become largely removed from the job that they were doing. For example, school teachers who gain promotion to head teacher have no teaching at all; nurses who reach management positions do no nursing; many sales managers do no selling.
5　Management is being seen increasingly as a trade or occupation – or indeed profession – in its own right, rather than something to be gained through promotion.
6　Because of the great changes in organisations, it is impossible to offer any certainty of promotion or succession to aspiring employees.

- Many organisations therefore offer flexibility and variety, and professional and technological opportunities, in place of management and promotion development activities. The best of these also enhance employee earnings so that they are not penalised financially.
- There is an increasing realisation that those who are good at a particular trade or profession should be kept in it, rather than being promoted away from it.
- Any movement from one occupation to another, especially movement from professional or technical occupations into management, must be underpinned by adequate and extensive training programmes.

23.11　Staff turnover

This comprises staff leaving voluntarily or being asked to do so because of some failing in their work or behaviour. A high staff turnover is costly in terms of efficiency and because of the expense of recruiting and training new staff. Nevertheless some staff turnover is healthy for an organisation because it prevents stagnation of ideas which fresh staff can introduce. However, the rate of turnover must not be excessive.

Among the reasons for staff severances can be:

1 Inadequate supervision.
2 Supervision seen by staff to be unreasonable.
3 Poor promotion prospects, lack of variety or opportunity.
4 Poor working conditions or inequitable pay.
5 Inadequate training which leads to lack of confidence.
6 Poor selection on recruitment.
7 Unsafe working conditions.
8 Inequitable distribution of work.
9 Boredom through lack of variety in job content or insufficient volume of work.
10 Business fluctuations.
11 Inappropriate management and supervision style.
12 Uncertainty of confidence in the future of the organisation.
13 Personality and professional clashes.
14 Bullying, victimisation and harassment.

The formula commonly used to measure labour turnover is:

$$\frac{\text{Number of departures}}{\text{Total workforce}} \times 100 = \text{Labour turnover \%}$$

This formula can be calculated for the organisation as a whole; or for its different departments, divisions and functions.

If labour turnover appears to be excessive, it is important for the reason to be investigated. This then becomes a basis either for remedial action, or for recognising that some categories of staff can only be retained for a certain period of time before they inevitably move on. Many organisations now conduct exit interviews, which are designed to ascertain the reasons why people leave.

23.12   Staff discipline

All organisations need to have rules of behaviour for staff which must be accepted by all, particularly in the areas of punctuality and absence, and also in terms of quality of output and performance. Codes of discipline have to be drawn up and written into staff service contracts. All organisations are required by law to have a written code of staff discipline; where one does not exist, standards established by the Advisory, Conciliation and Arbitration Service (ACAS) are deemed to exist. New recruits must be made aware of the code and the requirement for them to comply, and this is a key part of induction.

When it becomes necessary to discipline staff for any reason, the disciplinary code must always be followed. Failure to do this invalidates the disciplinary procedure, and no action may be taken against the individual. When subject to organisation discipline, individuals are always entitled to be accompanied by a work colleague or trade union representative; they are entitled to face any accuser and to state their case; and they are entitled to appeal against the outcome of the investigation.

The surest way to achieve and maintain good staff discipline is to devise a management style that ensures high work-force and organisational morale.

23.13   Staff dismissal

Dismissal occurs where an employer terminates the services of an employee for some reason. Dismissal may be:

(a) **Fair:** in which the employee is dismissed for some reason sustainable and supportable, and procedures and statutory obligations have been followed.

(b) **Unfair:** where either the employee was dismissed for no good reason; or where the employee was dismissed for an alleged good reason, but where procedures and contractual obligations were not fulfilled.

(c) **Wrongful:** where a fundamental breach of the employment contract on the part of the employer has occurred.

- All organisations maintain the sanction of dismissal as the final solution to a disciplinary problem. If this point is reached as the result of minor misdemeanours or lapses in performance, the employee must be given both ample time and support, and where necessary training, to remedy their performance before dismissal can be contemplated.
- Summary dismissal or instant dismissal occurs where the employee is discharged on the spot for some serious offence. Activities justifying summary dismissal include:
  1 Wilful misconduct at work.
  2 Proven dishonesty and breaches of the criminal law.
  3 Gross negligence in carrying out duties, including serious breaches of health and safety regulations.
  4 Disreputable acts in private life which may reflect badly on the organisation's reputation or prevent the member of staff carrying out their normal duties.
  5 Acts of gross insubordination.
  6 Threats of, or actual violence, to fellow members of staff.
  7 Bullying, victimisation and harassment.
  8 Unauthorised disclosure of business secrets to third parties.
  9 Persistent absenteeism or lateness.
  10 Any other substantial reason arising as the result of the precise circumstances of the situation.

Even where summary dismissal is contemplated, the individual affected must be given the opportunity to state their case; they are entitled to be represented at any hearing; they are entitled also to appeal against the decision.

The following should also be noted.

- Constructive dismissal occurs where an employer invites a member of staff to resign instead of being discharged, or where the employer makes the employee's continued employment untenable, for instance by requiring him to carry out tasks which he finds objectionable, or changing his work pattern to his significant disadvantage. For a member of staff to prove that constructive dismissal took place – i.e. that it was unfair or wrongful – they have to be able to prove that resignation was the only course of action open to a fair and reasonable person.
- Dismissal is always unfair when discrimination on the grounds of sex/gender, race, disability, marital status, or matters to do with maternity take place. Dismissal is also automatically unfair when an employee refuses to undertake activities that breach health and safety regulations; or when they exercise statutory employment rights.
- In some circumstances, employees may be dismissed under the terms of the 'statutory bar'. For example, a lorry driver who lost his driving licence for some reason would not be able to carry on working as a driver. For dismissal to be fair, however, the employee may be required to prove that no alternative work was available to the individual.
- When an employee is dismissed, or when they come to the end of a fixed-term contract, it is against the law for an employer to place any restriction on where they next go to work.

23.14 Redundancy

Redundancy occurs where a worker's services are no longer required because the need for the particular work has ceased to exist, because of technological changes, reduction in the volume of business or complete cessation of trading by the employer. It also covers the circumstances where an employee, instead of being made redundant, is transferred to another sector of the organisation and displaces another employee who is dismissed in consequence. This second employee is considered to have been made redundant.

In Britain, by virtue of the provision of the Employment Protection (Consolidation) Act 1978 a worker made redundant is entitled to compensation, known as redundancy pay, the minimum scales of which are laid down in this Act.

It should also be noted that unfair selection for redundancy normally constitutes unfair dismissal. By law, redundancies may only take place when all other avenues have been explored – such as short time working, reduced hours, temporary lay-offs, wage reductions, and so on.

23.15 Grievances

All organisations are required to have a procedure for the management of grievances. In all cases, it is usual for the grievance to be taken up initially with the worker's immediate superior. As with disciplinary matters, the member of staff is entitled to be represented by a work colleague or union representative. Where a collective grievance occurs, it is usual for this to be handled by a staff representative or trade union official on behalf of the group of workers involved.

- It is in an organisation's best interests that grievances are dealt with as quickly as possible. Grievances ignored or badly handled lead inevitably to discontent, and this may spread beyond the staff involved, adversely affecting wider morale.
- Minor disputes, grievances and squabbles are almost certain to take place, more or less as a fact of human behaviour! Managers and supervisors need to be aware of these, and also to recognise when these may become more serious.
- Serious grievances – especially allegations of bullying, victimisation and harassment – must always be dealt with as a matter of urgency. It is an organisational responsibility to ensure that these do not take place; and that where they do, the perpetrators are dealt with swiftly and effectively.

23.16   The employment life-cycle

This is the complete record of an employee from recruitment to cessation of employment. These records show the employment history of each worker and include details of training, pay and pay increases, promotions, absences and their causes, job grading and any merit ratings, performance appraisals, reprimands, attitudes and motivation. In this way a picture can be built up of the worker concerned. Hence, a record of his or her career progress and potential are provided so giving a guide to possible future training and educational programmes, which would benefit both the worker and his or her value to the organisation.

The final entry in an employment life-cycle record, will of course, be the date of leaving. This entry should also include the reason for the severance, e.g. retirement, voluntary leaving, dismissal and why, and any other relevant factors. This complete record should be retained for some time against the possibility of requests being made by third parties, such as other employers, for information about the worker. A usual demand is for a reference, and in this regard it should be noted that an employee or ex-employee has no right to demand a reference though it is usual for such a request to be met. Where a reference is given it must be true and accurate in the opinion of the past employer, without any suggestion of prejudice or malice.

It should also be noted, however, that any reference, however glowing, is no indication of future performance, however well the individual may have worked in the past.

23.17   Industrial relations

Industrial relations is concerned with the relationships between organisations, management and staff. It deals with conditions of service, the working environment, wages and salaries, and other terms and conditions of employment. Increasingly also, it deals with the broader issues such as health and safety at work, staff welfare, and hours and patterns of working.

- In Britain, industrial relations is traditionally viewed as being tripartite – a relationship between employers, staff representatives (especially trade unions), and the government. Employers and trade unions represented their own distinctive interest; and government became involved, historically as a large employer, and latterly because of extended legislation in the field of personnel and human resource management practice, and in terms of limiting and defining trade union influence. Too often, the relationship between employers and employees was adversarial, based on mistrust and conflict.
- The European Union recognised – and continues to recognise – the same players in industrial relations. However, the view is taken that this is very much a partnership – it is often called 'a social partnership' – in which the interests of all concerned are best solved by engaging in productive, harmonious and co-operative industrial relations.
- In Britain, the power and influence of the trade union has greatly been weakened in recent years. It is mainly due to the collapse of those industries in which trade unions were traditionally powerful – manufacturing, engineering, and primary industry and processes. Because of uncertainties in the employment market, however, many individuals choose to retain trade union membership as a form of employment protection insurance.
- Historically, the primary concern of industrial relations was collective bargaining. This took place at three levels – national; organisational; and plant (for individual site). Collective bargaining involved the establishment of universal standards for pay, terms and conditions of employment, and working arrangements. In recent years, organisations have sought to vary this approach, either through topping up national agreements (this is known as wages and conditions drift), or through introducing flexibility in working arrangements by agreement with the particular staff involved.
- Historically, organisations used to recognise a multiplicity and diversity of terms and conditions of employment for their different staffs. They also had agreements with trade unions whereby one category of staff would not be allowed to do the work of others (i.e. restrictive practices; restraint of trade; demarcation). The result was that much industrial relations was time-consuming, expensive and divisive. Today, therefore, employers are constantly seeking ways of updating and improving the instruments of their industrial relations as follows.

(a) **Single table bargaining:** whereby each category of staff, and any recognised trade unions, are invited or obliged to accede to a single set of terms and conditions of employment including pay scales.

(b) **Single union agreements:** whereby the employer is prepared to recognise one trade union only for the purposes of universal staff representation.

(c) **The non-union approach:** whereby the staff elect their own representatives, independent of any trade union, to represent their interests.

- The Social Charter of the European Union, to which the British government put its name in September 1997, will ultimately require all organisations to adopt a positive and harmonious approach and attitude to their workforce. The Social Charter is especially concerned with protecting, maintaining and developing individual rights; and drawing up ever-greater protections for those in work from redundancy and dismissal. Ultimately also, most organisations will be required to have work councils, giving employees the same status and importance as shareholders and their representatives.
- At local level, other than pay and conditions, the main industrial relations activity is dealing with disputes and grievances. These are often handled by joint consultative committees composed of representatives from management and staff. All manner of topics may also be raised with such committees, including safety, discipline, welfare and training. They also exists as one of the channels or media of communication; and when they work well, are a positive contributor to harmonious industrial relations.

23.18　Worker participation

The subject of worker participation in the organisation, particularly in the sphere of decision-making, was considered in Chapter 3; in 3.5 the question of actual worker directors was discussed as was joint consultation in 23.17 above. Both involve workers in the actual process of decision-making, though the latter in an advisory capacity only.

However, neither method involves workers financially, but a third proposition does, that of co-ownership. In its purest form it proposes that workers become actual shareholders in their companies, thus participating in the distribution of profits and having the power to vote at annual general meetings. The actual acquisition of shares by the workers poses a problem, especially as they can, if they work for a public company, purchase them through the stock market if they really desire to become co-owners.

- Two solutions have been successfully applied in practice. The first is to offer shares to workers at attractive prices; and the second is to award shares as bonus payments. The opportunity to share in the profits of their company is considered to encourage loyalty and a co-operative attitude in the workers and to provide a positive incentive for greater productivity.
- Although it is assumed that shares will have voting rights, some managements may view this with apprehension and in some cases shares issued to employees have no voting rights so that control remains firmly in the hands of the existing shareholders and management. In such cases it is considered that the fact of profit-sharing is sufficient participation and incentive. American company lost control to its work-force through the issue of shares with voting rights as bonuses, where the numbers of shares subsequently held by workers exceeded those held by the original owners, though in fact its profitability subsequently increased.

23.19 Trade unions

Membership of trade unions is no longer confined to workers in production, but extends to cover office workers, computer staff and even supervisors and managers. This is especially the case in local and central government, public services, transport, and primary and secondary industry. Such unionisation brings some benefits and some disadvantages to the organisation.

- **Advantages**
  (a) Time is saved in pay negotiations when dealing with a union as compared to dealing with individuals. This is particularly relevant in respect of supervisors and managers where it helps to promote equitable schemes of remuneration and to avoid inequalities and possible consequent resentment.
  (b) Where there is mutual respect – that is, where morale is good – employees can more easily be given a picture of the government's problems and thus obtain a better understanding of them through meetings with shop stewards and local union officials. Improved industrial relations should thus result.
  (c) Workers feel the strength of association and thus are able to have, through union representatives, constructive discussions on procedures relating to working practices, disciplinary measures and the like. Where relations are good, dissidents are often contained by the majority.
  (d) Co-operation with trade unions may help an organisation to meet more easily the obligations placed on employers by government regulations and statutes.
  (e) Changes in working practices and necessary redeployment of workers can be more easily effected if implemented with union co-operation. Where redundancies are inevitable union co-operation can be particularly helpful in obtaining fair compensation for those affected.
  (f) Joint consultation is made easier.

- **Disadvantages**
  (a) Managerial decisions may be delayed because of the lengthy discussions necessary at plant and local union level for those decisions to be implemented. Effective joint consultation can help minimise this.
  (b) A powerful union can perpetuate and intensify restrictive practices unnecessarily. An example would be the insistence on a qualified electrician to change the plug on a computer installation. This puts up costs and causes delays which create further costs.
  (c) Where more than one union operates on a site delays and disruptions may be caused by inter-union disputes.
  (d) Unreasonable demands may be made on management if a union is powerful, to the ultimate detriment of the organisation and even the industry.

There is no doubt that trade unions can contribute positively in all areas where they operate, provided their power is used reasonably and with discretion.

QUESTIONS

1 The chief management accountant of a firm is due to retire and a replacement has to be found.
   You are required to
   (a) explain the methods which may be used to recruit a replacement;
   (b) explain the means you would use to select the applicant most suitable for the post. (CIMA)

2 Discuss the policy issues which organisations should consider prior to recruiting personnel. (IAM)

3 You are required to explain the purpose and to describe the process of induction in respect of
   (a) a new employee joining the company;
   (b) a current employee transferred to a well-integrated group within the organisation. (CIMA)

4 What benefits might be expected to be obtained by a firm which makes a continuing investment in staff training? What forms might such training take? (IComA)

5 Discuss the application of manpower planning as a means of providing for managerial succession. (ICSA)

6 Describe the objectives of performance appraisal. How would you carry out the performance appraisal of a subordinate? (ICSA)

7 Describe a system of job evaluation. What are its advantages and disadvantages? (ICSA)

8 (a) Distinguish and, in each case, provide an example of:
      (i) summary dismissal
      (ii) unfair dismissal
      (iii) constructive dismissal.
   (b) Describe the procedure through which employees who consider they have been unjustly dismissed may seek to obtain redress. (IAM)

9 (a) Define 'Redundancy' as you understand it.
   (b) What are the main reasons why the dismissal of an employee may be 'unfair'? (IAM)

10 Outline and comment upon some of the grounds by which a contract of employment may reasonably or legitimately be terminated, or an employee dismissed. (ACCA)

▨ M **24** Management support services

Most large organisations include a management services function which is staffed by specialists in various fields to assist management in many aspects of its activities. Such specialists act in an advisory capacity only and have no executive powers. Usually they are grouped together in one unit whose head reports to the chief executive, or to a senior executive, who in turn is responsible to the chief executive for the activities of the management services staff. In some organisations, on the other hand, the different specialisms remain separate with their own leaders but responsible as before.

It is important that managers at all levels be aware of what services are available and how they can use them. This is part of the remit of all managers to continually seek ways of developing and improving their areas of responsibility.

24.1 Organisation and methods and work study

(a) Organisation and methods (O and M)

Commonly termed simply 'O and M', this is a group of techniques that seek to simplify office work and so to cut costs in this area. It has been said to be the application of common sense to reduce waste and, indeed, most of its operations are concerned with just that, the application of common sense to solve clerical problems. It can deal with the installation of complete new systems and procedures or with what is often called 'work simplification', the making of a particular task or series of tasks simpler or easier.

● Assignments are carried out by investigating what is currently done and questioning why, and though the organisation of the clerical procedures under review is of concern, the methods employed bear the greatest burden of investigation. By careful study the clerical workload is made lighter by reducing paperwork, eliminating redundant activities such as unnecessary manual copying from one document to another, reducing the movement of people and documents by improving office layout and generally cutting down wasteful clerical activities. Effective use of computerisation, including electronic data processing and storage, email, and the Internet, can make a major contribution here.

- Much O and M now involves clerical work study – that is the practice of detailed analysis and timing of tasks and subsequently setting standards of performance. Initially those concerned with office work claimed that it did not lend itself to work study techniques because most procedures were not repetitive enough. However, a very large proportion of the work done by office personnel has, in fact, been found to be suitable for work study techniques.

(b) Work study

Work study seeks to investigate and examine all aspects of works so as to improve efficiency and reduce waste of effort, thereby improving productivity. Work study has two parts, motion study and work measurement.

- Motion study examines in minute detail each aspect of a task with a view to avoiding unnecessary movement and reducing it where it cannot be eliminated. Economy of motion is the aim. This is sometimes achieved by reducing, for example, the extent to which an operator's arm must travel to move a control or manipulate material. In other cases the simultaneous use of both hands to accomplish part of a task instead of the use of one while the other is idle will effect an improvement in the economy of movement. How materials to be used are stacked and where is also a fruitful area for motion study, as is layout generally.
- The second part, work measurement, is self-explanatory. It is the practice of measuring how long the various elements making up a task take, and when these time measurements are added together they form a total time for the complete operation. The purpose is to establish how long a specified job should take a qualified worker to carry out at a given level of performance. There are two categories of work measurement: direct time study, which involves actually timing the job as it is performed, usually by means of a stop watch; and indirect timing. Techniques of indirect time study include synthetic timing, predetermined motion time study and analytical estimating, and they use elements of previous direct time studies and analytical estimates. These techniques are highly sophisticated and can be employed successfully only by experienced work study practitioners. Indirect methods can be used to provide reliable standards for jobs that are proposed but are not actually in operation. Finally, activities can be sampled on a statistically valid and reliable basis, and conclusions drawn.

(c) Implementing O and M and work study

O and M and work study are both put into practice in a similar fashion, which can be set down in seven main steps:

1 Select the job to be investigated.
2 Investigate and record the existing methods.
3 Examine critically the methods in use from the observations and records made.
4 Define and develop improved methods.
5 Establish performance standards for the new methods.
6 Install the new methods.

7 Maintain the new methods, making modifications as found to be necessary.

24.2 Operational research (OR)

Operational research (operations research in the USA), is the use of mathematics and mathematical models to assist management in arriving at management decisions.

- It is important to remember that OR cannot substitute for management, neither can it be a reason for management to abdicate the need for judgement in coming to decisions. What it can do is to present management with alternative solutions to problems and so allow judgement to take place on sound statistical and mathematical grounds rather than on the basis of experience and intuition. OR is useful only where all the elements of a problem can be quantified and expressed mathematically. It has no place in problem-solving involving sociological or psychological elements, and is only as accurate as the data it uses.
- The areas where OR has proved to be of most use are those concerning resource allocation (for example, machine-loading and transport-routeing), stock-control, production planning and scheduling, capital investment decisions and similar problems. It solves these problems through a number of mathematical techniques, among the most used being:

(a) **Linear programming** where comparisons can be made and evaluations formulated between different operations which have a straight line (linear) relationship between the variables within them. For example, lorry *A* may consume one gallon of fuel per mile transporting one ton and lorry *B* may consume two gallons of fuel carrying three tons over the same distance, fuel consumption being directly proportional in both cases to the load carried and the distance travelled. Where there exists such a relationship between methods then this is an area for linear programming.

(b) **Probability theory,** which is concerned with events where chance is, or appears to be, the determining factor in results. In fact in almost all cases the outcome is caused by a combination of a large number of circumstances which make a specific result probable but not absolutely predictable. Probability theory forms the basis of queueing theory, which is important in many areas of operations.

(c) **Queueing theory,** which is a technique applied to solving problems concerning the intervals and frequency of groupings of people or activities requiring attention. Examples are passengers calling at ticket offices, workers attending the stores for materials or tools, aircraft landing at airports and lorries wanting to load at loading bays. Queueing theory can offer solutions in regard to best intervals, costs, provision of facilities and other related problems.

(d) **Network analysis** (or the critical path network) is a technique of determining the critical elements in a sequence of operations so that the total programme can be completed in the least possible time. The method is to analyse the project into a network of activities (hence the term 'network analysis') which are plotted on a diagram. Those steps that are vital to the progress of the project, when connected together, form the critical path and cannot be delayed without detriment to the whole programme. Times for each step are indicated on the network and these, added together through the critical path, indicate the minimum time required for total completion. Other activities shown on the network diagram have less influence. Most networks are lengthy and complicated and are usually run on a computer.

Applications include long-term projects such as construction and civil engineering works, computer installations (from initial concept) and similar operations.

Critical path analysis (CPA) and programme evaluation and review technique (PERT) are the most widely used terms in network analysis. The main distinction between them is that CPA assumes reasonably accurate predictions of activity times whereas PERT accepts that such predictions are unlikely to be accurate and allows for this by taking into account three estimates: the shortest possible timings, normal timings and the worst timings likely to occur. Figure 24.1 shows a simple critical path network.

24.3 Management information systems

A management information system (MIS) can be defined as a formal system to provide all levels of management with all the relevant information they need with which to make appropriate decisions for the total control of an organisation.

- From this definition it will be observed that how the system should operate is not considered; only the fact that it should be formal is important. In other words the primary considerations for the installation of management information system are: who needs the information; what form it should take and what it should contain; whom the information is to go to; and what purposes it is to serve. It is irrelevant how the necessary data is to be processed, but in fact so voluminous is the information flow in a modern organisation that the use of a computer for processing is essential. The establishment of a data base in a computer system is of considerable advantage in connection with a management information system because it provides fast access to all the data and information within an organisation on all aspects of its operations.
- Management information is made available by means of various kinds of reports including statistical reports such as sales analyses, and control information such as budget variance reports. Ideally such information should be processed from data already in the system, but data must be acquired from external sources when necessary, for instance in cases involving market trends, general economic outlook and other external factors which may influence management decisions.
- To be properly effective, management information systems need to produce reports that are clear and accurate. Above all, these reports need to be under-

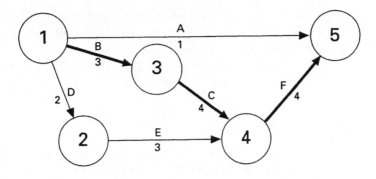

Key: Letters on lines = Activities
Numbers on lines = Times in days
Numbers in circles (nodes) = identification for use by computer only

Figure 24.1 A simple critical path network

standable and usable by the people for whom they are produced. In some cases, consideration must be given to the degree of accuracy, either because this is too costly, or because its attainment may cause unacceptable delay. Reports need to be as up-to-date as possible. Information systems and databases need to be fully flexible so that effective and accurate information can be produced when required. Management information systems are only effective if they serve the needs of the organisation (in the past, many organisations have suffered losses in efficiency and effectiveness because they have restructured themselves around inappropriate information systems. The tests of the effectiveness of management information systems are:

(a) Better management decisions.
(b) More effective utilisation of resources.
(c) Streamlined administration.
(d) Sounder quality of judgement, evaluation and analysis.
(e) Increased capacity in monitoring and evaluation of activities.
(f) More accurate corporate, departmental, divisional and functional planning.

24.4 Consultants

● Consultants are most frequently called in for the following reasons:

(a) To advise on ventures such as the installation of new plant, penetrating new markets or introducing new manufacturing methods.
(b) To restructure the organisation or management pattern, especially in times of rapid growth.
(c) To raise new capital.
(d) To advise on relocation.

(e) To sort out difficulties being experienced in functional areas where internal solutions have not been effective: these include stores control, marketing, profitability, O and M and so on.

(f) To endeavour to save a totally ailing concern. This is usually an act of desperation by the management and often the call comes too late for effective remedies.

- Many consultancy firms also provide specific problem-solving expertise in the following areas.
  (a) Finding specialist staff: this is called head-hunting or executive search.
  (b) Resolving personal and professional disputes: in other words acting as mediators or arbitrators.
  (c) Investigating new markets: and providing detailed market analyses, information and evaluation.
  (d) Dealing with technical and technological problems: for example, geologists are invited in by the oil industry to advise on the potential of new and existing oil fields; geotechnical consultants are called in by the building and civil engineering industry to advise on the strength and composition of particular land forms.
  (e) To make specific calculations.
  (f) To advise on employment practices.
  (g) To advise on specific factors: at present for example, there is a great deal of information required concerning the European Union, and different international markets and activities.

- Expert consultants provide excellent services. Their work and recommendations are based on their own expertise related to precise requirements of the organisation commissioning them. To be fully effective, they require the unqualified support of chief executive and senior management with whose authority they need to operate.

- Having said that, organisations should never be afraid of turning down consultant's recommendations if they are not happy with them, or if the recommendations do not stand up to the organisation's own judgement. Even where consultants have been extremely expensive, a recommendation should only be implemented if the commissioning organisation has full confidence in it.

QUESTIONS

1 How important is it that members of a Management Services Division should work closely with people from functional departments? How may such collaboration be achieved? (ICSA)

2 Explain what is meant by the term 'operational research' and describe a typical problem which might be solved, using this approach. (CIM)

3 (i) What do you understand by the term 'Management Information System'?
  (ii) Which characteristics should be embodied in effective 'Management Information Systems'? (IAM)

4 Describe what you understand by the phrase 'management information system'. In particular you should explain how the effective provision of information can assist management decision-making. (ICSA)

5 (a) Examine the purpose of:
   (i) a Gantt Chart
   and
   (ii) a Network Analysis Chart (Critical Path/Programme Evaluation and Review technique as used in operational planning).
   (b) Describe the circumstances that would be most appropriate to the use of each type of chart. (IAM)

6 'The great advantage of using consultants is that they are able to say things which the internal management could not say.' How far does this justify the use of consultants in business? (ACCA)

■ Ⅴ **25** The manager and change

Everywhere in the world, there is a revolution going on, a transformation of business and of the services needed and wanted by people. Whatever the merits of how activities were ordered and conducted in the past, new ways and methods are constantly being invented and implemented. The key to remaining effective in such an environment is having the quality, expertise and calibre of management available. One management authority, Graham Winch of University College London, indeed defines the priority of management as 'coping with change and uncertainty'.

25.1 Changes

These changes may be summarised as:

1 **Technological:** affecting all social, economic and business activities; rendering many occupations obsolete and creating new ones; and opening up new spheres of activity bringing travel, transport, distribution, telecommunication, industry, goods and services on to a global scale;

2 **Social:** the changing of peoples' lives from the fundamentals of life expectancy and lifestyle choice, to the ability to buy and possess items; to travel; to be educated; to receive ever-increasing standards of health care, personal insurance and information; to be fed; to enjoy increased standards of social security and stability;

3 **Economic and political:** resulting in changes in all government forms; the state of flux of the European Union and the adoption of super-national laws and directives; the creation of the single European currency; the collapse of the Communist Bloc and the USSR; the emergence of Taiwan, South Africa, Korea and Vietnam as spheres of political and economic influence; and the lesson and influences of Japan;

4 **Expectational:** in which the changes may be expressed as from a state of stability to a state of change itself or a state of flux. This includes the change from the expectation of working for one company or organisation; changes in occupation, training and profession; the requirement to constantly train and retrain throughout the working life. People also expect an ever-greater diversity of choice; and an ever-greater increase in the quality of what is on offer;

5 **Organisational:** driven by the changes indicated above, and the need to remain competitive in a global economy. Many organisations change their business (e.g. Virgin from music to air travel) and expect their staff to change with them. Hospitals in the UK are reconstituted as business units offering medical services at a price or charge and expect staff and patients to go along with this (right or wrong). Many nationalised industries and public utilities have been privatised – and this has caused change in organisational direction and strategy as the result. Finally, many organisations now find it necessary to locate their production at different places throughout the world for their own commercial advantage;

6 **Ethical:** in which organisations have ever-greater moral (as well as legal) responsibilities to their staff, customers and clients, to the environment, and to the community at large. There is also a broader dimension to this, for example, some sports goods and clothing retailers have located their production factories in some of the poorest countries of the world, and this has led to charges of exploitation.

Rather than passive acceptance or acquiescence, managers and organisations must assume responsibility for, and direction of, the change process and activities required to make it effective and successful.

25.2 Resistance to change

Resistance to change is a feature of all human behaviour, particularly where alterations to well- or long-established habits or routines are concerned. One of the most difficult aspects of introducing change is to carry all staff along with the change.

People will go along with change if they know, believe or perceive that it is in their interests to do so. It is therefore necessary to identify the barriers to change. These are certain to be raised by staff when they are faced with change, and so managers and supervisors need to be able to tackle them.

25.3 Barriers to change

Barriers to change may be classified as either operational or behavioural.

(a) Operational barriers

These are:

I **Location:** this is a barrier when, for whatever reason, it becomes impossible for the organisation to continue to operate in its current premises. Relocation has consequences for the resettlement of families, retraining and organisation development. Even when the new premises are close by, it may affect access, work and attendance patterns. For greater distances, the consequences of widespread disruption have to be addressed.

2 **Tradition:** this is a problem where there has been a long history of successful, steady-state work in specific, well understood and widely accepted ways. It is an especial problem where a whole community has grown around a particular industry or organisation (e.g. coal mining and pit villages).

3 **Success:** if the organisation is known or believed to be successful in its current ways of doing things then there is a resistance based on 'why change something that works?'

4 **Decline and failure:** this occurs where a given state of affairs has been allowed to persist for some time; and even though there is a general perception that things are wrong, or not as good as they once were, there is still a lack of will to do anything about it.

5 **Technology:** technological change disrupts patterns of activity, and professional and occupational identity. It has led to flexible working and away from traditional job titles, restrictive practices and demarcation. For many people who are to remain in their present job, there is still a necessity to be constantly trained and updated.

6 **Vested interests:** needs for organisational change are resisted by those who make a good living out of the status quo. These even include senior managers.

(b) Behavioural barriers

These are:

1 **Confidence in the future:** this is the most important barrier to be overcome; it creates heavy resistance where people are not properly informed of the proposals, and how these are to affect them.

2 **Lack of direction and purpose:** if organisations have not sorted out the bases and objectives of the changes that are proposed, they cannot expect either staff or customers to go along with them with any degree of confidence or understanding.

3 **Fear and anxiety:** these are human responses to concepts and situations that they do not fully understand. Those concerned with managing change have to recognise that they must alleviate fear and anxiety as far as possible.

4 **Perfection:** at the point at which change is proposed, suddenly everything concerning the status quo becomes 'perfect'. This is a very strong barrier to have to overcome because the status quo will, after all, have supported people well in the past.

   The extent and prevalence of these barriers will vary between situations. When facing any great change, however, the manager or supervisor will need to identify where these occur, and who is affected, as a prerequisite to effective planning for change.

● As a general rule, however, no change can be fully effective if the staff are not consulted and kept fully informed at all stages. Moreover, in the near future, this is certain to become a statutory requirement as greater staff involvement is required by European Union law.

25.4 Quality

A consequence of ever-increased customer expectations is attention to quality. People expect better quality products and services, evermore readily and conveniently available. Successful organisations have therefore had to pay close attention to the quality of every aspect of their activities.

- Customer satisfaction is now concerned both with the products or services offered, and also the ways in which they are delivered by the organisation. This is now recognised to cover the whole process from the acceptance of orders, through delivery and dispatch, to after-sales service. In many cases, this totality is instrumental in the general aspect of repeat business.
- Organisations have had to be concerned with staff excellence in terms of expertise, skills, knowledge and attitudes. This is, in turn, underpinned by a commitment, as far as possible, in terms of pay and rewards, continuity of employment, and variety and enhancement.
- Organisations themselves have had to take a direct responsibility to ensure that their products and services are constantly being improved.

25.5 Quality assurance

In manufacturing and industrial activities, quality of output is relatively easy to assure because, if necessary, each product or unit can be tested against the specification. Any that fall below this are simply rejected.

Quality assurance in service sectors, both public and commercial, is less easy to define because each transaction is based upon a human request rather than a finished item. In practice, it is achieved in the commercial service sectors by breaking down each component of the service into something which is either measurable absolutely, or into sub-categories for which minimum standards can be more easily defined.

For example, an insurance policy is the representation of a contract between one individual and the insurance corporation. It will state what coverage is given in relation to the individual's own circumstances and dispositions so that there is no doubt about the nature of the offering and expectation. Similarly, hotel ranking and grading systems represent a combination of ambience, facilities, room standard and location.

In public services, quality assurance now tends to be formalised by service level agreements and arrangements in which memoranda are drawn up specifying obligations and expectations on the part of the service users, consumers or purchasers, and their providers.

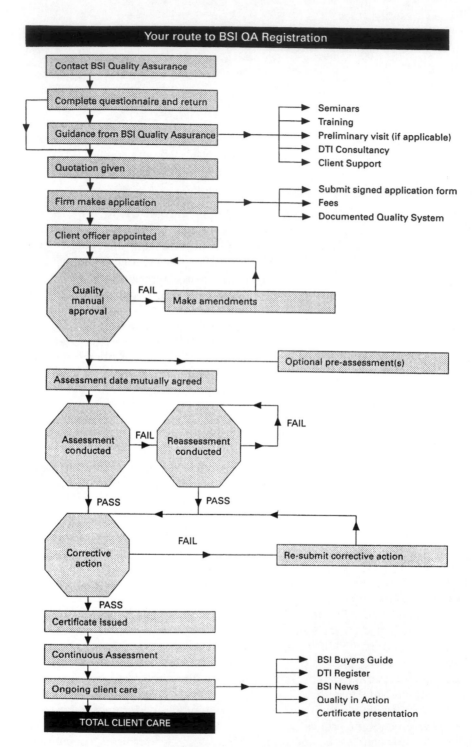

Figure 25.1 Quality assurance
Source: BSI Quality Assurance.

It is also possible to gain certification for quality assurance and many organisations in all sectors undertake to be assessed by an independent external organisation to British Standard 5750, the national standard for quality management systems. The standard (also known internationally as ISO9000 and at a European Union level as EN29000) provides a model management system that companies can use to help them install their own specific system. Once the management team are happy that their system meets all the requirements of the standard, they can then apply for assessment. The model for this assessment is given at Figure 25.1.

25.6 Current managerial issues

For the foreseeable future, the major issues facing organisations and their managers are as follows.

1   **Investment levels:** the best organisations are taking the view that much greater attention is required to investment in technology; investment in staff training and the maintenance of high-quality staff; and investment in continued customer service and satisfaction, as a prerequisite to long-term organisational well-being.

2   **Culture, attitudes and values:** the best organisations are increasingly adopting and requiring their staff to adopt distinctive ways of doing things, rather than being allowed to set their own standards. Organisations increasingly have their own distinctive and considered view of how they should best conduct the affairs.

3   **Business across cultures:** this especially applies to organisations operating in global markets. It applies also to a lesser extent to smaller organisations operating in a variety of localities.

4   **Strategy, policy and direction:** the capability to develop long-term clarity of purpose in all areas of activity, while maintaining the flexibility to take advantage of opportunities as they present themselves.

5   **Flexible patterns and methods of work:** this has led for example, to longer factory, shop, office, public and private facility opening hours based, in turn, on the recognition that customers will use organisation services when it suits them. As organisations have extended their activity times, so they have found that extra customers have come to them. This has, in turn, led to a great demand for short hours and other forms of part-time and off-site working and job opportunities for employees and potential employees.

6   **Ethics and morality:** there is an increasing realisation that there is a much greater propensity for consumers to use organisations in which they have confidence and that they can trust. This is based on the expectation of a long-term and continuously satisfactory relationship; and a much greater demand for work and staff relationships based on honesty and integrity rather than bureaucracy, barriers, procedures and in many cases, duplicity.

25.7   The professionalisation of management

Over the recent past, the nature of management has been transformed in both concept and approach. The basis of knowledge and expertise is becoming evermore widely understood and expected. All managers should at least have the basic knowledge and understanding indicated in these pages. Increasingly, as the nature of effective management in all spheres becomes more widely understood, and as organisations come to recognise the direct relationship between excellence in management and effectiveness of organisational performance, this will be seen as a beginning and not an end. The truly expert manager, moreover, will also have the same qualities of passion, conviction and commitment that other experts demonstrate in the pursuit of their chosen paths.

This is leading, in turn, to the increased professionalisation of management. The prevailing view has shifted away from technological expertise as the prerequisite to being an effective manager; and towards recognition that there is distinctive expertise required by those who manage, direct and supervise. While it remains true that technical and technological understanding are essential, especially for functional management activities, there is a distinctive body of skills, knowledge, attributes, behaviour and expertise that are both quite distinctive (as illustrated in these pages) and which should be held by all those who choose management as an occupation.

QUESTIONS

1 Consider whether major organisational changes need careful planning. How would you set about preparing to plan and implement a major change in an organisation? (ICSA)

2 Discuss the impact of changing technology on an organisation and its employees. (ICSA)

3 'The successful exploitation of new technology requires attention to the human resource.' Discuss. (ICSA)

4 Assume that you are the Facility Manager of a large national company occupying headquarters in a city centre. The company is reviewing its policy towards headquarters and related functions as part of a restructuring. The company is seeking reductions in corporate overheads which they feel are adversely affecting the company's competitiveness. [Among other things] the company decide to consider options to relocate. Identify the main options for the relocation. Suggest alternative ways of managing the project and propose the methods you will use to evaluate them. (IAM)

5 Why has 'facilities management' become more important in recent years? (IAM)

6 How many uses can you find for an ordinary plain paper clip? Name not less than fourteen.

7 By the use of appropriate examples, illustrate how social change is affecting management. (CIMA)

8 Explain what is meant by the following terms. In each case give two brief examples:
   (i) Changing work environments.
   (ii) Changing expectations and values in society. (IAM)
9 You are required to describe and assess the usefulness of
   (a) quality assurance;
   (b) quality circles. (CIMA)

■ ☑ Selected reading list

Mastering Basic Management is designed to be an introduction to the wide-ranging subject of management. For those who wish to further their studies the following short reading list will be of assistance. It is by no means exhaustive and most works will give guidance on further appropriate reading. In all cases the latest editions should be consulted, consequently no dates are given. Books already mentioned elsewhere are also omitted from the list.

General management

Adair, J. *The Action-Centred Leader* (London: Financial Society)
Adair, John, *Training for Leadership* (Farnborough: Gower Press)
Ansoff H. I., *Corporate Strategy* (London: Penguin Books)
Brech, E. F. L., *Principles and Practice of Management* (Harlow: Longman)
Cartwright R. *In Charge of Customer Relations* (Oxford: Blackwell)
Cartwright R. *In Charge: Managing People* (Oxford: Blackwell)
Drucker P. *The Practice of Management* (Harlow: Longman)
Handy C. B. *Understanding Organisation* (London: Penguin)
Harvey-Jones J. *Making it Happen* (London: Fontana)
Kanter R. M. *When Giants Learn to Dance* (New York: Free Press)
Kay-Ash M. *On People Management* (New York: Macdonald)
Lawrence P. A. *Management in Action* (London: Routledge)
Morita A. *The Sony Story* (London: Fontana)
Peters T. & Austin A. *A Passion for Excellence* (New York: Harper & Row)
Peters T. & Waterman R. *In Search of Excellence* (New York: Harper & Row)
Pettinger R. *Introduction to Management* (Basingstoke: Macmillan)
Pettinger R. *Managing the Flexible Workforce* (London: Cassell)
Semler R. *Maverick* (New York: Free Press)
Woodward J. *Industrial Organisation : Behaviour and Control* (Oxford: OUP)

Functional management

Armstrong M. *Human Resource Management* (London: Kogan Page)
Baker M. *Marketing* (London: Macmillan)
Cheatle K. *Code of Employment Practice* (London: NCVCCO)
Cartwright R. *In Charge of Finance* (Oxford: Blackwell)
Knott G. *Financial Management*, Professional Masters Series (Basingstoke: Macmillan)

Lockyer K. *Quantitative Production Management* (London: Pitman)
Packard V. *The Hidden Persuaders* (London: Penguin)
Porter M. E. *Competitive Strategy* (London: Macmillan)
Thompson J. L. *Strategic Management* (London: Chapman & Hall)

Management support services

Griseri P. *Managing Values* (London: Macmillan)
Pettinger R. *The European Social Charter : A Manager's Guide* (London: Kogan Page)
Trevor M. *Toshiba's New British Company* (London: Policy Studies Institute)

Index